Priestly Celibacy

Priestly Celibacy

Theological Foundations

Gary Selin

Foreword by J. Francis Cardinal Stafford

THE CATHOLIC UNIVERSITY OF AMERICA PRESS
Washington, D.C.

Library of Congress Cataloging-in-Publication Data

Names: Selin, Gary, 1964–

Title: Priestly celibacy : theological foundations / Gary Selin ; foreword by
J. Francis Cardinal Stafford.

Description: Washington, D.C. : The Catholic University of America Press, 2016. |
Includes bibliographical references and index.

Identifiers: LCCN 2015038132 | ISBN 9780813228419 (pbk. : alk. paper)

Subjects: LCSH: Celibacy—Catholic Church—History of doctrines. |
Priesthood—Catholic Church. | Lord's Supper—Catholic Church. | Catholic
Church—Clergy—Sexual behavior. | Priests—Sexual behavior.

Classification: LCC BX1912.85 .S45 2016 | DDC 253/.252—dc23 LC record
available at http://lccn.loc.gov/2015038132

To the Blessed Virgin Mary, Mother of Priests

CONTENTS

FOREWORD

The Author

Fr. Gary B. Selin, a diocesan priest, has been engaged in a book-length *"sacra conversatio"* concerning the origin and theological development of clerical celibacy. This "holy conversation" brings forward persons from the beginning of the Church to the present. His work is as useful as the theme is timely. The author himself is a thoughtful, gentle, and scholarly man of God. "Silence and work" are as integral to the rhythm of his ministry as they were to St. John of the Cross in the formation of Carmelites.[1] The author's experience in the formation and education of seminarians is extensive.

Selin's theological method is guided by the principle that reality is intelligible and true. He understands priestly celibacy as a gift, essentially related to the Eucharist. By acting in the Person of Christ, the Head of the body (*Presbyterorum Ordinis*, 2), the priest hands himself over forever to the service of God and of the Bride of Christ, His Church. This "renunciation in the supernatural order"[2] acts as a major musical key in the life of a priest, for it is given to the man as a free gift in perfect resonance with his own freedom. Because of the mutual freedoms, the gift received is a surpassing surprise from God, enabling the priest to act with holy simplicity in the Person of His Incarnate Son. God's gift of celibacy makes "the silent music" more accessible.

In four chapters together with an introduction and conclusion, Se-

---

1. Letter of St. John of the Cross to the Discalced Carmelite Nuns of Beas, 1587, *The Collected Works of St. John of the Cross*, trans. Kieran Kavanaugh, OCD, and Otilio Rodriquez, OCD (Garden City, N.Y.: Doubleday & Company, 1964), 688.

2. Karl Rahner cited by David W. Fagerberg, *On Liturgical Asceticism* (Washington, D.C.: The Catholic University of America Press), 2013, 80.

lin recaptures the sacred character of the priesthood. After meditating upon the major texts of the Catholic tradition, he pulls together various elements of authoritative teaching. His contribution is substantial to the long-overdue development of a coherent and systematic theology on the significance of perfect continence in priestly life and ministry.

The Content

Selin's presentation is rooted in the Bible and tradition. On exegetical and historical grounds, he insists that the origins of priestly celibacy commenced with the New Testament and was supported by papal and episcopal interventions. He reports on the June 16, 390, meeting of the Fathers of the Council of Carthage. They put into place a remarkable foundation for future theology. The prominence they gave to the liturgical context is particularly salient: "It is proper (*decet*) that the holy bishops and priests of God as well as the Levites, that is those who are in the service of the divine sacraments, observe perfect continence." The bishops concluded the decree with a climatic liturgical and ascetical singularity "so that they may obtain in all simplicity what they are asking from God." The more one meditates upon this text and acts upon it, the better one understands the "disciplined obedience"[3] of the new man in Christ. The bishops gathered in ancient Carthage realized that its content was "what the apostles taught and what antiquity itself observed."

Selin points out an unsettling historical reality. Over the past twenty-one centuries, with rare exceptions such as Johann Adam Möhler and Matthias Joseph Scheeben, the Church has not offered systematic reflection on the topic of priestly celibacy per se. In some centuries, especially more recent ones, Catholics stumbled badly over its origins and fumbled about its nature. What the author accomplishes builds upon the breakthrough of Pope Blessed Paul VI in his 1967 Encyclical Letter, *Sacerdotalis Caelibatus*. The pope, drawing upon the Vatican II Council, endorses three theological factors justifying priestly celibacy: the Christological factor represents the chief motive for the Church to hold fast to priestly celibacy modeled on the celibate life of Jesus; the ecclesiological factor enhances priestly pastoral charity; and the eschatological factor bears

3. Ibid., 26.

witness to the resurrection of the body. Selin highlights qualities that are easily overlooked—the comparative adverbs by which the Vatican II Council extols celibacy's "manifest suitability" to serve the "new humanity." The four are the following: *facilius* (more readily), *liberius* (more freely), *expeditius* (less encumbered), and *aptiores* (better fitted).[4]

In reviewing Jane Austen's *Emma*, Sir Walter Scott coined what Adela Pinch called a "conceit" in describing a typical reader of the novel: a "wandering traveler" who has no chance of having "his head turned." Pinch elaborated on Scott's insight. Scott was illustrating the motive of Austen's incorporating only the "ordinary" and "normal" of everyday life to illustrate the "new style of novel." By employing exclusively "ordinary details" to interpret the new epoch unfolding in post-Napoleonic, consumer-oriented England, Scott stated his perception of Austen's intentions: "The youthful wanderer may return from his promenade to the ordinary business of life without any chance of having his head turned by the recollection of the scene through which he had been wandering."[5] But Pinch's final interpretation of Austin as nihilistic is mistaken.

A different, revolutionary vision unfolded in the ancient Church that brings us closer to Alasdair MacIntyre's accurate judgment about Jane Austen's Christian identity. That vision continues in today's Catholic commitment to evangelization. Whenever Blessed Paul VI referred to the eschatological characteristics of priestly celibacy, he indicated that priestly celibacy was a perennial "head-turner" because in New Testament terminology, "the world has been turned upside down" (see Acts of Apostles 17:6) by Jesus's proclamation of the Kingdom of heaven.[6] What his encyclical pointed out was that the eschatological mystery

---

4. Vatican Council II, *Presbyterorum Ordinis*, n. 16.

5. Aptly cited by Adela Pinch in *Emma* by Jane Austen, ed. James Kinsley with an introduction by Adela Pinch (Oxford: Oxford University Press, reissued 2008), ix–x. Pinch calls attention to Scott's use of "a whole revolution of turns" found in *Emma*. Eschatology, of course, was not the point of reference of Scott, Pinch, or Austen; however, Scott's "wandering traveler" turning his head is an excellent metaphor for illuminating the Christian eschatological landscape. In contrast to Scott, Catholics have had the capacity also to underline the *kairos* (in the sense of "the extraordinariness") of the ordinary in light of the sacramentality of the world and of human beings created as male and female.

6. See biblical theme of C. Kavin Rowe, *World Upside Down: Reading Acts in the Greco-Roman Age* (New York: Oxford University Press, 2009).

vitalizing priestly celibacy has been given to the Church to "turn the head" of every "wandering traveler" in this land of unlikeness. A celibate priest has always been a divine exclamation point among ordinary and everyday things: "Acknowledge that you are strangers and exiles on the earth" (Heb 11:13).

Priestly celibacy carries forward and explicates the central mysteries: Trinity, Incarnation, and Redemption. A superb integrator, Selin uses the reality of lived celibacy to build bridges to other conciliar themes: pastoral charity, created and redeemed body, sacrament of marriage, poor church for the poor, eschatology, and so forth. The author highlights the ancient genealogy of nuptiality as a fountainhead of a Christian anthropology rooted in the Bible. This theological patrimony was later enriched by Origen, St. Bernard of Clairvaux, St. Thomas Aquinas, St. John of the Cross, and others.

The crucial theological motive of the bishops of the 390 Council when reiterating the necessity of clerical celibacy was the Eucharist. Selin later describes the relation between the Eucharist, to which the phrase of the Fathers of Carthage, "service of the sacraments," chiefly adverted, and perfect continence. "One of the most significant contributions ... is the highlighting of the Eucharist as the preeminent key for priestly celibacy.... Priestly mediation thus constitutes a specific difference that distinguishes celibacy from consecrated chastity. In particular, priestly mediation is centered on the Eucharist, which provides a solid foundation for theological development of the subject of priestly celibacy." Selin then draws upon a brilliant synthesis by Pope Benedict XVI in the Postsynodal Apostolic Exhortation of 2007, *Sacramentum Caritatis* (24).

Dynamically new and broadened anthropological foundations of priestly celibacy were developed by recent papal interventions, most notably by Pope St. John Paul II. Almost sixteen hundred years after the historic Council of Carthage, in weekly Wednesday audiences from 1979 to 1984 he elaborated on anthropological themes of the Vatican II Council. Presenting 129 generic reflections on the *Theology of the Body*, he described them as "catecheses," a weighty biblical word meaning "the communication of the living mystery of God."[7] His themes also were

---

7. Pope John Paul II, *Man and Woman He Created Them: A Theology of the Body*, trans. Michael Waldstein (Boston: Pauline Books and Media, 2006), 15. Citation is from Michael Waldstein.

biblical: "flesh" in the Johannine context of "the Word became flesh," "the union of man and woman as a 'great mystery'" in the tradition of St. Paul, commentaries on the *Canticle of Canticles* in the traditions of Origen, of St. Bernard of Clairvaux, and preeminently of St. John of the Cross. In contrast to the Enlightenment and post-Enlightenment eras, his catecheses did not reduce sex to a mere physical science. Rather, they were set within the anthropological mysteries of the Incarnation and the Redemption of the body. By coincidence, a few selective historical insights by Michel Foucault were also refurbished.[8]

In *Theology of the Body*, St. John Paul II gave precedence to the image of nuptial spirituality in St. John of the Cross. The Carmelite source may surprise some. Selin highlights the pope's reason. Man and woman are essentially relational in their incarnate love. Weekly papal discourses were seen as a cornucopia of original teachings in Carmelite spirituality. Generations of reflection will be required to make them our own again. Being grasped by Selin's systematic reflections makes possible the reader's grasp of the pope's teaching. St. Augustine's aphorism exposes the process of theological assimilation of Selin's book, *Capit ut capitur*—"one grasps in being grasped."

The pope also placed nuptiality of the body at the center of the Church's anthropology. Thirteen of the 1979–1984 catecheses addressed priestly celibacy. It was crucial that the pope thereby enfolded the meaning of priestly celibacy within the all-encompassing, Carmelite concept of nuptiality of the body. Finally, the major conciliar text used by St. John Paul II is found in *Gaudium et Spes* (24:3). His reflections are found in General Audiences 80–81.[9]

In 1992 the pope issued what Selin calls "John Paul's most significant teaching on the priesthood," the Apostolic Exhortation, *Pastores Dabo Vobis*. It was a long-expected document, and it met expectations. In his synthesis of the conciliar and postconciliar teachings on priestly

8. Michel Foucault, *Le souci de soi: histoire de la sexualité*, vol. III (Paris: Gallimard, 1984) (*The History of Sexuality*, vol. 3, trans. R. Hurley [New York: Pantheon, 1986]); "The Confession of the Flesh," reprinted in Colin Gordon, ed., *Power/Knowledge: Selected Interviews and Other Writings by Michel Foucault, 1972–1977* (New York: Pantheon Books, 1980). Cf. also *The Cambridge Companion to Foucault*, second ed., ed. Gary Gutting (Cambridge: Cambridge University Press, 2003, 2007).

9. John Paul II, *Man and Woman He Created Them*, 436–43.

celibacy, Selin underscores an unanticipated rehabilitation of the "ritual purity" arguments for priestly celibacy. Rather than rejecting those traditions as "discredited," Selin offers persuasive motives for keeping them. He asserts that they must be understood in light of the more recent and developed teachings of the Church's magisterium concerning priestly celibacy. Many sensed a liberation during the 1979–84 catecheses. They marked an epochal breakthrough. I read them with discerning admiration and used some of them in preparing a series of weekly articles in the Memphis diocesan paper. At last, I thought, the Church's pastors possess a theological discourse delivered in a personalist key that is worthy both of the conceptual polarities of "union and procreation" in the 1968 Encyclical Letter *Humanae Vitae* and of the splendid decree of the Council of Carthage in 390. Furthermore, Blessed John Paul II's *Theology of the Body* realized the explicit hopes of the V Ordinary Synod of Bishops in 1980 on "the Christian family."

Much remains to be done. A declining and decadent Western society has refused the papal initiatives. The culture faces enormous challenges as does the Church in limiting further contamination from it. The eclipse of human identity and dignity has been driven by ideologies such as *The History of Sexuality* by Michel Foucault and its translations into other languages during the late 1970s and 1980s, the advent of "gender" studies in academia, the hegemony of positivist law, the exponential growth of pornography, and the explosion of antimarriage worldwide, for-profit enterprises, and corporations.

The upheavals in sexual theory and practice are unprecedented. The revolution has been targeted to overturn normative relationships of the past, especially the foundational male-female and parent-child dyads. Marriage structures are being dismantled; they are considered by courts to be no more than museum trophies, skeletons of past "social constructs." The Eucharistic heart of the Church is being ripped out through the popular media's ridicule of the spousal relationship of Christ as Bridegroom to the Church, His Bride. Priestly celibacy has been caught up in the worldwide rage over the seeming incompatibility of love and adoration.[10] Thus, the original *parrhesia (freedom and*

10. This diagnosis of the root of modern chaos comes from years of reflection on the poetry of Wallace Stevens with insights from Helen Vendler's profound understanding of the

boldness in English) of Pope St. John Paul II in "being true in body and soul"[11] is more needed now than ever. Alert Christians are the sentinels in the new dark ages. Alasdair MacIntyre's coda to his similar, mortal diagnosis of contemporary culture is real, ominous, and shocking. "This time, however, the barbarians are not waiting beyond the frontiers; they have already been governing us for quite some time."[12] Selin's work appears at a *kairos*, "a decisive point of time."[13]

Two rarely cited texts from Edward Schillebeeckx, OP, confirm the rock-like solidness of the Christian tradition. Selin points out that St. John Paul II's teaching on celibacy was presented in a nuptial context. According to Schillebeeckx, nearly parallel historical studies yielded a welcome confirmation of his work in this field. He insisted that the married and priestly states complement and strengthen one another. The Dutch theologian acknowledged the singularly eschatological character of celibacy. When addressing the relation between the sacrament of marriage and priestly celibacy, Schillebeeckx concluded with an unexpected and preeminently pastoral insight. He first stated a historical fact: "The two states of life, marriage and celibate priesthood, were to have a mutually positive effect upon each other in Christianity."[14] Then he lit up his historical treatment of Christian marriage with a wake-up judgment: "We have reached the point where we are able fully to confirm the statement of the Protestant theologian, Max Thurian. 'When the vocation of celibacy is underrated, so is that of marriage.'"[15] These insights confirm Selin's conclusions.

Until the 1967 publication of *Sacerdotalis Caelibatus*, misinformation

---

poet in her *Wallace Stevens: Words Chosen Out of Desire* (Knoxville: The University of Tennessee Press, 1985), 10–28.

11. See Lecture at the Catholic University of America, "Pope Paul VI and Pope John Paul II: Being True in Body and Soul," J. Francis Stafford, November 13, 2008; found on the CNA website, http://www.catholicnewsagency.com/document.php?n=780.

12. Alasdair MacIntyre, *After Virtue*, second ed. (Notre Dame, Ind.: University of Notre Dame Press, 1984), 263.

13. Gerhard Delling, *Theological Dictionary of the New Testament*, vol. III, ed. Gerhard Kittel (Grand Rapids, Mich.: Wm. B. Eerdmans Publishing Company, 1965, 1982), 458.

14. Edward Schillebeeckx, OP, *Marriage: Human Reality and Saving Mystery*, trans. N. D. Smith (London: Sheed and Ward, 1978; originally published in 1965, 1978), distributed in the United States by Christian Classics, 131.

15. Ibid., 312.

and embitterment from the Reformation had obscured celibacy's fresh and revolutionary witness to the Kingdom of heaven. The confusion proved destructive. Erroneous deviations erupted again over priestly identity. In the 1960s and 1970s, the extent and depth of the crisis were publicly exposed by moral failures within the Church in both marriage and celibate clergy.

In the 1960s canonical and patristic scholars of both Eastern and Western Churches revisited the scholarship of the orientalist Gustav Bickell, and of Francis Xavier Funk. In the late nineteenth and early twentieth centuries, these two had engaged in a prolonged controversy on the origin and motives of clerical celibacy and set the stage for subsequent decades. This was more applicable to Funk, since Bickell withdrew prematurely from the controversy. In 1970 Roger Gryson supported Funk's thesis.

However, with the uncovering of the Paphnutius intervention at the Council of Nicaea as a fraud by F. Winkelmann in 1968, the discord over celibacy's origins has no longer been "the wind that lashes everything at once."[16] Bickell's conclusions have become more and more accepted. In other words, there is growing agreement that in the West the normative existence of perfect continence within the "clergy" goes back uninterruptedly to apostolic times. Although the celibate clerical witness in the East is considered also of apostolic origins, an erosion began after the fourth century until a breach took place at the 691 Council of Trullo. Cardinal Alfons Maria Stickler, canonist and historian, was active in the era of the Vatican II Council. His efforts were crucial in calling attention to the need for proper methodologies in studying the "canonical" history of "perfect continence" in the first three hundred years of Christianity. The distinction between law (*ius*) and norm (*lex*) was critical.[17]

From the vast and mostly neglected territory of celibacy, Selin has rightly given prominence to the extraordinary synthesis of Blessed Paul VI in 1967. He describes it as "the most comprehensive papal teaching on celibacy in the twentieth century and perhaps in history." Many

---

16. Wallace Stevens, *The Collected Poems of Wallace Stevens* (New York: Alfred A. Knopf, 1991), 358.

17. Alfons Maria Cardinal Stickler, *The Case for Clerical Celibacy: Its Historical Developments and Theological Foundations*, trans. Brian Ferme (San Francisco: Ignatius Press, 1995), 17–18.

were unaware of its significance, including myself. Perhaps his *Sacerdotalis Caelibatus* was lost amidst the momentous events accompanying the 1968 *Humanae Vitae*. Selin offers a similar explanation. Only with Selin's book have I discovered the 1967 encyclical's vast theological importance. Its contribution to understanding the historical development of priestly celibacy over the centuries, however, remains negligible.

In interpreting the history of the celibate clergy, I sought out historical resources. The search proved fruitless; the findings were meager and even useless. Libraries and bookstores were dead ends. Invariably, the only place where some light shone through was on bookshelves marked "consecrated life." But even there it was still pale. They were burdened with a drawback: the exclusive focus was on the vow in consecrated life. With the exception of the "ritual purity" motive, the search for the meaning of celibacy among diocesan priests led to a wasteland.[18]

Conversion and Celibacy

In the work of Blessed John Henry Newman, Selin discovered the fundamental importance of conversion in grasping the evangelical relation between priesthood and perfect continence. Newman elaborated a prelude in a series of relationships. "The doctrine of the Sacraments leads to the doctrine of Justification; Justification to that of Original Sin; Original Sin to the merit of Celibacy." Future researchers will need to unpack his rich but dense suggestive relations. St. John Paul II's teaching on the redemption of the body could be studied together with the central role of analogy in religious conversion found in two Jesuit theologians, Erich Przywara and Bernard Lonergan.

What might one expect from such research? It will be increasingly clear that an understanding of the celibate life of Jesus and its imitation from apostolic times by the "clergy" engaged in pastoral life presuppos-

18. Recently, I've become aware of several historical studies in Italian and German on changing structures of priestly ministry over two millennia. The authors have focused on dioceses and regions. British scholars have also been active in studying the structures of the "canonical" priesthood in medieval England and elsewhere. For example, Jerome Bertram, FSA, of the Oratory has published the Critical Texts with Translations and Commentary on *The Chrodegang Rules* (Aldershot: Ashgate Publishing Limited, 2005), an excellent study on the priesthood in medieval Continental Europe. The field is immense and complex. Vastly increased and intensified research in the history of the Catholic priesthood is imperative.

es a conversion of life. Przywara insists that each of the major "forms of a theory of knowledge ... bears within it a distinctly *religious substrate* ... a religious 'interiority of the interior.'"[19] He concludes, "The rhythm internal to a methodological theory of knowledge properly leads back to [Augustine]."[20]

Lonergan's insights on conversion converge on the centrality of Przywara's "inner sense of knowledge as such." He insists that conversion requires the individual's turn to a world "mediated by meaning," a conversion from "nature to spirit." This requires "a new understanding of oneself because, more fundamentally, it brings about a new self to be understood."[21] It involves an acceptance of one's historical horizons and the finiteness of one's freedom within that horizon. Finally, even though few are aware of its necessity, "the entire scope of ... analogy as a fundamental Catholic form"[22] is an essential prerequisite for religious conversion and an analogical glimpse of the transcendent God.

Lonergan cites also the experience of St. Augustine. The latter's conversion in 386 was followed by an extended retreat at Cassiciacum, where during dialogues with several friends; his mother, Monica; his eldest brother, Navigius; and Augustine's son, Adeodatus, he made a singular discovery that has been acknowledged to be a crucial step in converting to Christ. In the fifteenth book of *De Trinitate*, Augustine reported on the discovery of what he called the *verbum intus prolatum* (that which exists as an inner word). It was an epochal find. This "inner word" is the basis of the human capacity to make intelligible the gift from the other. Augustine accomplished this by mapping his own intellectual structure. Then, he made the momentous application by analogy of this discovery to the relations of the Three Persons within the interiority of the Triune God. While engaged in a search for Christ, others in holy dialogue were encouraged to make a similar exploration of their own interiority. Only by such a strenuous process does one discover the *verbum intus prola-*

19. Erich Przywara, *Analogia Entis: Metaphysics: Original Structure and Universal Rhythm*, trans. John R. Betz and David Bentley Hart (Grand Rapids, Mich.: William B. Eerdmans Publishing Company, 2014), 505.

20. Ibid., 508.

21. For these insights, I am indebted to Bernard Lonergan, *Doctrinal Pluralism* (Milwaukee: Marquette University Press, 1971), 33–34.

22. Przywara, *Analogia Entis*, 348 ff., esp. 353.

tum. Augustine's Cassiciacum dialogue assumes a community, engaging each participant in the process of interior discovery.

St. Augustine completes the process of ascertaining the relation of likeness/unlikeness or analogy between the generation of God's Word and the birth of "speech of spirit within spirit,"[23] the human inner word with a magnificent reflection. "But that word of ours, which has neither sound nor thought of sound, is the word of that thing which we inwardly speak by seeing it, and therefore, it belongs to no language; hence in this enigma there is a likeness, be it what it may, to that Word of God who is also God, since it is also so born from our knowledge as that Word who was also born from the knowledge of the Father."[24]

Lonergan is precise in describing the conclusion of the intellectual process. Analogy is central to conversion. He writes, "Imperfectly we grasp why God is Father, Word, and Spirit inasmuch as we conceive God, not simply as identity of being, understanding, thought, and love, but as that identity and yet with thought, because of understanding, and love, because of both, where 'because' means not the logical relation between propositions but the real *processio intelligibilis* of an intellectual substance."[25]

Conversion is inescapable for a Church imprinted indelibly with eschatology. Why is this so? The reason is that the Church is an evangelizing community. Consequently, the spiritual condition for accepting, practicing, and cherishing priestly celibacy requires the presence of a profound conversion not only by individual Christians but also by each local Church and each parish. A systemic, dialogic turn-about in Christ is required. Today, an antieschatological virus has penetrated into the Catholic imagination. Consequently, some have judged that a celibate, eschatologically witnessing clergy has become too enfeebled, anachronistic, and spiritless to cope with the earthly city that "loves itself in contempt of God" (adapted from St. Augustine).

23. Bernard J. Lonergan, *Verbum: Word and Idea in Aquinas*, second ed., ed. David B. Burrell, CSC (Notre Dame, Ind.: University of Notre Dame Press, 1970), x.

24. St. Augustine, *The Trinity*, trans. Stephen McKenna, CssR (Washington, D.C.: The Catholic University of America Press, 1963), 15, 14, 24, 487.

25. Lonergan, *Verbum: Word and Idea in Aquinas*, 213.

Conclusion

Selin's book is indispensable for those engaged in discussions on the topic of an "evangelizing Church," including her eschatological character. There is nothing comparable to it. It is essential for those engaged in conferences addressing "priestly celibacy." It serves as a *vademecum* for those engaged in rediscovering the identity of diocesan priests. To all interested in the eschatological witness of the parish and diocese, it offers the most recent, most comprehensive, and best-informed vision of the contributing role of the clergy. For all Christians in search of more than a notional grip on the "nuptial sacramentality" of redeemed creation, the author's grasp of the issue is invaluable. Jesus's celibacy was and remains essential for His threefold mission; it is equally crucial for those who act *in persona Christi*—"in the person of Christ."

Selin is clear that the Church cannot turn her back on a two-thousand-year-old teaching without threatening an historical break of immense consequences in the life of the Spirit. Schillebeeckx's aforementioned historical finding of the relationship between priestly celibacy and sacramental marriage should not be shrugged off.

Finally, the argument for celibacy's connection with priesthood is not merely extrinsic; it is greater than simple *convenientia* ("agreement"). These external designations are unworthy without something more. Selin is emphatic that light theologies won't work. They don't match up to the reach of a man's gift of a celibate life and heart to God and to the Church. He indicates that Pope St. John Paul II made reference to a "profound" connection between celibacy and ordination. He also cites the insistence of Cardinal William Levada, the former prefect for the Congregation for the Doctrine of the Faith, that "[being a priest and being celibate] form an integral whole in which the one reinforces the other." These insights respect the depth of the celibate vow.

From Selin's study, it is obvious that any lessening of support for priestly celibacy by the Church will aggravate the crisis not only of the faith of Christians in a world dominated by an enervating fatalism but also of the faith among secular priests. It will diminish the Church's witness to Christ, her Bridegroom. Finally, the drama of the witness of eschatological freedom within the Church will be in danger of being eclipsed. From Selin's overall research, it emerges that the celibate priest gives an irreplaceable, high-profile witness to the Christological, ecclesiological, and eschatological mysteries proclaimed by the Catholic faith. The priest's gaze upon Christ will sustain his people and himself in life's pilgrimage while he prays to the heavenly Bridegroom in communion with St. John of the Cross, "Let us go forth to behold ourselves in Your beauty."[26]

J. Francis Cardinal Stafford
Major Penitentiary Emeritus
Archbishop of Denver Emeritus

26. St. John of the Cross, *The Collected Works of St. John of the Cross*, 547.

Introduction

D URING A 2014 INTERVIEW with reporters on a flight returning from the Holy Land, Pope Francis responded to a question about the possibility of admitting married men to the candidacy for priesthood in the Latin rite: "The Catholic Church has married priests in the Eastern rites. Celibacy is not a dogma of faith; it is a rule of life that I appreciate a great deal and I believe it is a gift for the Church. The door is always open given that it is not a dogma of faith."[1] This response of the pope was similar to one that he gave to the same question asked of him, as archbishop of Buenos Aires, in 2012:

> For now, the Church remains firm on the discipline of celibacy. There are those who say, with a certain pragmatism, that we are missing out on more manpower. If, hypothetically, Western Catholicism would change on the issue of celibacy, I believe that it would be for cultural reasons (like in the Eastern Church), not as much as a universal option. For the time being, I am in favor of maintaining celibacy, with the pros and cons that it has, because it has been ten centuries of good experiences more often than failure. What happens is that the scandals are immediately seen. But tradition has weight and validity.... It is an issue of discipline, not of faith. It can be changed.[2]

While the pope affirmed that celibacy has been beneficial for the Church and indicated his personal preference that it be maintained, he also said that obligatory celibacy "can be changed." His comment has raised questions about the solidity of mandatory priestly celibacy for candidates for

1. Melinda Henneberger, "How About the Option of Priestly Celibacy?" *Washington Post*, May 28, 2014.

2. Jorge Mario Bergoglio and Abraham Skorka, *On Heaven and Earth: Pope Francis on Faith, Family and the Church in the 21st Century*, English ed. (New York: Random House, 2013), 48–49.

1

the priesthood in the Latin Church, particularly in view of it being an ecclesial discipline that is mutable.

Indeed, today there is a widespread discussion in the world and in the Catholic Church regarding priestly celibacy, particularly with reference to its mandatory character and usefulness in the Latin Church. Issues such as the lack of priestly vocations, the possible benefits of married Catholic priests, and the ecumenical reality of Protestant denominations with married ministers all seem to call into question the relevance of this centuries-old tradition. These issues highlight the widespread interest in priestly celibacy and underline its distinctiveness as a fundamental element in the history and spirituality of the ministerial priesthood.

A significant challenge in understanding the issue of priestly celibacy today is to find something more substantial than the "sound bite" theology offered in many popular accounts. Much of the discussion in the public forum revolves around sociological or pragmatic elements of celibacy, with few insights offered of a theological nature. Nevertheless, a richer account of priestly celibacy is available for those who seek a deeper understanding. This renewed insight, rooted in biblical and patristic meditations, has been developing substantially in the past fifty years through the influence of several official teaching documents of the Catholic Church, which in turn have provided a source for deep reflection by theologians.

Although the Catholic theology of priestly celibacy has advanced substantially since the 1960s, the understanding of celibacy prior to that time was rather limited in scope. For example, Pope Pius XII, while arguing for the suitability of celibacy for priests and for the evangelical counsel of chastity for religious in his encyclical *Sacra Virginitas* (1954), did not provide extensive arguments in favor of priestly celibacy that clearly differed for those used to justify the religious vow of chastity. Moreover, other magisterial documents of that time did not employ the full substance of the Catholic theological tradition but instead focused on two fundamental arguments: the superiority of celibacy over marriage and the need for the priest to maintain ritual purity.

On the other hand, the decree of Vatican II on the ministry and life of priests, *Presbyterorum Ordinis* (1965), presented a distinct theology of priestly celibacy that was broadly organized around a threefold scheme that highlighted its Christological, ecclesiological, and eschatological dimensions. This presentation of celibacy constituted a significant development in magisterial teaching. *Presbyterorum Ordinis* 16, for example, contained the first use of spousal language in support of priestly celibacy, while absent from the text were the arguments based on the superiority of celibacy over marriage and the need for the priest to maintain ritual purity.

Two years later, Blessed Pope Paul VI, in his encyclical letter, *Sacerdotalis Caelibatus* (1967), used the threefold dimension to develop further the reasons for the discipline of mandatory priestly celibacy in the Latin Church. His use of the ecclesiological dimension was especially helpful in inspiring some of the more creative developments in subsequent magisterial teachings. Finally, John Paul II, in the apostolic exhortation, *Pastores Dabo Vobis* (1992), employed the threefold dimension in order to highlight the pastoral fruitfulness of priestly celibacy.

This book aims at systematically presenting the riches of this developing Catholic theology on priestly celibacy, with a special focus placed on the development of the threefold scheme of priestly celibacy. It examines the scheme's internal consistency, magisterial authority, and theological value for the Church as a whole, as a way to a deeper understanding of the place of priestly celibacy in the ministry and life of the Church.

Because this study focuses on the theology of priestly celibacy in the Latin Church, it does not address the issue of married clergy of the Eastern Catholic or Orthodox Churches, both of which uphold the tradition of celibate bishops but differ on particulars concerning married and celibate deacons and priests.[3] Other topics not treated in this book are married priests in the Latin Church, such those in the Anglican ordinariate, and married permanent deacons.

With regard to the terminology used in this work, *continence* refers to the complete refraining from sexual intercourse, while *celibacy* signifies the willed state not to enter marriage.[4] *Chastity* indicates the moral

3. See Roman Cholij, *Clerical Celibacy in East and West* (Leominster: Fowler Wright, 1988); and Joseph J. Allen, ed., *Vested in Grace: Priesthood and Marriage in the Christian East* (Brookline, Mass.: Holy Cross Orthodox Press, 2001). The Second Vatican Council affirmed in *Presbyterorum Ordinis* 16 the lawful discipline of married clergy in the Eastern Churches.

4. According to the *Oxford Latin Dictionary, caelebs* ("unmarried; not having a spouse")

virtue that integrates sexuality within the person and is the proper use of one's sexual faculties in keeping with their particular states of life.[5] In magisterial documents, the state of *perfect chastity* is an expression used to describe the chastity to be practiced by those who are living a consecrated life in response to a specific calling from God; the word *perfect* signifies the *total* commitment to continence rather than the perfection of the virtue. *Cleric* signifies a man ordained to one of the higher orders (deacon, priest, and bishop), while *priest* denotes a presbyter as distinguished from a deacon or a bishop. *Priesthood* in general refers to the orders of the presbyterate and episcopate, although in some contexts only the former. Finally, *Magisterium* refers to the teaching office of the Catholic Church, that is, the bishops in communion with the successor of Peter, the bishop of Rome, whose task it is to give "an authentic interpretation of the Word of God, whether in its written form [Sacred Scripture] or in the form of Tradition."[6]

The structure of this book is organized as follows:[7] the first chapter considers three topics: (1) a summary of the biblical foundations of clerical continence and celibacy, (2) a review of the development of clerical continence and celibacy in the Latin Church from the early patristic era to the twentieth century, and (3) an overview of the theology of priestly celibacy in the twentieth century prior to the Second Vatican Council. This and subsequent chapters emphasizes the notion of celibacy as a *gift* of the Holy Spirit, and not only an ecclesial discipline.

The second chapter focuses on the renewal of magisterial teaching on priestly celibacy, principally in *Presbyterorum Ordinis* of Vatican II,

---

comes from the Sanskrit *kevalah* ("alone") and the Old English *hal* ("whole"). I have followed the definitions of *continence* and *celibacy* given by Edward Peters, "Canonical Considerations on Diaconal Continence," *Studia Canonica* 39 (2005): 147–80, fn. 1, at 147–48.

5. See *Catechism of the Catholic Church*, 2nd ed. (Washington, D.C.: United States Catholic Conference, 1997), articles 2337, 2348–50, and 2370. All citations from the *Catechism* are from this edition.

6. Vatican Council II, *Dei Verbum* 10, in Austin Flannery, ed., *Vatican Council II: The Conciliar and Post Conciliar Documents* (Northport, N.Y.: Costello, 1998), 387. All subsequent English translations of the Council documents are from this edition.

7. See Gary Selin, "On the Christological, Ecclesiological, and Eschatological Dimensions of Priestly Celibacy in *Presbyterorum Ordinis*, *Sacerdotalis Caelibatus* and Subsequent Magisterial Documents," STD diss., The Catholic University of America, Washington, D.C., 2011.

Sacerdotalis Caelibatus of Paul VI, *Pastores Dabo Vobis* of John Paul II, and some writings of Benedict XVI.

The third chapter consists of a thorough study of the threefold scheme of priestly celibacy in terms of its theological value for the Catholic Church, that is, as a way of understanding more thoroughly the place of celibacy in the ministry and life of the Church. The focus of this chapter is twofold: a study of the New Testament foundations of each dimension, followed by an elaboration of how each dimension can contribute to the development of an integral theology of priestly celibacy.

The fourth chapter proposes two synthetic theologies of priestly celibacy, each of which is centered on the Eucharist. One of the most significant contributions of this book is the highlighting of the Eucharist as the preeminent interpretative key for priestly celibacy.

The sustained controversy over obligatory priestly celibacy in the Latin Church attests to the importance of presenting a theology that can articulate well this seemingly obsolete clerical discipline. A review of contemporary literature shows that many works abound on the history, sociology, psychology and spirituality of priestly celibacy. However, very little has been offered in the way of a systematic theology per se. This book, therefore, fills a critical gap in the current theological literature on this important aspect of ecclesial ministry and life.

The Development of Clerical Continence and Celibacy in the Latin Church

T HIS CHAPTER provides a brief historical survey of the development of clerical continence and celibacy in order to prepare the way for a more systematic account in subsequent chapters. Although its focus is primarily on the discipline of celibacy, a more fundamental reality of celibacy in Catholic understanding appears along the way. That is, celibacy is a charism, or gift, given by the Holy Spirit to those men called to exercise the ministry of deacon, priest, or bishop in the Church. By giving proper attention to the charismatic quality of priestly celibacy, one will avoid the error of understanding it as merely a practice enforced by a disciplinary law; rather, it is a spiritual gift that offers the ordained minister a greater detachment from earthly ties that would prevent him from achieving a more intimate union with Christ. Among the benefits of enjoying this close union with Christ, the priest is freer to serve the faithful entrusted to him and he becomes a prophetic sign of future life in heaven.

The Biblical Foundations of Clerical Continence and Celibacy

CELIBACY IN THE OLD TESTAMENT was not prized as a noble calling and therefore was not a permanent or instituted state of life in Jewish culture. Because of the promise that God made to Abraham—that he would become the father of many nations—the Israelites looked on celibacy in a negative light, with marriage as the true source of fruitfulness and blessing. To remain unmarried and childless was to be the object of shame,[1] while bearing many children was a sign of divine blessing (see Gen 22:17; Ps 127:3–4).[2] Virginity in a bride, however, was the object of high praise (see Dt 22:14–29), and conversely, loss of virginity entailed a loss of honor (see 2 Sam 13:2–18; Lam 5:11). All priests were obliged to marry a virgin (see Lev 21:13f; Ezek 44:22).

The prophet Jeremiah was an exception to the divine mandate to marry (see Jer 1:4–10; 16:2–4). His celibacy symbolized the Lord God's withdrawal of the covenantal blessing: peace, love, and the virtues of an ideal married life that were forbidden to Jeremiah. God commanded Jeremiah to remain celibate so as to prophesy the imminence of Israel's chastisement. Under the influence of his predecessor Hosea, Jeremiah had a keen appreciation of the covenant between the Lord God and his people. When he saw that Israel did not listen to the warnings of God and that catastrophe was inevitable and the old covenant would come to an end, Jeremiah prophesied a new covenant (see Jer 31:31–34).

Temporary continence was nonetheless practiced for specific purposes. Levites and priests were required to practice ritual continence during their time of service in the temple (see 1 Sam 21:4–5), and all Jewish adult men were admonished to avoid sexual intercourse before worship (see Ex 19:15). Some men and women took the Nazarite vow (see Nm 6), which originally seems to have required some form of temporary continence.[3]

In the Hebrew tradition, the notion of ritual, or cultic, uncleanness was prevalent, and it excluded those affected, particularly a priest, from participating in communal worship. The *purity laws* were those laws in the Pentateuch that qualified certain actions, states of being, persons, or

---

1. See Sarah in Gen 16:1–2, Rachel in Gen 30:1, and Hannah in 1 Sam 1; concerning Jephthah's vow, see 11:37–50.

2. All scriptural citations are from *The New Revised Standard Version* (Nashville, Tenn.: Thomas Nelson, 1990), except those specifically indicated as being from the *Revised Standard Version, Catholic Edition* (Camden, N.J.: Thomas Nelson, 1966).

3. See Max Weber, *Ancient Judaism*, trans. Hans H. Gerth and Don Martindale (Glencoe, Ill.: Free Press, 1952), 94–95.

things as pure or impure. *Ritual purity* refers primarily to one's ability to participate in the cultic acts in the Temple, whereas *ritual impurity* signified a condition, usually temporary, that resulted from the normal cycle of human life: birth, disease, sexual activity, and death.[4] The married priest regulated his sexual activity by means of temporary continence for the sake of safeguarding ritual purity.

Later Judaism showed indications that the unmarried state was more highly regarded than before, as in the cases of Judith (see Jud 16:22) and Anna (see Lk 2:37), and celibacy became an instituted way of life with the appearance of the Essene community in the second century.[5] Yet despite this later development, there is no evidence of an institutionalized celibacy among the Israelites.

Within the New Covenant, however, there was a fundamental precedent for celibacy as a permanent state: the life of Jesus Christ. His celibacy is assumed in the traditions about him rather than being explicitly mentioned in the New Testament.[6] Some scriptural passages, however, do imply the celibacy of Jesus. The New Testament portrays Jesus as having no earthly ties. For example, no family member was present at his death except for his mother (see Jn 19:25). If Jesus had had a wife, presumably she would have been present or at least mentioned in this event and others in his life.

Furthermore, the manner of life that Jesus lived was compatible with his mission of evangelization but not with marriage. Jesus's chosen lifestyle expressed his mission, for he left his home and family in Nazareth in order to live as an itinerant preacher, consciously renouncing a permanent dwelling: "The Son of man has nowhere to lay his head" (Mt 8:20). Jean Galot argued that Jesus lived as an unmarried man for at least two reasons. First, it was appropriate that he whose mission was the spiritual engendering of a new humanity should abstain from

4. See John P. Meier, *Law and Love*, vol. 4 of *A Marginal Jew: Rethinking the Historical Jesus* (New Haven, Conn.: Yale University Press, 2009), 343–50. A more complete explanation of ritual purity will be given in chapter 3.

5. See J. Massingberd Ford, *A Trilogy on Wisdom and Celibacy*, The Cardinal O'Hara Series: Studies and Research in Christian Theology at Notre Dame 4 (Notre Dame, Ind.: Prentice-Hall, 1967), 28–43.

6. See John P. Meier, *The Roots of the Problem and the Person*, vol. 1 of *A Marginal Jew: Rethinking the Historical Jesus* (New York: Doubleday, 1991), 332–35.

bodily engendering; his fruitfulness and offspring belonged to the order of grace. Second, Jesus came to reveal God's love for all people. If Jesus had chosen to marry, he would have been bound to a particular love that would have concealed his universal love. His love for one woman would have distanced himself from all other women.[7]

Moreover, in the context of reaffirming the biblical teaching of the indissolubility of marriage (see Gen 1:27, 2:24), Jesus was asked by his disciples: "If such is the case of a man with his wife, it is better not to marry" (Mt 19:10). He answered them by describing three ways in which a person can be a *eunuch*: "Not everyone can accept this teaching, but only those to whom it is given. For there are eunuchs who have been so from birth, and there are eunuchs who have been made eunuchs by others, and there are eunuchs who have made themselves eunuchs for the sake of the kingdom of heaven. Let anyone accept this who can."

The noun *eunuch* occurs nowhere else in the New Testament with the exception of the story of the Ethiopian eunuch (see Acts 8:27–39). Of the three manners in which one is incapable of sexual activity, the third alone is voluntary: "eunuchs *who have made themselves* eunuchs." These people do so "for the sake of the kingdom of heaven," that is, for the Kingdom that Jesus was proclaiming and initiating (see Mt 4:17).

It is possible that Jesus was describing himself as such a voluntary eunuch for the sake of the Kingdom of heaven. Eunuchs were treated as outcasts in the Jewish community and were forced to live away from the Jewish people because it was considered improper for a man who had been deprived of his power to transmit life to come close to the God of life. Jesus, in using the word *eunuch*, may have been referring to himself as one considered as a eunuch and an outcast by his enemies, who also labeled him a glutton, a drunkard, a friend of tax collectors and sinners (see Mt 11:19), and a Samaritan with a demon (see Jn 8:48).[8] In speaking this way, Jesus was also stating that an unmarried person was no longer to be considered automatically as an outcast and sepa-

7. See Jean Galot, *Theology of the Priesthood*, trans. Robert Balducelli (San Francisco: Ignatius, 1985), 230–32.

8. See Francis J. Moloney, "Matthew 19, 3–12 and Celibacy: A Redactional and Form Critical Study /1/," *Journal for the Study of the New Testament* 2 (January 1979): 50–53, at 50–51, 235; see also Dt 23:1–2; Lev 21:17–20.

rated from God. Jesus can be seen as implicitly inviting his disciples to follow him in the state of being a "eunuch" for the Kingdom of heaven. He taught that there is a resurrection into a heavenly life in which there is no marriage (see Mt 22:30–32). It follows that celibacy, both his own and that of his disciples, was a prophetic lifestyle that bears witness both to the resurrection and to the Kingdom.

Noteworthy is that in Mt 19:11–12, Jesus spoke of one's choice to be a "eunuch for the sake of the kingdom of heaven" in terms of *gift*, rather than of an obligation or discipline: "Not everyone can accept this teaching, but only those to whom it is given" (Mt 19:11). This "teaching" is offered as a gift for those disciples whom Jesus calls to follow him. These words of Jesus form a foundation for the Catholic Church's perennial understanding of continence and celibacy as a gift (or charism) that is ordered to spiritual and ministerial fruitfulness.

It is in this Kingdom that Jesus would promise eternal life (see Jn 3:5, 17:3; Rom 6:23). In this context, a clear difference between Jewish and Christian notions of eternal life should be noted. In the Old Testament, it was imperative for the Jew to marry because there was no clear understanding of the resurrection of the body; Jews believed that they in some sense would survive death and live on through their offspring.[9] But with the Resurrection of Jesus, Christians can hope for an individual resurrection. Because Jesus rose from the dead and would bring to life those who died believing in him (see Jn 6:40 and 1 Thess 4:16–18), a Christian could in good conscience forego marriage for the sake of eternal life in the Kingdom of heaven. Jesus's own celibacy can thus be seen as a prophetic lifestyle, linked to his Resurrection.

As for the apostles, it is evident that Simon Peter was married because Jesus cured his mother-in-law at Capernaum (see Mt 8:14–15; Mk 1:29–31; Lk 4:38–39). Paul, on his part, wrote that he was celibate (see 1 Cor 7:7–8). The majority of fathers believed that he either had never been married or at least was a widower.[10] As for John, who was particu-

---

9. However, in later Jewish thought there are signs of belief in a resurrection: see 2 Maccabees 7, Lk 20:27–40, Mt 22:23–33, Mk 12:18–27.

10. See Ambrosiaster, *In Epistolam B. Pauli ad Corinthios Secundam*, 11, 2, in *Patrologia Latina* 17, 320a; Ambrose, *De Virginitate*, in *Patrologia Latina* 16, 315a; John Chrysostom, *In Epistolam ad Philippenses Argumentum et Homiliae* 1–15, 13, 3, in *Patrologia Graeca* 62, 279d.

larly beloved of Jesus (see Jn 13:23; 19:26; 21:7), several Church fathers attributed the special love of Jesus to John's state of perpetual virginity.[11] Other than Peter, Paul, and John, nothing substantial is known about the matrimonial status of the remaining apostles. The fathers believed that those apostles who were married on meeting with Jesus gave up their conjugal lives and practiced perfect and perpetual continence thereafter.[12] This apostolic continence or celibacy enabled them, among other things, to lead lives as itinerant preachers. Jesus promised great rewards to his disciples, including the Twelve, who had left their wives in order to follow him: "Peter said: 'Lo, we have left our homes and followed you.' And [Jesus] said to them, 'Truly, I say to you, there is no man who has left house or wife or brothers or parents or children, for the sake of the kingdom of God, who will not receive manifold more in this time, and in the age to come eternal life.'"[13]

The previously mentioned biblical sources, however, tell little concerning the lives of the apostles. What, then, did the apostles *teach* about marriage and the vocation to continence and celibacy? Paul provided the scriptural passages that justify celibacy for the lay, single Christian. In his first letter to the Corinthians (see 1 Cor 7:25–40), Paul counseled the unmarried faithful of Corinth to remain celibate, as he himself was (see 1 Cor 7:7–8), so that they might dedicate their time and energy more fully to serving Christ in his Church: "I want you to be free from anxieties. The unmarried man is anxious about the affairs of the Lord, how to please the Lord; but the married man is anxious about the affairs of the world, how to please his wife, and his interests are divided" (1 Cor 7:32–34a). Celibacy gives the freedom to be concerned about the "affairs of

11. See Epiphanius, *Panarion (Adversus Haereses)*, Haer. 58, 4, in *Patrologia Graeca* 41, 1016a; Jerome, *Adversus Iovinianum* I, in *Patrologia Latina* 23, 246b–c; Augustine, *Tractatus in Evangelium Ioannis*, 124, 7, *Corpus Christianorum* 36, 687. Jacobus de Voragine's *Golden Legend* (c. 1260) recounts a common belief in the Middle Ages that Jesus called the Apostle John to follow him on the day that John was to be married.

12. See Christian Cochini, *The Apostolic Origins of Priestly Celibacy*, trans. Nelly Marans (San Francisco: Ignatius, 1990), 83. According to Cochini, this patristic belief became part of the preaching in the great Christian centers as early as the end of the second and the beginning of the third century.

13. Lk 18:28–30 (*Revised Standard Version* translation). *Wife* is not listed in the parallel passages of Mt 19:27–30 and Mk 10:28–31, although a man who leaves his house and children would seemingly have to leave his wife, too.

the Lord" and thus "to please the Lord" with the whole heart (1 Cor 7:32). Paul nevertheless clearly emphasized that the call to celibacy is a counsel and not a precept.

The scriptural passages cited earlier, particularly 1 Corinthians 7:25–40 and Matthew 19:12, describe, as a Christian ideal, the theological and spiritual value of celibacy *in general*, which can be equally valid for any Christian who wishes to live a consecrated life. But these biblical citations do not seem to show any particular connection between celibacy and the *ministries* of the early Church.[14]

The Pastoral Letters, however, include a discussion of marriage and ecclesial ministry; that is, a candidate for the offices of bishop (*epískopos*), priest (*presbúteros*) and deacon (*diákonos*) must have been married only once. He must be a "man of one wife" (*mías gunaíkos ándra*; 1 Tm 3:2, 3:12; Ti 1:6). Exegetes have usually given one of two interpretations of "man of one wife": it prohibits either remarriage or polygamy.[15] The first interpretation holds that a candidate had been and could be married only once. Therefore, by implication, if his wife died, he could not marry again. The second view posits that the minister was forbidden to have more than one wife at the same time; this would simply be an exhortation to observe marital chastity. It is doubtful that this latter meaning is intended here, because polygamy was completely unacceptable in any case for Christians and such a man would have been excluded *a priori* from ministerial office. The first interpretation is therefore the more likely of the two.

According to Ignace de la Potterie, the juridical quality of the formula "man of one wife" indicates a specific criterion that Timothy and his assistants would keep in mind as they scrutinized candidates for office.[16] The ceremonious and formal sound of the formula implies a precise,

14. See Ignace de la Potterie, "The Biblical Foundation of Priestly Celibacy," in *For Love Alone: Reflections on Priestly Celibacy*, ed. Jose Sánchez (Slough, U.K.: St. Pauls, 1993), 13–30, at 14. This essay has been posted by the Congregation for the Clergy on the Vatican website: "The Biblical Foundation of Priestly Celibacy." *The Holy See*. http://www.vatican.va/roman_curia/congregations/cclergy/documents/rc_con_cclergy_doc_01011993_bfoun_en.html.

15. See Ignace de la Potterie, "'Mari d'une seule femme': le sens théologique d'une formule paulinienne," in *Paul de Tarse: apôtre du notre temps*, ed. Lorenzo de Lorenzi (Rome: Abbaye de Saint Paul, 1979), 619–38, at 619–23.

16. See ibid., 631–32, 636–38.

concrete legal demand of a fixed, technical, and stereotyped nature—screening out candidates for office who had been married more than once. Perhaps the reason underlying this rule is that remarriage was not particularly esteemed in late antiquity, and many early Church fathers considered second marriages as veiled adultery and disreputable.[17] This Pauline injunction, therefore, may have been a prudent measure of eliminating doubtful ministerial candidates.

In addition to these two common understandings of "man of one wife," some Church fathers posited a third reading, one that would enjoin sexual continence for married men on assuming ministry.[18] In order to explain this third patristic interpretation, de la Potterie gave the following argument: from the strictly biblical viewpoint, "man of one wife" is the only passage in the New Testament where an identical norm is laid down for the three groups of ministers and only for them. The phrase "man of one wife" is used to specify a requirement for *epískopos* (see 1 Tim 3:2), *presbúteros* (see Ti 1:6), *and diákonos* (see 1 Tim 3:12). It is never said of other Christians but is a requirement for these ministers in the exercise of their ecclesial ministry.

De la Potterie related these three passages to a fourth, 1 Timothy 5:9, which includes a complementary formula "woman of one husband" (*hénos andrós guné*). It refers to widows, at least sixty years old, who could become enrolled in an order of widows, provided that, among other things, they had been married only once. The formula "woman of one husband" does not simply apply to any Christian woman but only to an elderly widow who would exercise a ministry in the community, perhaps similar to that of a deaconess.[19] This prohibition against second

17. Clement of Alexandria, who was probably celibate, argued that only those Christians entered a second marriage who were incapable of continence because Paul allowed the second marriage for this reason (see 1 Cor 7:8ff). See Clement, *Stromata*, 3, 18, 107, 5–108, 2, in *Grieschische Christliche Schriftsteller* 2/4, 246, 5–20.

18. De la Potterie is not the author of this third interpretation of "man of one wife." While he has provided the specific argument outlined previously, the interpretation itself has patristic roots. See Ambrose, *Epistolae*, in *Patrologia Latina* 16, 1205b–c; Ambrosiaster, *In Epistolam B. Pauli ad Timotheum primam*, III, 12–13, in *Patrologia Latina* 17, 470b–71b; John Chrysostom, *Homiliae in I Tim. Prol.*, in *Patrologia Graeca* 62, 503f, and *Hom. 2, in Tit. I*, in *Patrologia Graeca* 62, 671; Eusebius of Caesarea, *De Demonstratione Evangelica* I, 9, in *Grieschische Christliche Schriftsteller*, 23, 43.

19. See de la Potterie, "The Biblical Foundation of Priestly Celibacy," 15.

marriages highlights the fidelity of a wife exclusively to her first and only husband, even beyond his death. As mentioned earlier, in antiquity remarriage bore the stigma of incontinence and this is clear in 1 Timothy 5:9–12 in Paul's words about widows. Younger widows frequently married again because they could not live continently. A widow who had been married only once should by this fact have already been tested with respect to continence. Marrying a second time is, for 1 Timothy 5:9, equivalent to being unable to live continently.

The validity of this argument depends upon the parallelism between the injunction for widows and that for the *epískopos, presbúteros*, and *diákonos* (see 1 Tm 3:2, 3:12; Ti 1:6) when the juridical sense of both phrases is compared. Because both phrases ("man of one wife" and "woman of one husband") are used in the context of ecclesial ministry, and because the latter phrase refers to the discipline of continence, by inference "man of one wife" would then require that a married cleric be bound to practice perfect sexual continence, that is, to live with his wife as though he had none (see 1 Cor 7:29), as well as forbidding a second marriage (digamy) on the death of his wife.[20] A widowed minister could not then remarry because he could not consummate his new marriage, on account of his commitment to continence. Moreover, as noted previously, second marriages were frowned on in the early Church, being seen by Christians as a sign of the inability to live in perfect continence.[21] As will be shown in the following, this third interpretation of "man of one wife" was used by Pope Saint Siricius and several fathers and subsequently became part of Catholic theological and canonical tradition.

The apostle Paul, on the other hand, seemed to argue for the continuation of the conjugal life for married apostles in 1 Corinthians 9:5: "Do we not have the right to take along a sister-woman [*adelphén gunaíka*], as do the rest of the apostles, and the brothers of the Lord, and Cephas?" What does this passage mean, and does the phrase *sister-woman* mean *wife*, as some translations render it?[22] In biblical Greek, *guné* generally

---

20. Ibid., 15–18.

21. See Cholij, *Clerical Celibacy in East and West*, 12–21.

22. See *New American Bible* and *Revised Standard Version*. The translation of 1 Cor 9:5 is my own.

means *woman*, although it can also signify *wife*. *Adelphé*, however, signifies *sister* and thus specifies here the type of woman that traveled with the Apostles: a *sister-woman* or *sister-wife*. There is agreement among the fathers about the interpretation of this phrase, namely, that it does not refer to women with whom the Apostles continued to live a conjugal life, but to women who served the material needs of their apostolic ministry, as did the women who followed Jesus (see Mt 27:55–56, Lk 8:2–3).[23] In cases where this *sister-woman* was also the wife of an apostle, her husband would be required to live with her "as a sister." With Paul, who wrote these words and was celibate, it is evident that his relationship with such a *sister-woman* would entail no conjugal activity.

With regard to the biblical roots of clerical continence and celibacy, the New Testament data concerning the regulation of the lives of the apostles and of early church ministers shows them as neither obliged to marry nor explicitly bound to observe the Old Testament regulations concerning ritual purity. Rather, the motivations for decisions in embracing the continent and celibate life are unique to the New Testament: (1) the example of Christ and Paul (celibacy); (2) the ostensible life of the married Apostles after their call to ministry (continence); (3) the vocation of the eunuch "for the Kingdom of heaven," which is understood to be a ministerial charism or gift; (4) the belief in Christ's Resurrection as the cause of the elect's resurrection; (5) Paul's counsel that an unmarried man be free of anxiety; and (6) one particular interpretation of the Pauline formula "man of one wife." The early Church drew from these New Testament themes in order to explain and promote clerical continence and celibacy.

The next section of this chapter is a study of the development of the *teaching* and *discipline* of clerical continence and celibacy in the Latin Church. Through the various texts that are studied, one can discern several elements of an underlying *theology* that flows forth from the teaching and supports the discipline. A question that merits reflection is whether the teaching and discipline were influenced by New Testament motivations such as those mentioned earlier or whether they

---

23. See Clement of Alexandria, *Stromata*, III, 6, in *Griechische Christliche Schriftsteller* 52, 220; Tertullian, *De Monogamia*, 8, in *Corpus Christianorum* II, 1239–40; Jerome, *Adversus Jovinianum* I, in *Patrologia Latina* 23, 245c–d; Cochini, *The Apostolic Origins of Priestly Celibacy*, 79–82.

were drawn from the Old Testament or other sources. The answer to this question may strengthen or weaken the foundations of the teaching, discipline, and theology of clerical continence and celibacy in the Catholic Church.

The first disciplinary decree in the Latin Church on clerical continence and celibacy occurred only in the early fourth century. It will be useful, however, to look at prior patristic writings that set the tone for the subsequent conciliar decrees.

Clerical Continence and Celibacy from the Patristic Era to the Second Vatican Council

WITH THE GROWTH of the Church in the postapostolic era, clerical life also developed. Although ample documentation points to the existence of celibate clerics in the early Church, it seems that many major clerics (bishops, priests, and deacons) were married.[24] There are at least three reasons why this may have been the case: (1) many Christians in the first generations of the Church were from a Jewish background and thus celibacy was not part of their culture; (2) in the pagan culture in which the majority of Christians lived, widespread sexual immorality greatly weakened marriage and family life and thus made it difficult for the Church to cultivate an environment in which celibacy could grow; and (3) the early Church wanted to emphasize the dignity of the married state against the heresies of the Encratites and Cathars.[25] As Christians successfully strengthened married life, a culture of virginal celibacy began to emerge.

What, then, are the origins of clerical continence and celibacy in the early Church? One view that has been influential, but that has been in rapid decline, was formulated in the nineteenth century by the German scholar Francis Funk. It has been elaborated more recently by Roger Gryson and can be summarized in the following manner.[26]

In the early Church, clerical celibacy was optional. Most of the apos-

24. See Roger Gryson, *Les origines du célibat ecclésiastique du premier au septième siècle* (Gembloux: Duculot, 1970), 42.

25. See Stefan Heid, *Celibacy in the Early Church: The Beginnings of a Discipline of Obligatory Continence for Clerics in East and West*, trans. Michael J. Miller (San Francisco: Ignatius, 2000), 61–64.

26. See Gryson, *Les origines du célibat ecclésiastique*, 203–4.

tles were married men, as were subsequent bishops, priests, and deacons, who were married and freely exercised their sexual rights in marriage. It is possible that from time to time some practiced voluntary
continence. As time went on, a movement inimical to marriage and the
body, influenced by pagan philosophies such as Stoicism and Neopla-
tonism, as well as the Encratite and Gnostic heresies, entered the life
of the Church so that, beginning with the second century, consecrated
virginity and later monasticism were increasingly encountered. In the
third century, this ecclesial development progressed, and an increasing
sacralization of Church office allowed foreign concepts of cultic or ritual purity to invade the Christian understanding of worship. Finally, in
the fourth century, with the Spanish Council of Elvira (305), this asceticism and sacralization joined forces in clerical discipline. What resulted
was the custom of both clerics and laypeople to abstain from marital
intercourse on days when the Eucharist was celebrated. In the Eastern
Church, married clerics could engage in marital intercourse with certain restrictions because the liturgy was not celebrated daily. On the
other hand, the introduction in the Latin Church of the daily celebration of the Eucharist toward the end of the fourth century led to the discipline of perfect and perpetual continence for major clerics.[27] This left
the door open for the gradual displacement of married by unmarried
clerics. Eventually, in the eleventh century, the Catholic Church made
the rule of celibacy binding on all major clerics of the Latin rite.[28]

There are several errors associated with the Gryson's theory, two
of which are his arguments that both anticorporeal philosophies and
ritual purity motivated the development of clerical continence in the
Latin Church.[29]

First, with regard to Encratism, a collective name for various anticorporeal movements: this did exist in the early Church in various re-

27. Ibid., 127, 197.

28. This summary of Gryson's theory has been aided by Heid, *Celibacy in the Early
Church*, 21.

29. See Gryson, *Les origines du célibat ecclésiastique*, 43, 203. Peter Brown and Lisa Sowle
Cahill also advanced similar theories. See Peter Brown, *The Body and Society: Men, Women, and
Sexual Renunciation in Early Christianity* (New York: Columbia University Press, 1988); Lisa
Sowle Cahill, *Sex, Gender, and Christian Ethics* (Cambridge: Cambridge University Press, 1996),
171–73.

gions. However, a direct influence of Encratite views on clerical life cannot be proved. On the contrary, Encratism existed as a strong force in the first centuries only in Asia Minor and Syria. Marcion and Tatian, two of the most prominent promoters of Encratism, were excommunicated in Rome because of their views, which included a strong ascetical tendency and the rejection of marriage.[30] Tatian moved to the region of Syria, the stronghold of the Encratite movement, shortly after his excommunication. In Syria around this time, perfect continence was required of all Christians and admission to baptism depended on it. This ascetical practice led to the eventual dissolution of existing marriages.

It seems unlikely that the Latin discipline of continence was introduced in order to keep up with the severe asceticism of the Syrians. Rome, the center of orthodoxy in the second century, clearly rejected the heresy and extreme asceticism of the Encratite movement. The latter, however, prodded the Latin Church to develop a sound, sober approach to asceticism and a balanced perspective on the body. As a result, the view of the Latin Church concerning the body ultimately influenced certain segments of the Eastern Church by introducing a more balanced discipline of continence.[31]

The popes continued to oppose rigorism, such as in the battle of two popes, Saint Callistus (d. 222) and Saint Pontian (d. 235), against the priest Saint Hippolytus (d. 236). Moreover, as Platonism became more popular with Christian thinkers, theologians in the West and the East recognized an unhealthy dualism in the Gnostic heresies that attacked the Church. Clement of Alexandria (ca. 150–ca. 215), for example, fought hard against this dualistic Gnosticism.[32] As a result, popes and the bishops of the Latin Church neither accepted these heretical ideas, nor did they attempt to impose them on the clergy and laity.

However, according to the theory popularized by Gryson, the severity of Rome, influenced by anticorporeal trends, suppressed the pristine, humane practice that is still maintained in the Eastern Church. Therefore, it was only by means of a law imposed on by the Latin hierarchy at

30. See Henry Chadwick, "Enkrateia," in *Reallexikon für Antike und Christentum* 5 (1962): 352–53.

31. See Heid, *Celibacy in the Early Church*, 62–64.

32. See Clement of Alexandria, *Stromata*, especially Book 3.

the end of the fourth century that major clerics were forced to maintain perfect and perpetual continence. Stefan Heid thus criticized this historical understanding:

Behind this *opinio communis* concerning a gradual intrusion of obligatory continence into the discipline for clerics, there is some sort of idea that in the beginning the clergy "naturally" made use of their marriage rights without specific regulations; the "unnatural" continence became widespread only gradually through the influence of ideas that were hostile to the body. It is considered improbable that an entire professional class would live more or less continently. At the same time this thesis is not infrequently associated with a particular image of the Church. If an ecclesiastical discipline of continence begins with an assembly of bishops, the one in Elvira, then this necessarily creates the impression that it was only gradually imposed from above against the vehement resistance from below.[33]

The second argument of Gryson claimed that clerical continence was motivated by an infusion into clerical life and liturgy of an exaggerated concern to preserve a Christian form of the Jewish notion of ritual purity, which, as described earlier, were laws in the Pentateuch that qualified certain actions, states of being, persons, or things as clean or unclean with regard to one's ability to participate in worship in the Temple. Gryson and others held that the desire to safeguard ritual purity was the primary motivation for married clerics to practice perfect continence and for unmarried men to embrace strict celibacy when entering ministry.[34] The concept of ritual purity, however, is complex and can be easily misunderstood through the use of modern categories foreign to the original sense of the term. One well-established fact about ritual purity in the Christian tradition, however, is its link with the Eucharist.[35] This connection raises a pertinent question: Was the daily celebration of the Eucharist the motivation for the introduction of clerical

33. Heid, *Celibacy in the Early Church*, 21–22. See also 15–18 on the legend of Paphnutius, an alleged father of Nicaea who, with the approval of the other bishops, advocated allowing married clergy to continue their conjugal lives. Although Gryson accepted the legitimacy of this historical account (see *Les origines du célibat ecclésiastique*, 87–93), the scholarly consensus today accepts the position of Winkelmann—that the story was fabricated. See Friedhelm Winkelmann, "Paphnutios, der Bekenner und Bischof: Probleme der Koptischen Literatur," in *Wissenschaftliche Beiträge der Martin Luther-Universität Halle-Wittenberg*, vol. I (1968): 145–53.

34. See Gryson, *Les origines du célibat ecclésiastique*, 197–204.

35. The relationship between priestly celibacy and the Eucharist is studied in chapters 3 and 4.

continence and celibacy in the Latin Church? Gryson maintained that perfect continence for the married cleric arose from the introduction of the daily celebration of the Eucharist in the West, while in the East the Eucharist was not celebrated daily, giving rise to periodic continence; that is, married clerics simply abstained from sexual intercourse the night before celebrating the Eucharist.[36]

Very little is actually known about the particulars surrounding the celebration of the liturgy in the early Latin Church, and there is not enough evidence to show conclusively that the daily offering of the Eucharist was the norm of the Latin Church in the fourth century. It was only at the end of the fourth century, at the very earliest, that the daily Eucharist started to become a widespread practice in certain particular churches within the Latin Church. This was considerably later than the first evidence of a widespread discipline of clerical continence, for example, the legislation of Elvira (305), which bound married clerics to perfect and perpetual continence.[37]

Daniel Callam has asserted that asceticism and virginity, rather than the desired protection of ritual purity, were the motivating factors behind the developing custom of the daily Eucharist: "Daily Mass should not be viewed as a cause, but as an effect, of clerical continence."[38] According to Callam, fourth-century asceticism did not view virginity and continence as effects of celebrating the Eucharist each and every day. Rather they were goods in themselves and necessary for a clergy who were expected to be models of prayer and Christian virtue. Early sources indicate that Mass was not celebrated every day in all places, and that "ritual purity is a subtle and complicated phenomenon involving fundamental religious instincts, the identity of the individual, the preservation of social order, and principles of hygiene."[39]

It is also unlikely that clerics of the Latin Church would suddenly,

36. See Gryson, *Les origines du célibat ecclésiastique*, 203–04.

37. Cyprian of Carthage (c. 208–258) referred to daily Mass in the 250s (see *Letter* 57), but it is not clear whether it was a universal practice or one that continued.

38. Daniel Callam, "The Frequency of Mass in the Latin Church, ca. 400," *Theological Studies* 45 (1984): 613–50, at 636.

39. Ibid., 636. The Church fathers on the whole accepted the ritual purity argument as a sound explanation of clerical continence and celibacy, and there is no evidence that they saw it as an expression of unhealthy Christian liturgical spirituality.

unreflectively, and obediently observe perfect continence by mandate of the popes and bishops, and there is no evidence of a widespread protest against such papal and episcopal mandates. Nor is it conclusive that the concern to protect ritual purity was intrinsically bound up with the daily celebration of the Eucharist and provided the primary motivation for clerical continence and celibacy, as Gryson claimed.[40]

With regard to the background to the fourth-century magisterial statements on clerical continence and celibacy in the Latin Church, very little documentation from the second and third centuries treats explicitly of clerical continence and celibacy. One of the few sources is Clement of Alexandria, who stated that a married cleric, having raised his children, had to live with his wife from the day of his ordination as with a *woman-helper* or *sister-woman*. Such a married cleric was called to live the life of the married apostle, as a perfect Christian without sexual relations.[41]

The prohibition of remarriage continued for major clerics in the Latin Church during this time. Some clerics certainly disregarded this discipline, but the prohibition remained. In the third century, the Eastern Church authorities are in fact stronger witnesses to a widespread discipline of clerical continence.[42] It is further significant that, although early documents attest to the existence of major clerics of the Latin Church with children, none of them states that these children were begotten after ordination. Rather, sexual intercourse by major clerics was not tolerated by the Church authorities and was subject to ecclesiastical sanctions.[43]

Such, then, are some of the references to clerical continence and celibacy in the second and third centuries. In the fourth century, however, the first conciliar legislation concerning a consistent practice of clerical continence and celibacy appears in the Latin Church. With the

---

40. See Gryson, *Les origines du célibat ecclésiastique*, 200, 203.

41. See Clement of Alexandria, *Stromata*, 3, 18, 107, 5–108, 2, in *Griechische Christliche Schriftsteller*, 2/4, 246, 5–20.

42. See *Didascalia Apostolorum* 4, in *Corpus Scriptorum Christianorum Orientalium* (*Scriptores Syri*), 176: 45, 15–46, 4; Eusebius, *Demonstratio Evangelica* 1, 9, 20ff, in *Griechische Christliche Schriftsteller Eus.* 6: 42, 33–43, 5; Origen, *Comm.* in Mt 14:22, in *Griechische Christliche Schriftsteller Orig.* 10: 337, 19–338, 7.

43. See Heid, *Celibacy in the Early Church*, 143.

lessening and eventual cessation of the persecution of the Church, provisional councils and synods were convened and record keeping was facilitated.[44] The regional Council of Elvira (305), although convened during continuing persecution, produced the first written law in the East or in the West with regard to clerical continence. In canon 33, the council required perfect continence for all married clerics under pain of deposition: "It has seemed good absolutely to forbid the bishops, presbyters, and deacons, that is, all clerics who have a position in the ministry, to have [sexual] relations with their wives and beget children. Whoever in fact does this is to be removed from the honor of the clerical state."[45] This disciplinary canon dealt with an infraction of an apparently existing observance. Neither it nor any other canon gave an explanation or justification for the law; it simply demanded obedience. It is therefore unlikely that it was an innovation that would have deprived married clerics of a long-established right.

Furthermore, it is a particular characteristic of law that the origin of a legal system consists in oral traditions, which only slowly receive a fixed, written form. Cardinal Alfons Stickler has given historical examples of this process:

It was only after centuries and for various sociological reasons that the Romans formulated in writing the law of the Twelve Tables. The German peoples only compiled their popular juridical system and customs in written form after many centuries of their actual existence. Up to that time, their law was unwritten and was handed on orally. No one would thereby affirm that, on this basis, their law (*ius*) was not obligatory and that its observance was left to the free will of the individual. Like the legal system of any large community, that of the early Church consisted for the greater part in regulations and obligations which were handed

44. The following summary on the development of the discipline of clerical continence and celibacy from the early Church until the early twentieth century relies on Roman Cholij, "Priestly Celibacy in Patristics and in the History of the Church," in *For Love Alone, Reflections on Priestly Celibacy*, 31–52, as well as Ray Ryland, "A Brief History of Clerical Celibacy," in *Priestly Celibacy: Its Scriptural, Historical, Spiritual, and Psychological Roots*, ed. Peter M. J. Stravinskas (Mt. Pocono, Penn.: Newman House Press, 2001), 27–44.

45. Council of Elvira, can. 33, in E. J. Jonkers, ed., *Acta et Symbola Conciliorum Quae Saeculo Quarto Habita Sunt* (Leiden: Brill, 1954), 12f; see Cochini, *The Apostolic Origins of Priestly Celibacy*, 158–61. All translations of texts of the councils and Church fathers are mine unless otherwise noted.

on orally, particularly during the three centuries of persecution, which made it difficult to fix them in writing.[46]

Thus, not only those norms that had been written down were obligatory, for the general sense of law (*ius*) is not equivalent to a norm (*lex*). Law is a legal obligation, whether it be established orally, handed on by means of custom, or already expressed in writing. A norm, however, is a statute or a rule established in written form and legitimately promulgated. It is probable, therefore, that certain ecclesial laws, including those dealing with clerical continence, were obligatory although not written down. Thus, the Second Council of Carthage (390), as will be seen, appealed to an unwritten law rooted in apostolic tradition to justify perfect and perpetual clerical continence.

In 314 Constantine called together the bishops of the empire at Arles to address the Donatist heresy. Canon 29 of this council forbade married bishops, priests, and deacons to have conjugal relations with their wives, under pain of deposition from the clergy. It is noteworthy that continence for married clerics was tied broadly to ecclesial ministry, which most probably embraced all three clerical ministries (liturgical, prophetic, and pastoral) rather than just one that was exclusively cultic.

The Council of Nicaea (325) likewise upheld the discipline of clerical continence for married clerics in canon 3, which forbade a cleric to live with any woman, with the exception of "his mother or sister or aunt, or of any person who is above suspicion."[47] The rationale behind this particular ruling seems to have been both to protect the chastity of the cleric and to avoid giving public scandal through an irregular living arrangement with a woman. The women living under the same roof with a cleric had to be above suspicion concerning the chastity of the cleric. The wife of a married cleric is not mentioned in this canon and does not fall in the category of any person "above suspicion."

In 384 Bishop Himerius of Spain wrote to Pope Saint Damasus (ca. 305–384) asking for help in dealing with married clergy who were having conjugal relations with their wives and begetting children. Damasus died

---

46. Alfons Stickler, *The Case for Clerical Celibacy: Its Historical Development and Theological Foundations*, trans. Brian Ferme (San Francisco: Ignatius, 1995), 18.

47. Council of Nicaea, canon 3; translation in Norman P. Tanner, ed., *Nicaea I to Lateran V*, vol. 1 of *Decrees of the Ecumenical Councils* (London: Sheed and Ward, 1990), 7.

before he could respond, and thus, his successor Siricius (ca. 334–399) stated in *Directa* (385) that married priests and deacons were bound by perfect and perpetual continence. Whereas the Levites were bound by temporary continence, the priests of the New Testament were bound by perpetual continence, which reflected the superiority of the New Law over the Old. Moreover, Siricius wrote that Christ wanted the beauty of the Church, whose Bridegroom he is, "to shine forth with the splendor of chastity, so that on Judgment Day, when he returns, he may find her without stain or wrinkle."[48]

In *Directa*, Siricius mentioned the Levitical priesthood in the context of liturgical sacrifice to imply that, as the Levites abstained from sexual intercourse in order to offer a worthy sacrifice, so too married clerics should abstain from their wives for the same reason. Siricius also stated that "[we] priests and deacons are bound together by an indissoluble law from the day of our ordination to put our hearts and bodies in sobriety and purity; may we be pleasing to God in all things, in the sacrifices we daily offer."[49]

The next year, Siricius, together with eighty bishops of the Roman Synod, issued *Cum in Unum* (386), in which they stated that those priests and deacons who after ordination beget children were acting against a law of perpetual continence that had bound major clerics from the beginning of the Church.[50] Siricius insisted that the question was not a matter of issuing new precepts but of reminding the clergy of rules that were long established. Some of the clergy had defended their continuing conjugal life by appealing to the biblical phrase "man of one wife" in 1 Timothy 3:2 (bishop), Titus 1:6 (presbyter), and 1 Timothy 3:12 (deacon). Siricius, however, argued that "man of one wife" did not mean that a married bishop in this case could continue conjugal relations after ordination but that a man married only once could be expected to live the life of perfect continence that was required after ordination: "[Paul] was not speaking of a man persisting in the desire

48. Siricius, *Directa*, in *Patrologia Latina* 13, 131b–47a, at 1139a; see Pierre Coustant, ed., *Epistolae Romanorum Pontificum* (Farnborough: Gregg Press, 1967), 623–38.

49. Siricius, *Directa*, in *Patrologia Latina* 13, 1139a.

50. See Siricius, *Cum in Unum*, in *Patrologia Latina* 13, 1160a–61a; Coustant, *Epistolae Romanorum Pontificum*, 655–57.

to beget children, but rather of maintaining future continence (*propter continentiam futuram*)."[51]

According to Siricius, having had only one wife was a requirement for receiving orders, because monogamy was seen as a sign that the candidate would have the capacity to practice perfect continence after ordination. Siricius also argued that the "daily necessities" of the married cleric's ministry necessitated his abstention from conjugal relations.[52] Although the *daily* necessities would include liturgical worship, they also embraced a broader clerical ministry, such as preaching and teaching. Nevertheless, the cultic element of the injunction points to the link between service in the sanctuary and ritual purity, which is a common theme in patristic writings on clerical continence and celibacy. In sum, Siricius used the Pauline formula "man of one wife" to defend clerical continence. However, he was not the first authoritative source to do so: the Syrian *Didascalia Apostolorum*, which dates back to the early third century, also utilized this particular reading of the text.[53]

Later in the century, the Second Council of Carthage was convened amid the crisis of the decline of the Church in North Africa. On June 16, 390, the bishops of northern Africa gathered under the presidency of Genethlius. The conciliar proceedings recorded the following: "Bishop Genethlius says: 'As was previously said, it is fitting that the holy bishops and priests of God as well as the Levites, i.e., those who are in the service of the divine sacraments, observe perfect continence (*continentes esse in omnibus*), so that they may obtain in all simplicity what they are asking from God; what the apostles taught and what antiquity itself observed (*ut quod apostoli docuerunt et ipsa servavit antiquitas*), let us also endeavor to keep.'" The bishops declared unanimously: "It pleases

51. Siricius, *Cum in Unum*, in *Patrologia Latina* 13, 1161a. A similar exegesis is found also in the writings of Church fathers contemporaneous with Siricius: Ambrose, Ambrosiaster, and Epiphanius of Salamis. See Ambrose, *Epistolae*, in *Patrologia Latina* 16, 1205b–c; Ambrosiaster, *In Epistolam B. Pauli ad Timotheum primam*, III, 12–13, in *Patrologia Latina* 17, 470b–71b; Epiphanius, *Panarion* [*Adversus Haereses*], in Karl Holl, ed., *Die Griechischen christlichen Schriftsteller der ersten drei Jahrhunderte*, vol. 31 (Leipzig: J. C. Hinrichs, 1922), 367.

52. See Siricius, *Cum in Unum*, in *Patrologia Latina* 13, 1160a.

53. See *Didascaliae Apostolorum Canonum Ecclesiasticorum Traditionis Apostolicae Versiones Latinae*, in Erik Tidner, ed., *Texte und Untersuchungen zur Geschichte der Altchristlichen Literatur*, vol. 75 (Berlin: Akademie-Verlag, 1963).

us all that bishop, priest, and deacon, guardians of purity, abstain from [conjugal intercourse] with their wives, so that those who serve at the altar may keep perfect chastity."[54]

The presiding bishop, Genethlius, thus said with the approval of his fellow bishops that the rule binding married bishops, priests, and deacons to practice perfect continence accorded with apostolic tradition. This is the strongest fourth-century witness to the *apostolic* tradition of clerical continence. Siricius's decretal *Cum in Unum* (386) had probably already reached the bishops of northern Africa and influenced their thinking. Interestingly, the constant presumption, even at the end of the fourth century, was that ministers were married, or at least a large number of them.

During the late fourth and early fifth century, several Eastern and Western fathers helped to spur the continual development of the theology of clerical continence-celibacy that echoed earlier conciliar statements, such as those of Elvira and the Second Council of Carthage. The teaching of Saint Epiphanius of Salamis (ca. 310–403) is significant insofar as he, an Eastern father, gave testimony to the unity of the Western and Eastern Churches on the matter of clerical continence, rooting it in divine Revelation. Referring to discipline of perfect continence, Epiphanius states that the Church "does not accept as deacon, priest, bishop and subdeacon, be he the husband of a single wife, the man who continues to live with his wife and to beget children. The Church accepts him who, as monogamist, observes continence or widowhood; this is observed above all wherever the canons of the Church are kept faithfully."[55] It is noteworthy that Epiphanius here commented on "man of one wife" in way similar to Siricius: that of requiring perfect and perpetual continence of the major cleric.

During this period several fathers in the Latin Church began to write in defense of consecrated virginity, as well as of clerical continence and celibacy. These teachings helped to strengthen the magisterial authority of the popes during this time. Among these fathers, Saint

---

54. Second Council of Carthage, *Corpus Christianorum* 149, 13; translation from Stickler, *The Case for Clerical Celibacy*, 24. See Cochini, *The Apostolic Origins of Priestly Celibacy*, 3–7.

55. Epiphanius of Salamis, *Panarion*, ed. Holl, 367; translation from Cholij, *Clerical Celibacy in East and West*, 20.

Jerome (ca. 347–420) stood out for his defense of clerical continence. In a letter written against Jovian, Jerome interpreted "man of one wife" in accord with Siricius and went as far as to liken an incontinent bishop to an adulterer: "You certainly would admit that he cannot be a bishop who continues to sire children during his episcopate. For if this is discovered, he will not be considered a husband but will be condemned as an adulterer."[56] Jerome seems to have accused the married bishop of adultery because the latter had acquired through ordination a new spouse, namely the Church. Jerome here used a spousal paradigm to buttress the argument for clerical continence and celibacy.

Jerome also referred to Paul's exhortation in 1 Corinthians 7:5–6— that spouses can practice periodic continence for the sake of prayer—in order to argue for perfect priestly continence. The priest must always pray because he must "always offer sacrifices for the people" and "[i]f he must always pray, he therefore must always abstain from the use of marriage."[57]

In 456 Pope Saint Leo the Great (ca. 400–461) wrote to Bishop Rusticus of Narbonne in answer to the question, "Of those [clerics] who minister at the altar and have wives, whether they are able licitly to have conjugal relations?" Leo responded in the negative, writing that once the ministers of the altar are ordained, they are no longer permitted to do so. Therefore, so that their union may change from carnal to spiritual "it is necessary that they, without sending away their wives, live with them as if they did not have them, so that conjugal love be safeguarded and nuptial activity cease."[58] Leo made it clear that bishops and priests were to live Paul's exhortation in a particular manner: "live with [their wives] as if they did not have them" (1 Cor 7:29). In most cases, these clerics had to separate from their wives, the latter being supported by the Church, either by entering a convent or by living in a community of women specifically established by ecclesial authorities.[59]

Up to the first half of the sixth century, the magisterial and patris-

---

56. Jerome, *Adversus Jovinianum* I, in *Patrologia Latina* 23, 257a.

57. Ibid.

58. Leo the Great, *Epistola ad Rusticum Narbonensem episcopum, Inquis. III, Resp.*, in *Patrologia Latina* 54, 1204a.

59. See Stickler, *The Case for Clerical Celibacy*, 34–35.

tic pronouncements on this issue dealt more with clerical continence rather than celibacy because many of the bishops, priests, and deacons were married. Around this time, however, an increasing number of bishops were selected from the celibate clergy in both the Eastern and Western Churches. For example, in 535 Emperor Justinian issued a law that required bishops to be either unmarried or separated from their wives.[60] As this and similar legislation took hold in the universal Church, the laws dealing with clerical marriage and continence began to be directed principally to priests and deacons.

Despite the gradual turn toward selecting celibate candidates for the episcopacy, the popes still had to deal with incontinent bishops. The early medieval period saw the widespread phenomenon of lay investiture bishops who were uncatechized in the Faith and worldly in their lifestyle. These bishops lived with their wives or concubines in plain sight and allowed their priests to live in a like manner. Many of these priests, living in the countryside and mired in poverty, supported themselves by farming, helped by wives and children. Consequently, they willed their benefices to their sons, which helped to establish a form of priesthood that was effectively hereditary.[61]

Clerical continence and celibacy in the early Middle Ages thus declined dramatically with many clerics living with either wives or concubines. From the sixth century until the Gregorian reform of the eleventh century, church authorities were constantly attempting to renew clerical life. The tone of the disciplinary measures taken by popes and bishops was one of reformation, rather than innovation. Collections of canons, such as the *Dionysiana* (ca. 500), reminded bishops of the discipline of earlier centuries. Around this time the *Penitential Books* of the Celtic Churches asserted the obligation to continence for those high clerics who had been previously married and imposed penalties on those who had conjugal relations with their wives after ordination.

60. See Justinian, *Novellae*, VI, c. 1, par. 7.

61. See Gerd Tellenbach, *The Church in Western Europe from the Tenth to the Early Twelfth Century*, trans. Timothy Reuter (Cambridge: Cambridge University Press, 1993), 90. My summary of celibacy in the Middle Ages is drawn in part from this work by Tellenbach, along with Stickler, *The Case for Clerical Celibacy*, 21–55, and Mary R. Schneider, "The Ancient Tradition of Clerical Celibacy," *Homiletic and Pastoral Review* (July 2007): 18–26.

In 653 the Council of Toledo barred clerics from having any form of public relationship with their wives or concubines. Penitential manuals and the *Capitularies* of the Frankish bishops also urged the conservation of clerical continence, as did several regional councils, diocesan synods, and the decrees of several popes. Saint Chrodegang (ca. 712–766), bishop of Metz, bound his cathedral clergy to communal life with him under a form of religious rule.[62] Chrodegang is considered one of the founders of the canonical life for priests, which later evolved into various communities of canons regular, who followed the *Rule of St. Augustine.* Canonical life made it easier for priests to live continently.

During this time the earliest legislation that permitted *periodic* continence for married clerics appeared at a regional council of the Eastern Churches, namely, the Second Council of Trullo (691–692).[63] This council upheld the traditional discipline that required bishops to be unmarried, or if married, to live apart from their wives, and also continued the ban on remarriage for all major clerics whose wives had died after their ordination. However, the bishops also introduced a law that was unprecedented in previous local or ecumenical councils. Canon 13 mandated that married priests, deacons, and subdeacons were not permitted to separate from their wives and were to observe periodic rather than perpetual continence. Trullo appealed to apostolic tradition and cited canons from the African Codex (419) to justify this legislation.[64] The reigning pope, Saint Sergius I (ca. 650–701), a Syrian by birth, did not accept the Trullan canons on clerical marriage, nor did his successor, John VII (ca. 650–707), who returned the Acts of the Trullan Synod unsigned. However, Adrian I (ca. 700–795), while rejecting the canons on clerical marriage, did accept with qualification other Trullan Acts that were free of anti-Roman canons.[65]

---

62. See John E. Lynch, "Marriage and Celibacy of the Clergy: The Discipline of the Western Church: An Historico-Canonical Synopsis," *The Jurist* 32 (1972): 14–38, at 35.

63. See Gryson, *Les origines du célibat ecclésiastique*, 120–26.

64. See canons 3 and 25 of the *Codex Canonum Ecclesiae Africanae* (419). Cholij argued that the Trullan Fathers, in canon 13, altered the African Codex in order to make their case: Cholij, *Clerical Celibacy in East and West*, 115–24, 179–92. See also Cochini, *The Apostolic Origins of Priestly Celibacy*, 405–10, and Heid, *Celibacy in the Early Church*, 311–15, who refers to canon 13 as a "momentous innovation."

65. Adrian I referred to the canons as though they pertained to the Third Council of Con-

Canon 13 of Trullo constituted a departure from the apostolic tradition of continence-celibacy that was codified at the Second Council of Carthage. In reflecting on the Trullan legislation, Cardinal William Levada wrote: "It is a common modern understanding of the history of celibacy to suggest that the practice of the early Church, at least until the decrees imposing celibacy 'in the strict sense' in the West, was that the early Church's practice was substantially that which later prevailed in the Eastern Churches, and that the practice of the West in requiring celibacy was a 'later' innovation. But recent historical studies have called this once prevalent view into question."[66]

With regard to the practice in the Latin Church, various councils and synods, such as those of Pavia (1022) and Burgess (1031), mandated perfect continence and banned major clerics from living with a woman. Those clerics who refused to separate from their wives were laicized. Moreover, children fathered after ordination were declared illegitimate and thus ineligible to receive orders. This legislation helped put an end to the hereditary priesthood. Around this time, the reform under Pope Nicholas II (ca. 990–1061) was aimed at correcting abuses in the Church, particularly simony, priests living in marriage (Nicolaitism), and lay investiture. The synodal legislation of Nicholas II in 1059 actually declared Nicolaitism to be a heresy and subsequent councils repeated his decrees. These reforms dealt with priests and deacons rather than bishops, who by this time were for the most part celibate. Nicholas II effectively used legates for the work of reform, including Humbert of Silva Candida, Hildebrand of Rome, and Saint Peter Damian. Hildebrand, as Pope Saint Gregory VII (ca. 1020–1085), and his immediate successors focused on correcting bishops who failed to reform their clergy with regard to abuses against celibacy and continence, as well as simony, lay investiture, and hereditary priesthood.

Among the many councils and synods of the eleventh and twelfth

---

stantinople: see Vitalien Laurent, "L'oeuvre canonique du Concile in Trullo (691–692), source primaire du droit de l'église orientale," *Revue des Etudes Byzantines* 23 (1965): 7–41, at 36, and Cholij, *Clerical Celibacy in East and West*, 7.

66. William Levada, "Celibacy and the Priesthood." *The Holy See*. http://www.vatican.va/roman_curia/congregations/cfaith/documents/rc_con_cfaith_doc_20111121_levada-celibacy-priesthood_en.html.

centuries called to enforce, among other things, the discipline of clerical continence and celibacy, the most significant were the First Lateran Council (1123) and the Second Lateran Council (1139). Lateran I made into universal law the prohibition of priests, deacons, and subdeacons cohabiting with their wives or concubines. Canon 7 stated that these clerics were forbidden to live with wives or concubines and to cohabit with other women, except those whom the Council of Nicaea permitted to dwell with them solely on account of necessity, namely "a mother, sister, paternal or maternal aunt, or other such persons, about whom no suspicion could justly arise."[67]

On the other hand, Lateran II declared that marriages contracted after ordination would be null and void: "matrimonium non esse censemus."[68] In doing so, the council was reemphasizing the law of clerical continence and the prohibition of the celibate cleric to marry or the married cleric to marry again after ordination.[69] Often Lateran II is wrongly interpreted as having introduced for the first time the general law of *celibacy*, with only unmarried men being admitted to priestly ordination. Yet what the council actually did was to reemphasize the law of *continence*.[70]

Subsequent legislation continued to deal with issues relating to the ordination of married men. The primary sources for these laws were the *Quinque Compilationes Antiquae*, which were compiled between 1187 and 1227, and the decretals of Pope Gregory IX (ca. 1145–1241). These decretals formed part of the *Corpus Iuris Canonici*, a canonical work completed in the fourteenth century by eminent canonists such as Saint Raymond of Peñafort (ca. 1175–1275). These sources indicate that from the time of Pope Alexander III (ca. 1100–1181), married priests were not, as a rule, allowed to possess benefices nor to bequeath a benefice.

67. First Lateran Council, canon 7, in Tanner, *Decrees of the Ecumenical Councils*, vol. 1, 191. These bishops thus interpreted canon 3 of Nicaea as excluding wives from the category of women "about whom no suspicion could justly arise."

68. Second Lateran Council, canon 7, in Tanner, *Decrees of the Ecumenical Councils*, vol. 1, 198.

69. Ibid. The Fourth Lateran Council (1215) reaffirmed the legislation of the Second Lateran Council: see canon 14, Tanner, *Decrees of Ecumenical Councils*, vol. 1, 242.

70. "Ut autem lex continentiae et Deo placens munditia in ecclesiasticis personis et sacris personis dilatetur," Second Lateran Council, canon 7, in Tanner, *Decrees of the Ecumenical Councils*, vol. 1, 198.

Young wives of priests and the wives of bishops had to agree at the time of ordination to enter a convent.[71]

In 1322 Pope John XXII (1249–1334) declared that no married man could be ordained unless he had full knowledge of the obligations of church law. If a wife had not given her free consent to his ordination, the husband, even if already ordained, was to reunite with his wife and thus be barred from exercising his priestly ministry.[72] This irregularity of the married man was not due to the marriage bond per se but rather to the assumption of the unwillingness or reluctance of the spouses to separate. The rights of the wife, fully respected by church law, may have hastened the eventual universal practice, established after the Council of Trent, of ordaining only unmarried men. Hence, the Gregorian Reforms did not mandate universal celibacy for priests of the Latin Church, but simply enforced existing laws concerning perfect and perpetual continence for major clerics.

Despite the conciliar and pontifical legislation that emanated from the Gregorian Reforms, priestly concubinage continued to be a problem in the Latin Church. This led to calls for easing of the rules enforcing clerical continence and celibacy during the centuries between the Gregorian Reforms and the Council of Trent. Even respected churchmen such as Panormitanus at the time of the Council of Basle (1417–1437) called for the mitigation of the rules enforcing clerical continence and celibacy, as did Erasmus and secular rulers with political goals in mind: Charles V, Ferdinand I, and Maximilian II. For their part, Martin Luther and Ulrich Zwingli made the abolition of clerical continence and celibacy one of the central tenets of their reform but linked this goal with the abolition of the Catholic theology of the sacramental priesthood.[73]

In answer to the Protestants, the bishops of the Council of Trent, during the third and final period of the council (1562–1563), rejected calls for

71. See Aemilius Friedberg, ed., *Corpus Iuris Canonici*, 2 vols. (Graz: Akademische Druck— U. Verlagsanstalt, 1955), III, 32, c. 6. The relevant sections are: Liber III, tit. 1 (*De Vita et Honestate Clericorum*), tit. 2 (*De Cohabitatione Clericorum et Mulierum*), tit. 3 (*De Clericis Coniugatis*), tit. 32 (*De Conversione Coniugatorum*), Liber IV, tit. 6 (*Qui Clerici vel Voventes Matrimonium Contrahere Possunt*). Gratian's earlier *Decretum* (ca. 1140) also contains many texts on celibacy and continence.

72. See John XXII, "De voto et voti redemptione," Titulus VI, cap. un., *Extravagantes Iohannis XXII*, in *Corpus Iuris Canonici*.

73. See Lynch, "Marriage and Celibacy of the Clergy," 189–212, at 206.

the mitigation or abolition of the rules for clerical continence and celibacy. In session 23 (July 15, 1563), they established seminaries to prepare young men for the priesthood and for the celibate life (canon 18).[74] This was a key strategy for enforcing strict celibacy. In session 24 (November 11, 1563), they reaffirmed the prohibition of clerical marriage (canon 9)[75] and rejected the thesis that the marital state was superior to the celibate state (canon 10).[76] Concerning the Tridentine legislation, Roman Cholij wrote: "The discipline of continence by this time had meant in practice that only an unmarried man would be ordained. This is also shown in the discussions of the Council, for example when one theologian, Desiderius de S. Martino, concerned by the shortage of priests, suggested the possibility of ordaining married men provided the wives gave consent and that they and their husbands lived in continence. But the measure was not deemed expedient."[77]

Although these Tridentine decrees did not have an immediate impact on priestly formation, they helped gradually to establish the universal practice of ordaining only unmarried men. Canon 18 of session 23 of Trent obliged all dioceses to establish seminaries for the education of future priests and allowed for the admission of boys (*pueri*) as young as twelve years.[78] This monumental decision was gradually implemented throughout the Church, and for the most part, it steadily eliminated married men from the priesthood in the Latin Church. The popes during this time, however, had to deal consistently with priests who married after ordination. Priests, for example, who had married during the French Revolution were required either to renounce their civil marriage (invalidly contracted) or to allow the Church to sanate the invalidity. In the first case, they could be readmitted to priestly ministry; in the second, they were permanently barred from it.

Various voices continued to call for the Catholic Church to relax the law of celibacy. But these pressures notwithstanding, the popes upheld

74. See Council of Trent, canon 18, in Norman P. Tanner, ed. *Trent to Vatican II*, vol. 2 of *Decrees of the Ecumenical Councils* (London: Sheed & Ward, 1990), 750–55.

75. See Council of Trent, canon 9, in Tanner, *Decrees of the Ecumenical Councils*, vol. 2, 755.

76. See Council of Trent, canon 10, in Tanner, *Decrees of the Ecumenical Councils*, vol. 2, 755.

77. Cholij, "Priestly Celibacy in Patristics and in the History of the Church," 47.

78. See Council of Trent, canon 18, in Tanner, *Decrees of the Ecumenical Councils*, vol. 2, 750–53.

mandatory priestly celibacy through various authoritative teachings, such as Gregory XVI (1765–1846) in *Mirari Vos* (1834) and Pius IX (1792–1878) in *Qui Pluribus* (1848). After the First Vatican Council (1869–1870), the schismatic Old Catholics abolished clerical celibacy, much to the consternation of their sympathizer, Ignaz von Döllinger (1799–1890).[79]

Around this time, the resurgent Thomism of the late nineteenth and early twentieth centuries followed the tradition of associating clerical celibacy with ritual purity, greater freedom for prayer, and the undivided heart. The scholastic theologians of this time, who tended to be more analytical and logical rather than analogical and mystical in outlook, did not add much to the justifications that had been advanced by theologians writing since the Council of Trent. Ritual purity, the superiority of consecrated virginity over marriage, and freedom from the cares of marriage and family were the arguments preferred by both the Magisterium and theologians.

The Theology of Priestly Celibacy prior to the Second Vatican Council

IN THE PREVIOUS SECTION, the majority of the texts studied have dealt with the *discipline* of clerical continence and celibacy as expressed through various patristic and magisterial texts. The emphasis on the discipline, however, should not eclipse a more fundamental reason or motivation given by Christ for the practice of clerical continence and celibacy. That is, the vocation to continence and celibacy is a *gift*, or charism, freely bestowed by the Holy Spirit on the man who is called to serve in the Catholic Church as a deacon, a priest, or a bishop.

In this study of the *discipline* of clerical continence and celibacy, an accompanying *teaching*, or *doctrine*, that has supported the discipline of the Latin Church has appeared along the way. The following section will shift the focus from the ecclesial discipline to the development in magisterial *teaching* on priestly celibacy, as well as taking note of a *theology* that arises through the reflections of several significant theologians.

---

79. See Stanley L. Jaki, *Theology of Priestly Celibacy* (Front Royal, Va.: Christendom Press, 1997), 191.

Hence, the writings of several popes and theologians of the late nineteenth and early twentieth centuries are studied in light of their contributions to the renewal of Catholic teaching and theology of priestly celibacy leading up to the Second Vatican Council.

The first significant theologian writing on celibacy in the late nineteenth century was Johann Adam Möhler (1796–1838), who penned in 1828 a creative, although polemical, work against some proponents of optional celibacy.[80] Möhler focused mostly on defending priestly celibacy, and therefore, his work was more apologetic than theological. Möhler contended that it is celibacy that signifies the irreducible independence of the church with regard to the state. Celibacy belongs to a different order from the one expressed in civil society, for the priest's celibacy places him above the ends that society pursues. Celibacy proclaims that the state is something different from the church and that earthly power is not a goal.[81] Möhler was also concerned that the attack against clerical celibacy forms part of a plan to keep the pope distant from the Catholic Church in Germany. Although the state might treat the bishops as subordinates, it has to concede that the pope is a sovereign power independent of all governments. That the pope approves priests in their celibacy effectively protects them from being regarded as servants of the state.[82]

Matthias Scheeben (1835–1888) advanced the notion that the priest has a maternal role in the Church. In *The Mysteries of Christianity* (1865), he argued that the priest embodies within himself a mystery of sacerdotal maternity in that new life comes about through his sacramental ministry:

In a part of its members the Church, as his Bride, was meant to be a true mother to the children who were to be reborn to him as Bridegroom, so that the heavenly rebirth of the human race might correspond to its natural generation, and the organization of the God-man's family might conform to the family of the earthly man. To this end [Christ] weds a part of the members of the Church in a special way, entrusts to their keeping the mystical resources belonging to the Church in

80. See Johann Adam Möhler, *The Spirit of Celibacy*, trans. Cyprian Blamires (Chicago: Hillenbrand, 2007).
   81. Ibid., 86–87.
   82. Ibid., 92–93.

common, and overshadows them beyond all others with the power of the Holy Spirit, so that they may bear him children and bring them into closer fellowship with Himself. This is the great mystery of the maternity of the Church in her priesthood.[83]

Scheeben claimed that the task of ministerial priests is to bring Christ to birth anew in the Church through the power of the Holy Spirit, both in the Eucharist and in the hearts of the faithful. He drew a comparison between the maternal roles of the Blessed Virgin Mary and of the priesthood: the miraculous conception of Christ and his birth from the womb of Mary is the model and the basis of the further spiritual conception and birth of Christ in the Church through the priesthood:

As Mary conceived the Son of God in her womb by the overshadowing of the Holy Spirit, drew him down from heaven by her consent, and gave him, the Invisible, to the world in visible form, so the priest conceives the Incarnate Son of God by the power of the same Spirit in order to establish him the bosom of the Church under the Eucharistic forms. Thus Christ is born anew through the priesthood by a continuation, as it were, of his miraculous birth from Mary; and the priesthood itself is an imitation and extension of the mysterious maternity that Mary possessed with regard to the God-man.[84]

For Scheeben, the Holy Spirit is the active principle by whom the priest, in his maternal priesthood, conceives new life from Christ the Bridegroom. Scheeben interestingly identified the priest in his sacramental ministry as acting in the person of the bridal Church, rather than in the person of Christ the Bridegroom. Scheeben's theology of the priesthood is unique in terms of its bridal association of the Church and the priest with Christ the Bridegroom and is a rich development of the nuptial dimension of the priesthood and, consequently, forms a foundation for an ecclesiological dimension of priestly celibacy.

Blessed John Henry Newman (1801–1890) defended priestly celibacy against attacks by Anglican theologians. Writing as an Anglican in 1845 in *An Essay on the Development of Christian Doctrine*, Newman saw priestly celibacy as firmly embedded in Catholic tradition:

83. Matthias Joseph Scheeben, *The Mysteries of Christianity*, translated by Cyril Vollert (St. Louis: B. Herder, 1947), 546.
    84. Ibid., 546–47.

The doctrine of the Sacraments leads to the doctrine of Justification; Justification to that of Original Sin; Original Sin to the merit of Celibacy. Nor do these separate developments stand independent of each other, but by cross relations they are connected, and grow together while they grow from one. The Mass and Real Presence are parts of one; the veneration of Saints and their relics are parts of one; their intercessory power and the Purgatorial State, and again the Mass and that State are correlative; Celibacy is the characteristic mark of Monachism and of the Priesthood. You must accept the whole or reject the whole; attenuation does but enfeeble, and amputation mutilate.[85]

This teaching of Newman that celibacy is the characteristic mark of the priesthood is built on his prior claim that the doctrine of original sin reveals the merit of celibacy. The logical starting point toward the rationale of the celibate priesthood is original sin, which deeply affected the proper use of sex. The role of the priesthood is to mediate human redemption from this sinful, fallen state.[86] Celibacy in some manner is an instrument of healing in the area of human sexuality.

With regard to the history of clerical celibacy, one important exchange occurred in nineteenth century Germany, when Franz Funk (1840–1907) and Gustav Bickell (1838–1906) disputed the origins of clerical celibacy. Funk, a historian of the early Church, maintained that the ecclesial law mandating celibacy for priests in the West was a twelfth-century development that had very little to do with the nature of the priesthood itself.[87] Bickell, an orientalist, argued against a merely disciplinary view of priestly celibacy in favor of one founded on biblical and theological reasons.[88] Funk's view, which prevailed for the remainder of the nineteenth into the twentieth century, disproportionately influenced scholarship on the origins of priestly celibacy up to the Second Vatican Council. Bickell's

85. John Henry Newman, *An Essay on the Development of Christian Doctrine* (London: Basil Montagu Pickering, 1878), 94.

86. See Jaki, *Theology of Priestly Celibacy*, 163.

87. See Franz X. Funk, "Der Cölibat keine apostolische Anordnung," *Theologische Quartalschrift* 61 (1879): 208–47; see summary by Cochini, *The Apostolic Origins of Priestly Celibacy*, 32–36. Funk's views were influential upon subsequent scholarship, especially as transmitted through Vacandard in his essays: Elphège-Florent Vacandard, "Les Origines du célibat ecclésiastique," in *Études de critique et d'histoire religieuse*, 1st ser (5th ed.: Paris, 1913), 71–120, and "Célibat," in *Dictionnaire de théologie catholique* 2 (Paris, 1905): 2068–88.

88. See Gustav W. Bickell, "Der Cölibat eine apostolische Anordnung," *Zeitschrift für Katholische Theologie* 2 (1878): 26–64.

position, however, gained greater prominence in the postconciliar years and influenced magisterial teaching during the pontificate of John Paul II.

The Funk-Bickell debate was the last instance of significant scholarly research on priestly continence and celibacy in the nineteenth and the beginning of the twentieth century. Serious scholarship on priestly celibacy during this time period, for all intents and purposes, receded into the background. Between the Funk-Bickell debates and significant magisterial teaching on priestly celibacy in the 1930s, however, there emerged canonical legislation that concretized the clerical praxis in the Latin Church in the early twentieth century.

That is, in 1917 Pope Benedict XV promulgated the first universal code of canon law for the Latin Church. In the section dealing with the obligations of clerics, canon 132, §1 treated the obligation of clerical celibacy: "Clerics constituted in major orders are prohibited from marriage and are bound by the obligation of observing chastity, so that those sinning against this are guilty of sacrilege, with due regard for the prescription of canon 214, §1."[89] This canon referred to all clerics in major orders, not only to priests. A cleric made a promise of celibacy when he received the order of subdeacon, which was considered a major order.[90] Hence, subdeacons, deacons, priests, and bishops were bound by the obligation to observe "chastity," which in this context meant perfect and perpetual continence for all major clerics. Edward Peters comments on particular nuances of the chastity and continence in the 1917 Code in comparison with the 1983 Code:

It must be recalled first that, in accord with sound moral theology, a man who is not married lives chastely only by observing, among other things, continence. To call upon a man who is not married to live chastely, therefore, *was* to call upon him to live continently. A survey of commentaries on the 1917 Code supports the interpretation that what is called "continence" in law today was called "chastity"

89. *The 1917 or Pio-Benedictine Code of Canon Law in English Translation with Extensive Scholarly Apparatus*, ed. and trans. Edward Peters (San Francisco: Ignatius, 2000), 68. Canon 214, § 1 enabled a man, who was ordained to major orders under grave fear, to seek dispensation from celibacy and the recitation of canonical hours.

90. The Second Lateran Council (1139) established the subdiaconate as a major order and extended the legislation on continence and celibacy to include subdeacons: see Second Lateran Council, canon 7, in Tanner, *Decrees of the Ecumenical Councils*, vol. 1, 198.

in the former law and, as is true of modern canon law, that two related but distinct obligations in regard to clerical continence (or chastity) and clerical celibacy were set forth in the 1917 Code.[91]

Thus, clerical chastity implied two obligations: abstinence from marriage (celibacy) and the living of perfect chastity (continence).

Clerics under the 1917 Code were almost always celibate. In rare cases, however, a married man could be ordained to the priesthood through special papal dispensation.[92] Such married clerics were bound to live with their wives in perfect and perpetual continence. Commentaries on the 1917 Code pointed out the illicitness of married clerics having conjugal relations after ordination: "As regards a man *already married* … with a dispensation such a man may be licitly and validly ordained, but he is then forbidden to use the marriage rights, though the marriage remains valid."[93]

Aligned with the concept of the illicit use of marriage by a married cleric is the illegitimacy of children born of such a cleric. Canon 1114 declared the illegitimacy of a child born to a parent who was under solemn religious vows or ordained to major orders, thus reaffirming the prohibition against a major cleric's use of marriage after the reception of orders: "Those children are legitimate who are conceived or born of a valid or putative marriage unless the parents, because of a solemn religious profession or the taking up of sacred orders, had been, at the time of the conception, prohibited from using the marriage contracted earlier."[94] The concept of illegitimacy of a child born of a married priest may seem foreign and even cruel to the contemporary mind. But among other reasons, the 1917 Code retained this precept in order to emphasize the grievousness of the cleric's transgression of clerical chastity.

Other than the 1917 Code, early-twentieth-century magisterial doctrine did not offer much reflection on priestly celibacy. In fact, it is not

91. Peters, "Canonical Considerations on Diaconal Continence," 157.

92. For example, Pierce Connelly of Philadelphia had to separate from his wife, Cornelia, prior to his priestly ordination in the Catholic Church; see Juliana Wadham, *The Case of Cornelia Connelly* (New York: Pantheon, 1957), 39–40.

93. T. Lincoln Bouscaren and Adam Ellis, eds., *Canon Law: A Text and Commentary, 4th Edition* (Milwaukee, Wisc.: Bruce, 1966), 115.

94. English translation from Peters, *Pio-Benedictine Code*, 384.

until Pope Pius XI that one finds the first significant twentieth-century magisterial teaching on priestly celibacy.[95]

In 1932 the French theologian Gaston Lecordier wrote a spirited defense of traditional magisterial teaching on priestly celibacy.[96] Lecordier sought to refute an argument by a theologian identified as J. M. T., who, in his efforts to strengthen the magisterial teaching on the issue, defended priestly celibacy according to a natural law argument versus the traditional stance that relies on considerations of suitability (*raisons de convenance*).[97] J. M. T. advanced the notion that the human person experiences shame or modesty (*pudeur*) as a type of reflexive reaction to the final cause of the marital act: a child conceived in original sin. This feeling of shame would therefore legitimize the practice of perfect continence and affirm its superiority over marriage. Furthermore, because the practice of perfect continence would free one from shame, ecclesiastical celibacy in particular could be seen as a triumph over the feeling (*sentiment*) of shame. Lecordier for his part argued that J. M. T. went well beyond the bounds of what is universally held in dogmatic and moral theology. Although J. M. T. used some arguments of Augustine, he does not exercise the same reserve and care as did the Universal Doctor. Lecordier pointed out that J. M. T. did not have a clear understanding of *pudeur* and that he praises celibacy so highly that the flesh is disparaged by contrast: marriage leads to works of sin and death. His positions that marriage dispose one "to sin and death" and that woman is more impure than man are but two of several errors that fall outside of the boundaries of acceptable Catholic teaching on marriage and the family.[98]

Lecordier concluded by stating that the traditional magisterial de-

95. The twentieth-century predecessors of Pius XI contributed minimally to magisterial teaching on priestly celibacy, such as Pius X, "Haerent Animo," *Acta Apostolicae Sedis* 41 (1908): 545–79, at 555–57, and Benedict XV, "Ad R.P.D. Franciscum Kordac, Archiepiscopum Pragensem, Coetum Episcoporum Convocandum Statuens," *Acta Apostolicae Sedis* 12 (1920): 33–35.

96. See Gaston Lecordier, "Une récente apologie du célibat ecclésiastique," *Revue apologétique* 561 (1932): 685–700.

97. See J. M. T., *Le célibat d'aprés une loi naturelle* (Paris: Editions de Pierre-Prat, 1932). Lecordier provided no page numbers of the length of the work by J. M. T., whom Lecordier did not specifically identify beyond his initials.

98. See Lecordier, "Une récente apologie du célibat ecclésiastique," 690–91.

fense of priestly celibacy based on the reasons of fittingness are suffi-
ciently formulated to provide a reasoned and satisfactory account, even
though they fall short of demonstrative arguments. Unlike the ques-
tionable views of J. M. T., the magisterial teaching is circumspect, balanced, and reverential toward both marriage and the celibate life.[99] The
ideas of J. M. T. manifest an anticorporeal philosophy that resembles
elements of the Manichaean heresy.

The encyclical letter *Ad Catholici Sacerdotii* (1935) of Pius XI is perhaps the best representative of early-twentieth-century pontifical teaching on the ministerial priesthood.[100] In the encyclical, the pope desired
that the faithful appreciate the sublimity of "the Catholic Priesthood and
its providential mission in the world" and that priests themselves have a
deeper understanding and esteem of their vocation (see n. 6).

Within the context of the piety of a Catholic priest, Pius XI broached
the topic of priestly celibacy: "For from piety springs the meaning and
the beauty of chastity."[101] After treating of the obligation of clerics in the
higher orders of the Latin Church to observe perfect celibacy, the pope
drew on the wisdom of the ancients to justify the necessity of priestly
ritual purity:

A certain connection between this virtue [chastity] and the sacerdotal ministry
can be seen even by the light of reason alone: since "God is a Spirit," it is only
fitting that he who dedicates and consecrates himself to God's service should in
some way "divest himself of the body." The ancient Romans perceived this fitness;
one of their laws which ran *Ad divos adeunto caste*, "approach the gods chastely,"
is quoted by one of their greatest orators with the following comment: "The law
orders us to present ourselves to the gods in chastity of spirit, that is, in which are
all things, [n]or does this exclude chastity of the body, which is to be understood,
since the spirit is so far superior to the body; for it should be remembered that
bodily chastity cannot be preserved unless spiritual chastity be maintained."[102]

99. Ibid., 700.

100. See Pius XI, *Ad Catholici Sacerdotii*, in *The Papal Encyclicals 1903–1939*, ed. Claudia
Carlen (Ann Arbor, Mich.: Pierian, 1990), 497–516; *Acta Apostolicae Sedis* 28 (1936): 5–53; English translations from the Carlen edition.

101. Pius XI, *Ad Catholici Sacerdotii*, n. 40. In this document, Pius XI used *chastity* synony-
mously with chaste *celibacy*.

102. Ibid., n. 42.

Pius XI appealed to ancient Roman thought on ritual purity to justify priestly celibacy. This appeal to natural reason, rather than to theology, may indicate that the pope wanted to show that celibacy was not against human nature and that, consequently, celibacy, lived according to supernatural motives, did no harm to the celibate individual.

Pius XI proceeded to state that the New Testament priesthood, being much superior to that of the Old Law, demanded a still greater purity (cf. nn. 42–43). He then briefly summarized the historical development of priestly celibacy: the law of ecclesiastical celibacy, whose first written traces presupposed a still earlier unwritten practice rooted in the Gospel and apostolic preaching, dated back to canon 33 of the Council of Elvira (cf. n. 43). He took pains, however, not to be seen as disapproving the different discipline that legitimately prevailed in the Eastern Church.[103] On the other hand, concerning the Second Council of Carthage (390), which ruled that married clergy were bound to practice perfect continence because it accorded with apostolic tradition, Pius XI stated that this law made obligatory what might be termed "a moral exigency that springs from the Gospel and the apostolic preaching" (n. 43).

Having summarized the thoughts of Church fathers, such as Saints Ephrem and John Chrysostom, on the beauty and dignity of celibacy (cf. n. 44), Pius XI then praised clerical celibacy because of the "incredible honor and dignity" of the priesthood. Referring to the liturgical office of the priest, the pope said that the priest has a duty that is in a certain way "higher than that of the most pure spirits" who stand before the Lord. He emphasized the priest's need to be totally dedicated to the things of the Lord and detached from the things of the world in order to dedicate himself to prayer because his mission is the salvation of souls. Is it not then fitting that the priest keep himself free from the cares of a family, which would absorb a great part of his energies (cf. n. 45)? The cares of the family and the need to please his wife would prevent the married priest, as a minister of God, from praying as he ought. Priestly celibacy, Pius XI believed, safeguards the time and energies of the priest so that he can be free to pray and minister to the Church.

Pius XI also justified celibacy on the grounds of ritual purity: the

103. Ibid., n. 47.

physically and spiritually chaste priest who dedicates and consecrates himself to God's service should in some way "divest himself of the body" (n. 42) and remain pure and free from conjugal relations. A greater "purity" was needed for the New Testament priesthood than for the Levitical priesthood. The noble ministry of the celibate priest reaches its culmination in the liturgy wherein he has to be pure in body and soul in order to offer up prayers that are pleasing to God. Furthermore, the pope emphasized the importance of the priest being free from the cares of the world and family so that he might dedicate his time to prayer. Finally, Pius XI stated that sacerdotal celibacy corresponds better to the desires of the Sacred Heart of Jesus and to his purposes with regard to priests.[104] Although he linked celibacy with this Christological image, he stopped short of declaring that celibacy enabled the priest to be an icon or image of Jesus Christ.

Ad Catholici Sacerdotii contained at least two themes that had been part of the magisterial teaching for centuries: (1) celibacy relates to the priest's freedom from the cares of marriage and the family in order to act better as a mediator; (2) celibacy is a means of protecting ritual purity. These two dimensions can be traced to the patristic era. Pius XI, however, did not link celibacy to other themes that appear in patristic and scholastic writings (as will be shown in the following chapter), such as the celibate priest living in imitation of the celibate Christ (see Lk 18:28–30), the significance of being an image of Christ the Bridegroom of the Church (see Eph 5), and the eschatological dimension of being a "eunuch for the kingdom of heaven" (see Mt 9:12).

In 1950 Pope Pius XII issued the apostolic exhortation, *Menti Nostrae*, which was directed to the clergy.[105] In his brief treatment of the reasons for celibacy, Pius XII emphasized the liberating effects of celibacy and the need for priests to renounce "the things of the world" in order to have care only for "the things of the Lord."[106] The attractions of the world were dangerous to the priest, for he could become absorbed by their charm, which would divide his heart, as Paul warned in 1 Cor-

104. Ibid.
105. Pius XII, *Menti Nostrae* (Washington, D.C.: National Catholic Welfare Conference, 1951); *Acta Apostolicae Sedis* 42 (1950): 657–702; English translations are from this edition.
106. Pius XII, *Menti Nostrae*, n. 20.

inthians 7:32–33. The priest must also grow in the virtue of chastity so that he might become, together with Christ, more of "a pure victim, a holy victim, an immaculate victim" (see n. 21). The pope here cited the Roman Canon, thus implicitly linking celibacy to the sacred liturgy. Furthermore, the pope cautioned the priest against having excessive familiarity with women, for unchastity in thought, word, and action would make him too impure to celebrate the sacred liturgy: "'Watch and pray,' mindful that your hands touch those things which are most holy, that you have been consecrated to God and are to serve Him alone."[107]

In this exhortation, Pius XII followed the thought of Pius XI in emphasizing two motivations for priestly celibacy: (1) the priest acquires freedom from distractions arising from marriage and worldly concerns so that he can concentrate his time and energy on his ministry for the sake of a greater ministerial fruitfulness, and (2) the priest gains a purity of body and soul that will enable him worthily to offer liturgical worship.

Several years later, Pius XII wrote the encyclical letter *Sacra Virginitas* (1954) to explain and defend consecrated virginity in general.[108] This was his most authoritative teaching on the topic for both priests and all those faithful—male or female religious, consecrated virgin, or cleric—who had taken some form of promise or vow to renounce marriage and sexual relations. The pope's treatment of priestly celibacy thus falls within the broader subject of consecrated virginity.

Pius XII listed two reasons why Christian men and women are attracted to consecrated virginity (see nn. 20–24). First, the renunciation of marriage frees one from its obligations so that the heart is not divided between the love of God and the love of spouse. Persons who desire to consecrate themselves to God's service embrace the state of virginity in order to be more freely at the disposition of God and more fully devoted to the good of neighbor.[109] Second, men and women are drawn to the state of virginity because of the many advantages in the spiritual life that come from renouncing all sexual pleasure (see n. 21). The pope pointed out that such pleasure, when it arises in the context

---

107. Ibid., n. 23.

108. See Pius XII, *Sacra Virginitas*, in *The Papal Encyclicals 1939–1958*, 239–53; *Acta Apostolicae Sedis* 46 (1954): 161–91.

109. Pius XII, *Sacra Virginitas*, n. 20.

of the chaste use of marriage, is ennobled and sanctified by the sacrament of Matrimony. But as a result of the fall of Adam, the subrational faculties of human nature no longer obey right reason and thus may involve the person in "dishonorable" actions. Pius XII here quoted Saint Thomas Aquinas, who taught that the pleasure associated with the use of marriage keeps the soul from "full abandon to the service of God."[110]

Pius XII then turned to the matter of priestly celibacy. In an argument similar to that given for consecrated virginity in general (cf. n. 20), the pope points out that the Catholic Church demands that the sacred ministers of the Latin Church observe perfect chastity for two reasons: (1) to acquire spiritual liberty of body and soul and (2) to be freed from temporal cares so as to engage fully in apostolic ministry (cf. n. 22). These two reasons, however, are not proper to the priestly state alone. Pius XII therefore highlights a third reason that is unique to the sacerdotal life: the priests' renunciation of marriage was related to their service at the altar (cf. n. 23). The pope set up an analogy between the priests of the Old Testament and those of the New: as the Levites had to abstain from the pleasures of marriage during their service in the Temple for fear of being declared impure by the Law (cf. Lev 15:16–17; 1 Sam 21:5–7), so, too, should the priests of Jesus Christ be in a state of perfect "chastity" because every day they offered the sacrifice of the Mass. Accordingly, priestly celibacy is most fitting for the good of the church because "holy virginity surpasses marriage in excellence" (n. 24).

Pius XII justified celibacy based on the priest's need to safeguard ritual purity. But over and beyond this argument, which was based on the sacred liturgy, the pope used arguments that were equally applicable to the religious charism of virginity: (1) spiritual freedom of body and soul and (2) freedom from worldly concerns in order to engage fully in apostolic ministry. Thus, Pius XII did not give reasons for priestly celibacy that differ greatly from those for religious virginity. This underdeveloped notion of priestly celibacy in *Sacra Virginitas* can be explained partially by the general audience to whom the letter was addressed: those in the religious life, clerics in major orders in the Latin Church,

---

110. See Thomas Aquinas, *Summa Theologiae*, II–II, q. 186, a. 4, in *Sancti Thomae Aquinatis Opera Omnia*, vol. X, Leonine edition (Rome: Ex Typographia Polyglotta S. C. de Propaganda Fide), 1889.

members of secular institutes, members of the lay faithful who make a private promise or vow of chastity (cf. n. 6), and "all of these beloved sons and daughters who in any way have consecrated their bodies and souls to God" (n. 7). Nevertheless, the portions of the encyclical that do address priestly celibacy reflect the need for a teaching that is more *priestly* in notion.

Although the Magisterium during this time acknowledged the superiority of the virginal state over marriage, which in turn justified priestly celibacy as put forth in *Sacra Virginitas* of Pius XII, its arguments were always carefully nuanced in order to praise the dignity and beauty of the marital state. Despite the limitations of its teaching during this time, the Magisterium was careful to emphasize the greater dignity of the virginal life without denigrating marriage and the acts proper to it.

In 1955 Max Thurian, a member of the Taizé Community, compared the married and celibate ways of life in *Marriage and Celibacy*.[111] This work did not deal with priestly celibacy as such but was focused on marriage and celibacy as vocations of the Christian faithful in general. According to Thurian marriage is an *indirect service* of God and the Church whereas celibacy facilitates *direct service*. This singularity of purpose characteristic of voluntary celibacy is how the state came to be seen as existing "for the sake of the kingdom of God." Through being solely directed toward the Kingdom, the celibate Christian acquires a resemblance to Christ, not only on the spiritual level but also on the physical and practical levels. Thus, it is a state of life that is especially adapted to the service of the Kingdom: "Like Jesus, the Christian celibate can be engaged entirely, spiritually and humanly, in the ministry. He is not a celibate in order to be more tranquil but to resemble Christ in his work for the Kingdom. All his energies and preoccupations must tend to a living preaching of the Gospel in order to hasten the return of Christ, if he wants to live in the truth of his state."[112]

Thurian here underscored both the Christological and the eschatological dimensions of celibacy. The Christian embraces celibacy in order to imitate and resemble Christ in his work for the Kingdom (the Chris-

---

111. See Max Thurian, *Mariage et Célibat* (Neuchâtel and Paris: Delachaux & Niestlé, 1955).
112. Ibid., 134; translation mine.

tological significance) and hastens the second coming of Christ, which is the goal of Christian preaching and witness (the eschatological significance). Although Thurian emphasized the great dignity of the celibate life, he also cautioned against despising married life. Rather, the celibate forgoes conjugal love in order to be entirely at God's disposal without restriction in service and prayer, and therefore remains available to extend the love of Christ to all people.[113]

In *What Is a Priest?* (1957) Joseph Lécuyer provided a description on the importance of the celibacy of Christ as an example and inspiration for the priest.[114] Lécuyer pointed out that because Christ came to announce and inaugurate the Kingdom of heaven, his disciples, especially the priests, should want to give the same prophetic witness in their own lives: "Would they not be led to do as he did, and to abstain on earth from any other marriage, so as to consecrate themselves entirely to preparing for that wedding banquet of which the Eucharist is the Sacrament?"[115]

Like Thurian, Lécuyer underlined two dimensions of priestly celibacy: (1) the Christological notion in that the celibate priest is a representative of Christ the Bridegroom and (2) his eschatological mission of preparing the faithful for the marriage feast of the divine Bridegroom. In addition, Lécuyer stated that imitation of the celibacy of Jesus Christ is the primary motivation for his celibate disciples themselves to live that state of life. This is a simple yet important point since the acknowledgment of Christ's own celibacy has been often omitted from scholarly discussions about the suitability of priestly celibacy in the Latin Church.

In *The Celibacy of the Priest* (1960), Wilhelm Bertrams contributed two arguments for celibacy that are distinctly priestly.[116] First, Bertrams argued that a priest, whose priesthood participates in the one Priest-

---

113. Ibid., 153.

114. See Joseph Lécuyer, *What Is a Priest?* trans. Lancelot Sheppard (New York: Hawthorn, 1959).

115. Ibid., 91–92. Lécuyer was a key contributor to the Vatican II document on the ministerial priesthood (*Presbyterorum Ordinis*) and supervised the drafting on the section on celibacy: see Yves Congar, *Mon Journal du Concile*, vol. II (Paris: Cerf, 2002), 443, 511.

116. See Wilhelm Bertrams, *The Celibacy of the Priest: Meaning and Basis*, trans. Patrick Byrne (Westminster, Md.: Newman Press, 1963).

hood of Christ, is commissioned to lead human beings to union with God. If the priest is to lead, it follows that he must already have "arrived" at that union of supernatural love insofar as it is possible here on earth. This means that the priest is a good priest to the extent that he loves God: an exclusive devotion to God must shine forth in his life. Bertrams wrote that "[t]he person who, by virginitas, gives up marital love, which completes him in a human way, dedicates thereby his life to God, to make it full of His love."[117] It cannot be otherwise for the priest. As dedicated to God, the priest is free for the works of love as he promotes the salvation of souls; therefore his office of divine mediator, the exercise of which demands Christian mercy, exists for the service of others.

Second, Bertrams employed a Christological argument for priestly celibacy as based on the eucharistic sacrifice. He reasoned that the priest represents Christ as both Priest and Victim in the offering of the sacrifice of the Mass. To offer the total sacrifice of his life along with Christ, the priest is called to take on virginity-celibacy, which itself is a participation in the Cross of Christ: "Without the undertaking of virginitas the representing of Christ by the priest would lack something for its perfection. The celebration of the Holy Sacrifice is, on that account, for the priest a continual appeal to take on celibacy, and not just externally—merely as a single state."[118] Celibacy must become the consecration of the entire man for the service of God, be a spiritual sacrifice in the sense of an act of divine adoration. If the very nature of virginity almost necessarily leads to a vow of perpetual chastity, the celebration of the Holy Sacrifice calls for the vow in a very special way.

Priestly celibacy, therefore, is intimately connected with the highest act of the *munus sanctificandi* of the priest and presupposes that he consciously identifies himself with Christ as victim in the eucharistic sacrifice. Bertrams, however, did not limit the meaning of celibacy to the offering of the Mass, for the celibate priest is also Christ's representative to those faithful committed to him, in his parish. As Christ belongs to all people—not to one alone—so the priest as Christ's representative belongs to all, a state that necessarily excludes marriage for him.[119] This

117. Ibid., 37.
119. Ibid., 113, n. 6.

118. Ibid., 39.

argument of Bertrams is strongly Christological and links the celibate priest to the salvific mission of Christ. There is also implicitly present an ecclesiological perspective insofar as the celibate priest belongs to every member of the Church, as Christ wholly belongs to his bridal Church (see Eph 5). The priest's celibacy enables him to represent more clearly Christ the Bridegroom and frees him from marital and paternal ties that would prevent him from imitating Christ's total dedication to the Church.

Odo Casel (1886–1948), in *The Mystery of the Church*, a work published posthumously in 1961, explored the nuptial dimension of the priesthood. He was particularly astute in pointing out the significance of liturgical signs as symbols of an ecclesiological or spousal notion of the priesthood.[120] Casel argued that all liturgical activity of the Church flows from the relation of the Church as Spouse to Christ, her Head and Bridegroom. It is especially in the liturgy that the Church manifests herself as the "Bride of the Lamb" (Rev 21:10), who entirely belongs to her Bridegroom, and as Mother nourishes and forms in her own life what she received from him, and transmits it to her children.[121]

The bridal Church is protected and guided by the Bridegroom's visible representative, the bishop. Casel explained that the ancient liturgical blessing of the bishop's ring carries with it a profound theological expression of this bridal relationship: "In the consecration of a bishop, for instance, the new bishop is given a ring with these words: 'Receive this ring, symbol of faithfulness; preserve intact the Bride of God, that is, the Holy Church, adorned with unchangeable faithfulness.' The bishop, who represents Christ the High Priest, is married in eternal faithfulness to the virginal bride of God."[122] Casel here drew on a patristic tradition that described the bishop as wedded to his particular local church.[123] As Scheeben had done before, Casel developed a notion of the *ecclesiological-spousal* dimension of the priesthood, which would be introduced later into the magisterial teaching of Vatican II on priestly celibacy.

---

120. See Odo Casel, *Mysterium der Ekklesia: von der Gemeinschaft aller Erlösten in Christus Jesus. Aus Schriften und Vorträgen* (Mainz: Matthias Grünewald, 1961).

121. Ibid., 80.

122. Ibid., 81; translation mine.

123. See, for example, Epiphanius, *Advers. Haer. Panar.*, 59, 4, in *Patrologia Graeca* 41, 1024.

In 1961 Lucien Legrand published an article that explored the eschatological notion of celibacy.[124] For Legrand, celibacy is a "prophecy in action, a foreboding of the end, a public proclamation of the fleeting character of this world" and is directed to the Kingdom of heaven as to a final cause. In biblical language, "the Kingdom of heaven" is synonymous with "the Kingdom of God" because the word *heaven* was used by the Jews as a substitute for "God" as a way of avoiding the pronouncement of the divine name. The Kingdom of heaven, in which the blessings of salvation would be realized, was at the center of Jesus's preaching. It is "the life of the age to come" ("eternal life" in Johannine terms) and signifies the new resurrected life that the Jews had desired, the prophets had foretold, and the apocalyptic writers had described. Legrand underlined the "already but not yet" characteristic of celibacy, stating that virginity is an anticipated realization of the final transformation: "Eschatological life has begun to stir in [celibates] and that life will be, and can already be now, a life which has gone beyond the necessity and the urge of procreation."[125] Although Legrand in his essay dealt with celibacy in general, he did not link it to the priesthood. His treatment of the eschatological dimension, however, contributed to the development of the theology of celibacy in the early 1960s. As was indicated earlier, the magisterial teaching on priestly celibacy in the years prior to Vatican II lacked a rich theological depth and thus was ready for renewal. It was through the efforts of theologians such as Legrand that a more profound theology was formed from which the bishops and their periti would draw at the Second Vatican Council.

In 1962 on the eve of the council, Bertrand de Margerie published a defense of the magisterial teaching on priestly celibacy. De Margerie was prompted in part by a provocative article written by a Dominican priest, Raimondo Spiazzi, who argued that the historical evidence for the discipline of clerical celibacy was inconclusive.[126] In order to sup-

---

124. See Lucien Legrand, "The Prophetical Meaning of Celibacy," *Review for Religious* 20 (1961): 330–46.

125. Ibid., 343.

126. See Bertrand de Margerie, "Luzes Antigas e Novas sobre o Celibato," *Revista Eclesiástica Brasileira* 22 (1962): 616–37, and Raimondo Spiazzi, "Annotazioni," *Monitor Ecclesiasticus* 84 (1959): 369–409.

port his arguments to the contrary, de Margerie drew on the texts from *Sacra Virginitas* of Pius XII, but he also put forth his own contributions, one of which addresses the popular notion that the imposition of priestly celibacy in the Latin Church constitutes a violation of personal liberty. Proponents of this theory saw celibacy as a charism freely given by the Holy Spirit and thus beyond the Church's authority to dictate through its canon law.

De Margerie's primary tenet was that the Church has the right to require celibacy for priests and that the exercise of this right does no harm to the free will of candidates. He pointed out that, first and foremost, the Church does not prohibit anyone who is free of impediments from marrying. In other words, no Catholic layman is "obliged" to become a priest. If, however, a man should freely make the decision to embrace the priesthood, it is in his best interest to submit to the law of celibacy because the Church judges this discipline to be more useful for the perfection of this particular state of life.[127]

Moreover, de Margerie also underlined two elements that are part of any authentic priestly vocation: the divine and the ecclesiastical. The latter element is the point of contention for those who struggle with the law of celibacy in the Latin Church: "The Sacrament of Orders was not entrusted by Christ with regard to the conditions of its administration, to the subjective wills of individuals, but to the hierarchy. And there is no complete and objective divine vocation where there is no ecclesiastical vocation, or when the candidate does not consent to build up the Church (which is the role of the priest) in a manner in conformity to the will of this same Church. The priesthood, the priestly vocation, is ecclesial or it is not a vocation."[128]

The basic premise, then, is that the vocation to the priesthood is of and for the church, or it is not an authentic vocation. De Margerie emphasized that one should not drive a wedge between the visible and invisible ruling elements of the Church, that is, the Magisterium and Christ.

The final magisterial teachings on priestly celibacy prior to Vatican were given by Pope Saint John XXIII. First, in his encyclical letter *Sacerdotii Nostri Primordia* (1959), which dealt with the life of Saint John

127. See Margerie, "Luzes Antigas e Novas," 623.
128. Ibid.; translation mine.

Vianney, the pope directed his teaching to "those in sacred orders," and urged clerics to devote their attention to the "wonderful example of this holy man" who once shared in their priestly work and now served as their heavenly patron (n. 5).[129] The primary purpose of the letter was to encourage the clergy to foster divine friendship with Christ the Lord and grow in it, for this was the main source of the joy and fruitfulness of any priestly work (cf. n. 7).

From the life of this saint, John XXIII drew some lessons for all priests, particularly in the area of priestly chastity (cf. nn. 20–25): the importance of voluntary mortification of the body (cf. n. 20), detachment from external things in order to acquire and protect chastity (cf. n. 20), the difficulty of the mission of a diocesan priest who has to live in a society that is infected by a looseness in morals and unbridled lust (cf. n. 21), the need for priests who work alone in the midst of temptations against chastity to dedicate their whole life to perfecting this virtue (cf. n. 22), and the practical truth that the ascetical life makes a priest more ready and eager to attend to the needs of his brethren (cf. n. 25). Thus, the pope substantially repeated the thought of his predecessors with regard to the freedom from external things that the priest needs in order to (1) acquire and protect chaste celibacy and (2) be better prepared to attend to the needs of those whom he serves. Interestingly, he did not utilize arguments based on ritual purity or the superiority of the celibate life to marriage.

Second, in an address to the participants of the Roman Synod of January 26, 1960, John XIII spoke of cries coming from priests throughout the universal church regarding priestly celibacy:

First of all we lament that, in order to repair a small piece of her lost beauty, some, indulging in a sort of hallucination, think that the Catholic Church wants, or deems it opportune, to stand down from the ecclesiastical law of celibacy, which through the course of centuries was and is the outstanding and most resplendent ornament of the priesthood. Indeed, the law of sacred celibacy and the care that is to be given that it might be diligently kept is always brought back to our mind by the memorable and glorious struggles of those times in which the Church of God was called to engage in dire combats and which brought forth a threefold

<hr/>

129. John XXIII, *Sacerdotii Nostri Primordia*, in *The Papal Encyclicals 1958–1981*, 21–37; *Acta Apostolicae Sedis* 51 (1959): 545–79.

triumph: For this is the mark of the victory of the Church of Christ: striving to be *free, chaste, and universal.*[130]

By 1960 the protests coming from priests and others were enough to move the pope to make this defense of priestly celibacy. These voices for change in the existing discipline of celibacy in the Latin Church would grow louder during the Second Vatican Council.

In his teachings, John XXIII credited celibacy with providing for the priest the wherewithal to dedicate his life totally to the Church, free from spiritual and physical distractions that would draw him away from his prayer and ministry. However, John XIII did not draw from the fullness of Catholic tradition in his teaching on the suitability of obligatory priestly celibacy in the Latin Church. Although at the time this approach was deemed sufficient, the bishops and theologians at the Second Vatican Council sought richer themes and a better synthesis.

Summary

AN EMINENT PRIEST SCHOLAR, Christian Cochini, whose meticulous studies have helped to recover an understanding of the apostolic roots of clerical continence and celibacy, has written:

The Augustinian principle, desiring that "what has been kept by the entire Church and was always maintained, without having been established by the councils, [is] regarded as quite rightly as having been transmitted only by the apostolic authority," seems to find in the discipline of celibacy-continence for the higher ranks of clergy, as practiced during the early centuries, an adequate and justified application. Let us conclude that the obligation demanded from married deacon, priests, and bishops to observe perfect continence with their wives is not, in the Church, the fruit of belated development, but on the contrary, in the full meaning of the term an unwritten tradition of apostolic origin that, so far as we know, found its first canonical expression in the 4th century. "*Ut quod apostoli docuerunt, et ipsa servavit antiquitas, nos quoque custodiamus*"—"What the apostles taught, and what antiquity itself observed, let us endeavor also to keep." The affirmation of the Fathers of Carthage will always remain an essential link with the origins.[131]

---

130. John XXIII, "Virtutes Dignitati Sacerdotum Necessariae: Caput, Cor et Lingua," *Acta Apostolicae Sedis* 52 (1960): 221–30, at 226; translation mine.

131. Cochini, *The Apostolic Origins of Priestly Celibacy*, 439.

The statement of the Second Council of Carthage remains one of the most solid witnesses to this apostolic tradition of clerical continence and celibacy. Since the fourth century, Catholic doctrinal, theological and disciplinary tradition has developed several insights and explanations of the *charism* and *discipline* of clerical continence and celibacy, among which are ritual purity, the superiority of celibacy to marriage, a greater facility in ministering to the Church, and a life in imitation of Christ. The two most common arguments were probably those based on ritual purity and the superiority of the celibacy over marriage, about which Joseph Komonchak commented, "These [two] motives prevail in the disputes at the time of the Gregorian Reform, at the Council of Trent, and in the nineteenth century controversies. In fact, there is a remarkable similarity in the arguments brought forth on both sides of the debate from the fourth century to the twentieth."[132]

These two traditional explanation for priestly celibacy—ritual purity and the superiority of the celibate life to marriage—were omitted from the conciliar and postconciliar documents of Vatican II that dealt with priestly celibacy. Despite the omission, the two arguments can still be considered helpful in explaining priestly celibacy, provided they are expressed in a manner that accords with Catholic teaching.

Moreover, magisterial teaching on priestly celibacy before Vatican II tended to be expressed in a negative manner: celibacy frees a priest from those things that hinder him from love of and service to the faithful of the Church. While this perspective is valid, the positive dimensions of priestly celibacy, such as the good of a dynamic spiritual paternity, must also be articulated. While celibacy helps the priest to attain liberation *from* earthly responsibilities tied to marriage, it also facilitates freedom *for* attaining a closer identification with Christ.

A corrective to this somewhat negative emphasis comes with the emergence of a threefold dimension of celibacy (Christological, ecclesiological, and eschatological), the elements of which were articulated at the Second Vatican Council and subsequently developed by Paul VI. The threefold dimension provided a needed emphasis on the other-directed dimensions of priestly celibacy and stimulated a renewal of

132. Joseph Komonchak, "Celibacy and Tradition," *Chicago Studies* 20, no. 1 (1981): 9–10.

⌒⌒⊃ 2

The Renewed Magisterial Teaching on Priestly Celibacy

T HE RENEWAL of theology of priestly celibacy in the twentieth century began with the writings of several theologians, presented in the last chapter, and was reflected and extended to some extent in pontifical teaching from Pius X to John XXIII. With the promulgation of *Presbyterorum Ordinis* (1965) of Vatican II and *Sacerdotalis Caelibatus* (1967) of Paul VI, however, there arose a rich doctrine that substantially develops the Catholic understanding of priestly celibacy as a *gift* that is to be cherished, nurtured, and protected by the Church. The reformulated teaching emphasizes certain biblical and patristic themes, such as the celibate priest being an icon of Christ, the Bridegroom of the Church. This teaching is "renewed" insofar as it is rooted in New Testament themes and incorporates patristic insights on the nature of priestly celibacy.

The focus of this chapter is the rich teachings of the Magisterium during the second half of the twentieth century. These teachings in turn have helped to stimulate further reflection on the part of theologians. Such is the dynamic interplay between magisterial teaching and the work of theologians. As the International Theological Commission has described, "[t]heology investigates and articulates the faith of the Church, and the ecclesiastical magisterium proclaims that faith and authentically interprets it."[1]

1. International Theological Commission, *Theology Today: Perspectives, Principles, and Criteria* (Washington, D.C.: The Catholic University of America Press, 2012), 34.

The Second Vatican Council

Lumen Gentium 42

The Dogmatic Constitution on the Church, *Lumen Gentium* (1964), contains a chapter on the call to holiness, which addresses various ways in which the People of God can grow in sanctity.[2] Among these ways for fostering sanctification are the evangelical counsels, which Jesus proposed for his own disciples' observation. The counsel of consecrated virginity holds a particular pride of place:

Likewise the Church's holiness is fostered in a special way by the manifold counsels which the Lord proposed to his disciples in the Gospel for them to observe. Towering among these counsels is that precious gift of divine grace given to some by the Father (cf. Mt 19:11; 1 Cor 7:7) to devote themselves to God alone more easily with an undivided heart (cf. 1 Cor 7:32–34) in virginity or celibacy. This perfect continence for love of the kingdom of heaven has always been held in high esteem by the Church as a sign and stimulus of love, and as a singular source of spiritual fertility in the world.[3]

"Perfect continence" is singled out as preeminent among the other counsels. *Continence* in this context refers to the unmarried or celibate state rather than the abstinence from conjugal relations by a married cleric. With regard to *virginity* and *chastity* in this context, Francisco Egana wrote that

[a]lthough the concept of chastity is distinct from that of celibacy, an analysis of the context in which the ecclesiastical documents use the words shows clearly that the Church uses indiscriminately the expression "virginity," "perfect chastity," and "celibacy" to express that "precious gift of divine grace given to some by the Father to devote themselves to God alone more easily with an undivided heart for the Kingdom of Heaven" (*LG* 42). Traditional canonical doctrine identifies both expressions defining the celibacy of the clergy "the obligation to observe perpetual and perfect chastity." In any case, unquestionably—even from a conceptual point of view—chastity includes celibacy.[4]

2. See Vatican Council II, *Lumen Gentium*, chapter 5, nn. 39–42.

3. Ibid., n. 42.

4. Francisco Egana, "Religious and the New Rite for the Ordination of the Deacon," *Consecrated Life* 17, no. 2 (1992): 98–121, at 105.

It is significant that in *Lumen Gentium* the bishops did not employ the Tridentine teaching on the superiority of virginity over marriage, and thus steered clear of a direct comparison of virginity-celibacy and marriage.[5] Rather, they focused on perfect continence as a sign and stimulus of divine charity and on its being a source of spiritual fecundity in the world. This positive attitude represented a shift in the Magisterium's presentation of virginity-celibacy and its relation to marriage. Subsequent texts of Vatican II would continue the theme of how marriage and celibacy are able to coexist in harmony, each enjoying its proper dignity.[6]

Perfectae Caritatis 12

Along with *Lumen Gentium* there were two other conciliar documents that mentioned either consecrated chastity or celibacy: *Perfectae Caritatis*, the decree on the renewal of religious life, and *Optatam Totius*, the decree on the training of priests, both of which were promulgated on October 28, 1965.

Because *Perfectae Caritatis* has to do with the renewal of the religious life, its focus is limited to members of religious communities who are bound by the evangelical counsels. Article 12 deals with consecrated chastity for religious *as a group*, with no distinction being made between men and women. For this reason, there is no mention of celibacy for those members of religious orders who are ordained as deacons or priests. Thus, *Perfectae Caritatis* 12 gives a more general treatment of chastity, as this following passage attests: "Chastity 'for the sake of the kingdom of heaven' (Mt 19:22), which religious profess, must be esteemed an exceptional gift of grace. It uniquely frees the heart of man (cf. 1 Cor 7:32–35), so that he becomes more fervent in love for God and for all men. For this reason it is a special symbol of heavenly benefits, and for religious it is a most effective means of dedicating themselves wholeheartedly to the divine service and the works of the apostolate. Thus, for all Christ's faithful religious recall that wonderful marriage

5. See canon 10, *Canons on the Sacrament of Marriage*, Session 24 (November 11, 1563), in Tanner, *The Decrees of the Ecumenical Councils*, vol. II, 755.

6. See Joseph Komonchak, "The Council of Trent at the Second Vatican Council," in *From Trent to Vatican II: Historical and Theological Investigations*, ed. Raymond Bulman and Frederick Parrella (Oxford: Oxford University Press, 2006), 61–80, at 75.

made by God, which will be fully manifested in the future age, and in which the Church has Christ for her only spouse."[7] The text concentrates on the liberation that chastity gives to the religious for a more fervent love for God and neighbor ("it uniquely frees the heart of man"). The formulation of religious chastity in positive, rather than negative, terms gives this teaching a certain *ad extra* dynamism: freeing the heart for service, rather than simply withdrawing whatever can impede a person from holiness. It also adds an eschatological dimension of chastity ("for the sake of the Kingdom of heaven") insofar as the evangelical vow of chastity enables the consecrated religious to be a prophetic witness of the Kingdom of heaven. In addition, this text refers to an ecclesiological dimension insofar as consecrated religious form part of the bridal Church in relation to Christ the Bridegroom ("for all Christ's faithful religious recall that wonderful marriage made by God ... in which the Church has Christ for her only spouse").

Perfectae Caritatis does not describe the religious life as a "state of perfection," in part because the council fathers wanted to avoid giving the impression that marriage was not a sufficient means for attain the perfection in charity and holiness. Joseph Komonchak wrote, "It would appear that in its treatment of celibacy, or consecrated virginity, as in its treatment generally of the religious life, Vatican II was concerned to avoid referring to such a vowed life as a 'state of perfection,' as if other Christians are not called to perfection. If the religious life were to be recommended as something that belongs to 'the Church's life and holiness,' it would not be on the grounds of singling it out and elevating it to a superior status."[8]

The Pastoral Constitution on the Church in the Modern World, *Gaudium et Spes*, which was promulgated several weeks later (December 7, 1965) also sought to avoid giving the impression that marriage lacked the sufficient means for attaining Christian holiness. Not only does *Gaudium et Spes* praise the marriage bond, but it also describes marital sexual intimacy as a noble and honorable act that enriches the spouses in joy, gratitude, and married love.[9]

7. Vatican Council II, *Perfectae Caritatis*, n. 12.

8. Komonchak, "The Council of Trent at the Second Vatican Council," 75.

9. See Vatican Council II, *Gaudium et Spes*, n. 49.

Perfectae Caritatis 12, for its part, reaffirms the rich Catholic teaching on the excellence of the consecrated chastity "for the sake of the Kingdom of heaven," which refers to its eschatological significance. On the other hand, it says nothing about the manner in which an ordained priest who has taken religious vows might differ from a nonordained religious with regard to the eschatological dimension.

Optatam Totius 10

Optatam Totius treats of the formation of seminarians in the Latin Church.[10] Article 10 emphasizes for the most part the practical elements of the formation of seminarians in the "venerable tradition" of priestly celibacy as laid down by the regulations of the Latin Church. It also points to the need for candidates for the priesthood to know and esteem Christian marriage, a sacrament that represents the love which exists between Christ and the Church (see Eph 5:32). Seminarians, however, are also to recognize the "greater excellence of virginity" (*praecellentia virginitatis*) and to be consecrated to Christ so that they could offer themselves to the Lord with a deliberate and generous choice and a total surrender of body and soul. Although this phrase does not explicitly state that virginity is of "greater excellence" than *marriage*, the text implies this comparison. This understated but clear claim regarding the superiority of virginity to marriage contains a footnote that cites Pius XII, who in *Sacra Virginitas* defended the Tridentine teaching that anathematized anyone who denied that celibacy or consecrated virginity was superior to marriage.[11]

Optatam Totius 10 also includes a brief theological synopsis of priestly celibacy. The text describes several dimensions of celibacy that are to be incorporated into the teaching and formation of seminarians:

Students who follow the venerable tradition of priestly celibacy as laid down by the holy and permanent regulations of their own rite should be very carefully

10. The conciliar documents on the priesthood and priestly formation, namely *Presbyterorum Ordinis* and *Optatam Totius*, deal primarily with the diocesan priesthood. There is no extended focus on the meaning of the priesthood in the religious life. See Kenan Osborne, "Priestly Formation," in *From Trent to Vatican II: Historical and Theological Investigations*, 117–35, at 127.

11. See Pius XII, *Sacra Virginitas*, n. 32. Interestingly, the council fathers did not use pro-celibacy arguments in *Optatam Totius* 10 based on the concept of ritual purity.

trained for this state. In it they renounce marriage for the sake of the kingdom of heaven (cf. Mt 19:12) and hold fast to their Lord with that undivided love which is profoundly in harmony with the new Covenant; they bear witness to the resurrection in a future life (cf. Lk 20:36) and obtain the most useful assistance towards the constant exercise of that perfect charity by which they can become all things to all men in their priestly ministry.[12]

The text lists several theological justifications for priestly celibacy, three of which stand out. Although not explicitly named as such, these three reflect a significant grouping of concepts that recur frequently in later magisterial documents: (1) "[Priests] renounce marriage for the sake of the kingdom of heaven (cf. Mt 19:12)" and "bear witness to the resurrection in the future life (cf. Lk 20:36)" (the eschatological dimension), (2) "hold fast to their Lord with that undivided love which is profoundly in harmony with the new Covenant" (the Christological dimension), and (3) "obtain the most useful assistance towards the constant exercise of that perfect charity by which they can become all things to all men in their priestly ministry" (the ecclesiological dimension).

These three perspectives on priestly celibacy provide new insights into priestly celibacy. The overall theme is positive and dynamic: celibacy enables a priest *to be* and *to do*, rather than simply *negating* an earthly good from his life, such as marriage. These three dimensions emerged as guiding concepts in later magisterial teaching on priestly celibacy. *Optatam Totius* 10 constitutes a significant development of magisterial teaching insofar as priestly celibacy is presented under a threefold, positive dimension. On the other hand, *Optatam Totius* 10 also includes a trace of the teaching of Trent, that is, the "greater excellence" of virginity. This blend of old and new magisterial teachings indicates that the bishops desired to follow a hermeneutic of continuity that recognized legitimate development of doctrine without repudiating previous magisterial teaching.

Presbyterorum Ordinis 16

The Decree on the Ministry and Life of Priests, *Presbyterorum Ordinis,* is divided into three chapters: (1) on the priesthood in the Church's mis-

---

12. Vatican Council II, *Optatam Totius*, n. 10.

sion, (2) on the ministry of priests, and (3) on the life of priests.[13] Chapter 3, on the requirements for the life of the priest, deals with humility and obedience, celibacy, and voluntary poverty. Article 16, which deals with celibacy, can be divided into three principal sections.

Priestly Celibacy in General   The first section of article 16 addresses celibacy in general: "Perfect and perpetual continence for the sake of the kingdom of heaven was recommended by Christ the Lord (cf. Mt 19:12). It has been freely accepted and laudably observed by many Christians down through the centuries as well as in our own time, and has always been highly esteemed in a special way by the Church as a feature of priestly life. For it is at once a sign of pastoral charity and an incentive to it as well as being in a special way a source of spiritual fruitfulness in the world."[14] The phrase that describes perfect and perpetual continence as "a sign of pastoral charity and an incentive to it as well as being in a special way a source of spiritual fruitfulness in the world" follows closely what is said in *Lumen Gentium* 42.

The text further adds an explanation of the relationship between the priesthood and celibacy that takes into account the tradition of the Eastern Churches: "It is true that [celibacy] is not demanded of the priesthood by its nature. This is clear from the practice of the primitive Church [cf. 1 Tm 3:2–5; Ti 1:6] and the tradition of the Eastern Churches where, in addition to those—including all bishops—who choose from the gift of grace to observe celibacy, there are also many excellent married priests."[15] The first sentence reflects the common Catholic understanding that celibacy is neither part of the essence of the ministerial priesthood nor necessary for its function. This sentence serves as an introduction to a brief discussion of married priests in the Eastern Churches.

The text goes on to state that the council in no way intended to alter the discipline of the married priesthood which "is lawfully practiced in the Eastern Churches." Married priests are to persevere in their holy vocation so that they might continue fully and generously to give them-

13. See Vatican II, *Presbyterorum Ordinis*, nn. 2–21.
14. Ibid., n. 16.
15. Ibid.

selves to the flock commended to them. There are no references made to the married priest's wife and none to the Christian upbringing of his children.

Theological Dimensions of Priestly Celibacy   The second principal section of article 16 deals with the appropriateness of celibacy for priests and contains the three aspects of priestly celibacy that first appeared in *Optatam Totius* 10 but now in a more developed form: the Christological, ecclesiological, and eschatological dimensions. Neither *Presbyterorum Ordinis* 16 nor *Optatam Totius* 10 uses these three terms *as such*, but the concepts are nevertheless present in the text. The Christological dimension indicates the priest's union with Christ:

> There are many ways in which celibacy is in harmony with the priesthood. For the whole mission of the priest is dedicated to the service of the new humanity which Christ, the victor over death, raises up in the world through his Spirit and which is born "not of blood nor of the will of the flesh nor of the will of man, but of God" (Jn 1:13). By preserving virginity or celibacy for the sake of the kingdom of heaven (cf. Mt 19:12) priests are consecrated in a new and excellent way to Christ. They more readily cling to him with undivided heart (cf. 1 Cor 7:32–34) and dedicate themselves more freely in him and through him to the service of God and of men. They are less encumbered in their service of his kingdom and of the task of heavenly regeneration. In this way they become better fitted for a broader acceptance of fatherhood in Christ.[16]

This text states two facets of priestly celibacy that join the priest closely to Jesus Christ: *mission* and *consecration*.[17] With respect to *mission*, the whole priestly ministry is dedicated through celibacy to the service of a new humanity, which Christ brought forth through His Spirit in the world and which has its origin "not of blood, nor of the will of the flesh, nor of the will of man but of God" (Jn 1:13). Implicit in this statement is the belief that the celibate priest can give himself more fully to his mission if he is free from care for a wife and children. With regard to *consecration*, celibate priests are consecrated to Christ in a "new and excellent

---

16. Ibid.

17. See Friedrich Wulf, "Chapter III: The Life of Priests (Articles 12–16)," in *Commentary on the Documents of Vatican II*, vol. IV, ed. Herbert Vorgrimler, 191–239, at 285 (New York: Herder and Herder, 1969).

way" and "more readily cling to him with undivided heart" (see 1 Cor 7:32–34). Thus, they can give themselves more freely in and through Christ to the service of God and humanity and are better fitted for a "broader acceptance of fatherhood in Christ." The primary orientation is to Christ rather than to the Church, with the priest's spiritual paternity springing directly from his union with the Lord.

The second dimension, the ecclesiological, refers to the priest in his relationship with the Church and in bringing the faithful closer to Jesus Christ: "By means of celibacy, then, priests profess before men their willingness to be dedicated with undivided loyalty to the task entrusted to them, namely that of espousing the faithful to one husband and presenting them as a chaste virgin to Christ. They recall that mystical marriage, established by God and destined to be fully revealed in the future, by which the Church holds Christ as her only spouse."[18] This text uses the Pauline imagery from 2 Corinthians 11:2: "I feel a divine jealousy for you, for I betrothed you to Christ to present you as a pure virgin to her one husband." Paul described the Church in Corinth as a chaste bride whom he, as her father, had prepared and presented to Christ. Through his marriage with the Church, Christ inaugurated a new and unique relationship between God and humanity. Although the council fathers used nuptial imagery in describing the celibate priest as the father of the bride, they did not apply to the celibate priest the imagery of Christ the Bridegroom of the Church.

The third dimension, the eschatological, identifies the celibate priest as a prophetic witness to the heavenly realities that will never pass away: "Moreover they [celibate priests] are made a living sign of that world to come, already present through faith and charity, a world in which the children of the resurrection shall neither marry, nor be given in marriage."[19] The celibate priest as a living sign of the future Kingdom of God reminds the faithful of that Kingdom and of the fact that they will be taken up into the eternal marriage between Christ and his Church.

The Law of Celibacy   Following a brief survey of the genesis of laws regulating celibacy, this section of article 16 contains an approval and

18. Vatican Council II, *Presbyterorum Ordinis*, n. 16.
19. Ibid.

confirmation of the discipline of the Latin Church and a petition for the whole Church to pray that priests be faithful to this gift: "[The council] feels confident in the Spirit that the gift of celibacy, so appropriate to the priesthood of the New Testament, is liberally granted by the Father, provided those who share Christ's priesthood through the sacrament of Order, and indeed the whole Church, ask for that gift humbly and earnestly."[20] The text notes the foundational notion of celibacy as a *gift* and points out that prayer is the means by which the priest is able to receive the gift of celibacy and to live it faithfully. God the Father will liberally grant it because of its fitting connection with the priesthood of the New Testament.

This section concludes with an exhortation for celibate priests to persevere in their state of life, holding fast to it with courage and enthusiasm, while keeping before their eyes the great mysteries that are signified and fulfilled in it. Given that many people consider perfect continence to be impossible, priests are exhorted to pray humbly and perseveringly for the grace of fidelity. In addition to prayer, priests are admonished to incorporate asceticism into their lives.

Presbyterorum Ordinis 16 is the most complete statement on priestly celibacy by Vatican II and contributes significantly to the development of magisterial teaching on this subject. It employs an abundance of biblical and patristic themes, much more so than did the preconciliar magisterial teaching of the twentieth century. Among the conciliar themes one notices the emergence of three specific dimensions of priestly celibacy: the celibate priest's union with Christ (the *Christological* dimension), his service to the Church (the *ecclesiological* dimension), and his prophetic witness to heavenly life (the *eschatological* dimension). This triad serves as a summary of the multilayered significance of sacerdotal celibacy.

Presbyterorum Ordinis 16 does not follow *Optatam Totius* 10 in referring to the *praecellentia* of celibacy vis-à-vis marriage. Rather, the text strives to state something equivalent through different language: "By preserving virginity or celibacy for the sake of the kingdom of heaven priests are consecrated in a new and excellent way to Christ. They more readily (*facilius*) cling to him with undivided heart and dedicate

---

20. Ibid.

themselves more freely (*liberius*) in him and through him to the service of God and of men. They are less encumbered (*expeditius*) in their service of his kingdom and of the task of heavenly regeneration. In this way they become better fitted (*aptiores*) for a broader acceptance of fatherhood in Christ."[21] Priestly celibacy is praised more quietly here by means of four comparatives (*facilius, liberius, expeditius, aptiores*).[22] In choosing this mode of expressing the excellence of the celibate life, the bishops avoided words that would suggest a clear correspondence with the Tridentine teaching on the superiority of virginity to marriage. This ostensible aversion of the council fathers in evoking an association with Trent on this issue in *Presbyterorum Ordinis* 16 may also have been an operative influence upon the formulation of *Optatam Totius* 10. Although *Optatam Totius* 10 speaks of the greater excellence of virginity (*praecellentia virginitatis*) it does not make an explicit comparison between virginity and marriage.

Presbyterorum Ordinis 16, therefore, is the principal locus for the renewal of magisterial teaching on priestly celibacy at the Second Vatican Council. In the other conciliar texts that deal with chastity or celibacy,[23] there is comparatively little doctrinal development, with the clear exception of *Optatam Totius* 10. Despite its brevity, the rich account of priestly celibacy in *Presbyterorum Ordinis* 16 provides a foundation for further doctrinal development. In some respects, it can be seen as an outline for a more complete presentation to be given at a future date. In fact, Pope Paul VI would issue such a presentation a year and a half after the promulgation of *Presbyterorum Ordinis*.

Paul VI and *Sacerdotalis Caelibatus*

A FULLER DEVELOPMENT of conciliar teaching on priestly celibacy may have been limited in part by the prohibition of Paul VI against any

---

21. Ibid. Rather than "less encumbered," a more accurate translation of *expeditius* is "more expeditiously." Hence the phrase is better translated "they more expeditiously minister to his Kingdom."

22. See Komonchak, "The Council of Trent at the Second Vatican Council," 75.

23. See *Lumen Gentium*, n. 29, 42; *Perfectae Caritatis*, n. 12; *Orientalium Ecclesiarum*, n. 17.

further discussion among the bishops about the retention of obligatory priestly celibacy in the Latin Church. While the pope directed his prohibition against those who were questioning the wisdom of the Latin discipline, he may have inadvertently discouraged a fruitful exchange of ideas on celibacy in the remaining time of the council.

On October 11, 1965, Paul VI decided to intervene in the discussion concerning clerical celibacy among the fathers at Vatican II by imposing a moratorium on further discussion on the floor that dealt with changes to the law of celibacy in the Latin Church. Various bishops, including Melkite Patriarch Maximos IV Sayegh, had been planning to open a debate on the value of celibacy and were eager to advance the idea of married clergy in the Latin Church.[24] The earlier conciliar debate concerning the ordination of married men to the permanent diaconate in *Lumen Gentium* 29 had encouraged some bishops to raise similar points in the schema on the priesthood, for as soon as the question was raised—whether men ought to be admitted to a restored diaconate without any obligation to celibacy—the question of the celibacy of priests was also raised.[25]

The intervention of Paul VI on October 11 consisted in having a letter written by him to be read to the bishops. In the letter, the pope wrote of his awareness of the plans of several council fathers to publically question the discipline of obligatory celibacy for priests in the Latin Church. In view of this matter that "demands great prudence and carries such great weight," Paul VI asked those bishops who felt it to be their duty, to express their views in writing to the Presidential Council, which in turn would pass them on to him for consideration. Explaining his action, Paul VI wrote, "It is our purpose, so far as we are able, not only to preserve this providential, sacred, and ancient law, but also to strengthen its observance by calling the priests of the Latin Church back to a consciousness of the causes and reasons which today, indeed

---

24. See Mauro Velati, "Completing the Conciliar Agenda," in *The Council and the Transition: The Fourth Period and the End of the Council, September 1965–December 1965*, vol. V of *History of Vatican II*, ed. Giuseppe Alberigo and Joseph A. Komonchak, 185–274, fn. 133, at 233 (Maryknoll, N.Y.: Orbis and Leuven: Peeters, 2006); Anthony P. Kowalski, *Married Catholic Priests: Their History, Their Journey, Their Reflections* (Mequon, Wisc.: Caritas, 2004), 18–20.

25. See Wulf, "Chapter III," 280.

today most of all, require that the law itself be held by all to be deeply meaningful, and that they consecrate themselves fully to Christ and his love alone, and that they all devote themselves only to the service of the Church and the souls of men."[26] The pope further stated that priests of the Latin Church needed to reflect on the causes and reasons of celibacy, which must be held to be deeply meaningful. In other words, it is not enough for priests to accept the ecclesial law of celibacy, but they also must consider its underlying reasons. Here the pope gave the motive and the impulse for a richer and deeper magisterial teaching on celibacy.

The fruit of this deeper consideration of priestly celibacy came in the form of Paul VI's own encyclical letter, *Sacerdotalis Caelibatus*, which he issued on June 24, 1967, one-and-a-half years after the closing of the Second Vatican Council.[27] The pontiff presented in the encyclical the most comprehensive papal teaching on priestly celibacy in the twentieth century, perhaps in the entire history of the Catholic Church. Unfortunately, this encyclical remains largely unknown in popular and academic circles, although it is the most complete magisterial exposition to date on priestly celibacy. One reason for its relative obscurity could be that in the following year Paul VI released his monumental encyclical, *Humanae Vitae*. The controversy surrounding *Humanae Vitae* may have distracted the faithful from much of the pope's previous teaching on priestly celibacy.

In the opening paragraph of *Sacerdotalis Caelibatus*, Paul VI underlined celibacy as an ecclesial *gift* that must be cherished and protected: "Priestly celibacy has been guarded by the Church for centuries as a brilliant jewel, and retains its value undiminished even in our time when mentality and structures have undergone such profound change."[28] Yet,

---

26. Paul VI, "Epistula Summi Pontificis Pauli VI ad em.mum P.D. Eugenium card. Tisserant Praesidem Consilii Praesidentiae Ss. Concilii," in *Acta Synodalia Sacrosancti Concilii Oecumenici Vatican II*, vol. IV/I, 40 (Vatican City: Typis Polyglottis Vaticanis, 1970–1988); translation mine.

27. See Paul VI, *Sacerdotalis Caelibatus*, in *The Papal Encyclicals 1958–1981*, 202–21; *Acta Apostolicae Sedis* 59 (1967): 657–97. All subsequent English translations of the encyclical are from this official English edition. This approved translation, however, has some deficiences, which I will correct by placing bracketed words into the text.

28. Paul VI, *Sacerdotalis Caelibatus*, n. 1.

amid the modern expression of opinions there is a persistent pressure from some clergy and laity alike for the Church to reexamine this discipline on account of the difficulty or even impossibility of living it.

Before beginning his teaching on priestly celibacy, the pope acknowledged that he was addressing this issue in view of his intervention at Vatican II:

This state of affairs is troubling consciences, perplexing some priests and young aspirants to the priesthood; it is a cause for alarm in many of the faithful and constrains us to fulfill the promise we made to the Council Fathers. We told them that it was our intention to give new luster and strength to priestly celibacy in the world of today. Since saying this we have over a considerable period of time earnestly implored the enlightenment and assistance of the Holy Spirit and have examined before God opinions and petitions which have come to us from all over the world, notably from many pastors of God's Church.[29]

His teaching, accordingly, would not be a reworking of former magisterial arguments, but an earnest attempt to present a profound understanding of celibacy for the contemporary world. Before giving his presentation, however, Paul VI listed some of the more common objections to priestly celibacy: (1) The New Testament does not openly demand celibacy for ministers, but rather proposes it as a free act of obedience to a special vocation or to a spiritual gift (see Mt 19:11–12). Jesus did not make it a prerequisite in choosing the Twelve, nor did the apostles impose it on the leaders of the first Christian communities (see Tm 3:2–5, Ti 1:5–6). (2) The Church fathers founded their arguments for celibacy and continence on an overly pessimistic view of the human condition or on a somewhat distorted notion of the purity necessary when dealing with sacred things. In addition, the old arguments are no longer in harmony with the different social and cultural milieus in which the Church today, through her priests, is called on to work. (3) It is wrong to exclude from the priesthood those who have been called to the ministry without having been called to celibacy. This is to identify wrongly the gift of the vocation to the priesthood with that of perfect continence or celibacy as a state of life for ecclesial ministers. (4) Celibacy aggravates the shortage of priests. (5) A married priesthood would remove the occasions of

29. Ibid., n. 2.

infidelity, waywardness, and defections of celibate priests. It would also enable priests to witness more fully to Christian living through marriage. (6) Celibacy is against nature, and physically and psychologically detrimental to the development of a mature and balanced human personality. Celibate priests often become hard and lack human warmth and are bound to live a life that leads to bitterness and discouragement. (7) Celibates passively receive this state of life, and hence, they neither understand its complexities nor have the full freedom to choose it.[30]

The pope recognized that the sum of these objections would appear to render obsolete the tradition of clerical celibacy in the Latin Church. In response, he cited the example of saints and faithful ministers of God whose lives of sacred celibacy were the greatest witness to the necessity of preserving this gift. He saw that celibate clerics could live lives of courageous self-denial and spiritual joyfulness with exemplary fidelity and relative facility. In view of these positive fruits, Paul VI concluded, "We cannot withhold the expression of our admiration; the spirit of Christ is certainly breathing here."[31] The pope therefore resolved that the law of celibacy should continue to be linked to ecclesiastical ministry.

What, then, about the distinction between the call to the priesthood and the obligation to live a celibate life: should Church authority impose the law of celibacy upon those who have freely responded to the priestly charism given to them by the Holy Spirit? Paul VI responded:

[We acknowledge that] the gift of the priestly vocation dedicated to the divine worship and to the religious and pastoral service of the People of God, is undoubtedly distinct from that which leads a person to choose celibacy as a state of consecrated life. But the priestly vocation, although inspired by God, does not become definitive or operative without having been tested and accepted by those in the Church who hold power and bear responsibility for the ministry serving the ecclesial community. It is therefore the task of those who hold authority in the Church to determine in accordance with the varying conditions of time and place, who in actual practice are to be considered suitable candidates for the religious and pastoral service of the Church, and what should be required of them.[32]

---

30. See Paul VI, *Sacerdotalis Caelibatus*, nn. 5–11.

31. Ibid., n. 13.

32. Ibid., n. 15.

In this careful formulation, the pope argued that church authority has a divine mandate to test and accept candidates according to their suitability for orders and that the Latin Church is justified in seeking suitable candidates only from the ranks of the celibate.

Paul VI's purpose for this encyclical, then, was to set forth the fundamental reasons for celibacy in a manner more suited to the understanding of the contemporary person. In pursuit of this end, he stated an important point of principle: "Consideration of the 'manifold suitability' (cf. *Presbyterorum Ordinis* 16) of celibacy for God's ministers is not something recent. Even if the explicit reasons have differed with different mentalities and different situations, they were always inspired by specifically Christian considerations and after they have been thoroughly examined one can arrive at the underlying reasons. These can be brought into greater evidence only under the influence of the Holy Spirit, promised by Christ to His followers for the knowledge of things to come and to enable the People of God to increase in the understanding of the mystery of Christ and of the Church."[33]

A most intriguing phrase of this statement, that the "explicit reasons" given in the past in favor of celibacy were "always inspired by specifically Christian considerations," implies that Paul VI had in mind two of the most recent arguments of his papal predecessors: ritual purity and the superiority of celibacy over marriage. The pope, however, neither gave examples of how such pro-celibacy arguments of the past were inspired by "specifically Christian considerations" nor indicated what were the more fundamental reasons underlying them.

Paul VI then described the nature of the ministerial priesthood, which can be understood only in the light of the newness of Jesus Christ, the eternal Priest.[34] Each priest participates in the one priesthood of Christ, to whom he looks as model and ideal. It is true that Christ brought forth a new creation through His Pascal mystery (see 2 Cor 5:17; Gal 6:15), thus giving a new meaning to matrimony, raising it to the dignity of a sacrament, a symbol of His own union with the Church. But

---

33. Ibid., n. 18. I have modified the offical English translation of the penultimate sentence ("Semper tamen innitebantur in sententiis vere christianis, quibus penitus perspectis ad rationes perveniebatur altiores"), particularly by translating *rationes* as *reasons* rather than *motives*.

34. Ibid., n. 19.

Christ also introduced into time a *new* form of life that is divine and that radically transforms the human condition (see Gal 3:28). Celibacy manifests this new way of Christian life: "Christ, Mediator of a more excellent Testament, has also opened a new way, in which the human creature adheres wholly and directly to the Lord, and is concerned only with Him and with His affairs; thus, he manifests in a clearer and more complete way the profoundly transforming reality of the New Testament."[35] As the celibacy of Christ signified his total dedication to the service of God and humanity, the freedom from the bonds of flesh and blood would perfect the dignity and mission of the sacred ministers sharing in His priesthood.

Paul VI next introduced the dimensions of priestly celibacy according to a threefold dimension, or scheme: Christological,[36] ecclesiological,[37] and eschatological.[38] Here the pope explicitly used these three terms and joins them together as a triad.

First, the Christological dimension refers to the celibate priest in his union with the celibate Christ in his priestly life and mission. The priest's acceptance of celibacy for the sake of the Kingdom of heaven, which together with the Gospel (see Mk 10:29–30) and the name of Christ (see Mt 19:29) motivate him to accept the burdens of the apostolate, facilitates his closer participation in the life of Christ. The newness of life that Christ ushered in is shared in a very particular way by his ministers: "[This] is the mystery of the newness of Christ, of all that He is and stands for; it is the sum of the highest ideals of the Gospel and of the kingdom; it is a particular manifestation of grace, which springs from the paschal mystery of the Savior. This is what makes the choice of celibacy desirable and worthwhile to those called by our Lord Jesus. Thus they intend not only to participate in His priestly office, but also to share with Him His very condition of living."[39] The priest's response to the celibate life is an answer of love to the love which Christ manifested so clearly (see Jn 3:16, 15:13). Rightly then, Vatican II considered celibacy "as a symbol of, and stimulus to, charity";[40] it stimulates the priest to a

---

35. Ibid., n. 20.

37. Ibid., nn. 26–32.

39. Ibid., n. 23.

36. Ibid., nn. 19–25.

38. Ibid., nn. 33–34.

40. Vatican Council II, *Lumen Gentium*, n. 42.

charity that is open to all. Celibacy is not an end in itself, but it is a way by which the priest becomes an example of Christ's total dedication to his mission of salvation, and it thereby effects his growth in charity and sacrifice. In sum, the bond between the priesthood and celibacy is seen as "the mark of a heroic soul" (*fortissimi animi index*) and the imperative call to unique and total love for Christ and the Church.[41]

Next, priestly celibacy contains an ecclesiological significance, which refers to the priest's ministry in the Church and for the Church. Paul VI described this dimension with imagery from the Ephesians 5: "'Laid hold of by Christ' (Phil 3:12) unto the complete abandonment of one's entire self to Him, the priest takes on the likeness of Christ most perfectly, even in the love with which the eternal Priest has loved the Church His Body and offered Himself entirely for her sake, in order to make her a glorious, holy and immaculate Spouse."[42] The celibate priest becomes likened to Christ, Head and Bridegroom of the Church. The priest also manifests the virginal love of Christ for the Church and the spiritual fecundity of this marriage, by which the children of God are born, "not of blood, nor of the will of the flesh" (Jn 1:13).

Moreover, the priest's total service of Christ and of his Mystical Body increases his ability to pray. Free from the distractions of an earthly family, the celibate priest increases in his ability to listen to the word of God and to meditate prayerfully. Like Christ himself, the priest is wholly intent on the things of God and of the Church (see Lk 2:49; 1 Cor 7:32–33), living in the presence of God in order to intercede for the faithful (see Heb 9:24, 7:25). The Divine Office in particular is a profound means of helping the priest to join his prayer with that of the Church.[43]

Paul VI continued his treatment of the ecclesiological significance of priestly celibacy by stating that the celibate priest acquires a greater richness of meaning and sanctifying power in his own efforts at growth in holiness through the ministry of grace and that of the Eucharist. In the Eucharist, the priest places on the altar his entire life. Part of this sacrificial offering is the way in which the priest dies daily to himself.

41. See Paul VI, *Sacerdotalis Caelibatus*, n. 25.
42. Ibid., n. 26.
43. Ibid., nn. 27–28.

By giving up the love of a family of his own for the love of Christ and his Kingdom, he finds a fruitful life in Christ.[44]

Because the priest represents Christ to the community of the faithful committed to his charge, it is appropriate that he be a fitting icon of Christ. In this context, Paul VI developed the notion of the priest as an image, or icon, of the celibate Christ:

> In the community of the faithful committed to his charge, the priest represents Christ. Thus it is most fitting that in all things he should reproduce the image of Christ and follow in particular His example, both in his personal and in his apostolic life. To his children in Christ, the priest is a sign and a pledge of that sublime and new reality which is the kingdom of God, of which he is the dispenser; he possesses it on his own account and to a more perfect degree, and nourishes the faith and hope of all Christians, who because they are such, are bound to observe chastity according to their proper state of life.[45]

This passage underlines clearly the Christological dimension ("the priest represents Christ"), which is also closely linked with the ecclesiological dimension insofar as the priest is said to acquire through celibacy the ability to become an image of Christ's total and exclusive love for the members of the Church. Because *Presbyterorum Ordinis* 16 did not use the notion of the celibate priest as an icon of Christ the Bridegroom, Paul VI here enriched the ecclesiological dimension by using this perspective inspired by Ephesians 5:25-27.

The pope also emphasized the practicality of celibacy insofar as it provides the priest with the maximum efficiency and the best disposition, mentally and emotionally, for the continuous exercise of a perfect charity. This singular availability permits him to spend himself wholly for the welfare of all, in a fuller and more concrete way.[46] The guarantee of freedom and flexibility in the pastoral ministry allows the priest to give to the faithful the fullness of that which is due to them (see Rom 1:14).

Finally, Paul VI dealt with the eschatological significance of priestly celibacy. The celibate priest bears a twofold prophetic witness that (a) all earthly goods are transitory and (b) the blessed in heaven will be taken up into the eternal marriage between Christ and his Church. Sacerdotal

---

44. Ibid., nn. 29-30.   45. Ibid., n. 31.
46. Ibid., n. 32.

celibacy reflects the Kingdom of God, which is present already on earth in mystery and which will reach its perfection only with the final coming of the Lord Jesus. The pilgrim Church constitutes the seed and beginning of this Kingdom.

The eschatological dimension is inspired by the words of the Lord Jesus that "in the resurrection they neither marry nor are given in marriage, but are like angels in heaven" (see Mt 22:30). In the world, one becomes so involved with earthly concerns and the desires of the flesh that heavenly realities are often forgotten. Priestly celibacy-continence acts as an antidote to this earthly attitude insofar as it reminds the faithful of the rewards of heaven and testifies to the progress of the People of God toward the final, heavenly goal of their earthly pilgrimage: "This continence, therefore, stands as a testimony to the necessary progress of the People of God toward the final goal of their earthly pilgrimage, and as a stimulus for all to raise their eyes to the things above, where Christ is seated at the right hand of God and where our life is hidden [with Christ in God until it also appears with Him in glory]."[47] Priestly celibacy proclaims the presence on earth of the final stages of salvation (see 1 Cor 7:29-31) and anticipates the fulfillment of the Kingdom of heaven.

Of the three dimensions of celibacy presented in *Sacerdotalis Caelibatus* by Paul VI, the eschatological is the least proportioned to the priesthood itself; that is, its characteristics are similar to those attributed to the chastity of consecrated religious as outlined in *Perfectae Caritatis* 12. Because Paul VI made no significant distinctions between consecrated virginity and priestly celibacy from an eschatological perspective, further theological development of the eschatological dimension of *priestly* celibacy seems called for.

The remainder of the encyclical letter deals with celibacy in the life of the Church, human values, priestly formation, priestly life, defections from the priesthood, the bishop's role as father toward his priests, and the role of the faithful in encouraging the priest in his celibate life.[48] Within these remaining sections, three elements are of particular importance for this study. First, in his short account of the history of the

47. Ibid., n. 34.
48. Ibid., nn. 35-97.

development of priestly celibacy, Paul VI simply stated that in Christian antiquity the Church fathers and ecclesiastical writers testified to the spread of the voluntary practice of celibacy by sacred ministers. He neither posited that celibacy was of apostolic origin nor suggested it to be a later development.[49]

Second, Paul VI dealt with the sensitive issue of the discipline of the Eastern Churches.[50] Having recognized that the legislation of the Eastern Church governing married and celibate clergy was a long established tradition, the pope then made a statement that is generous in its ecumenical implications: "If the legislation of the Eastern Church is different in the matter of discipline with regard to clerical celibacy, as was finally established by the Council of Trullo held in the year 692, and which has been clearly recognized by the Second Vatican Council, this is due to the different historical background of that most noble part of the Church, a situation which the Holy Spirit has providentially and supernaturally influenced."[51] Paul VI here stated that the Trullan legislation manifested a legitimate development of clerical life—the married priesthood—insofar as the Holy Spirit influenced the customs of the Eastern Church "providentially and supernaturally." The pope's statement can be reconciled with previous magisterial pronouncements, insofar as the Magisterium has recognized the legitimacy of the married priesthood.[52] It is not clear, however, if the pope was also referring to the creation of the Eastern legislation on *periodic continence* for married major clerics, which was codified in canon 13 of the Council of Trullo and was a departure from the traditional clerical discipline concerning perfect and perpetual continence for major clerics.

Continuing his treatment, Paul VI pointed out that the Eastern Churches allow only celibate priests to be ordained bishops and that priests themselves cannot enter into marriage after their priestly ordination. This tradition indicates that these Churches possess to a certain extent the principle of a celibate priesthood, of which the bishops possess the summit and fullness.[53] Paul VI then defended the legitimacy

---

49. Ibid., n. 35.   50. Ibid., nn. 38–40.
51. Ibid., n. 38.
52. See Vatican Council II, *Presbyterorum Ordinis*, n. 16.
53. See Paul VI, *Sacerdotalis Caeliabatus*, n. 40.

of the discipline of the Latin Church against those who charge that it is a corruption of an early, original norm: "It is unthinkable that for centuries she has followed a path which, instead of favoring the spiritual richness of individual souls and of the People of God, has in some way compromised it, or that she has with arbitrary [and insolent] juridical prescriptions stifled the free expansion of the most profound realities of nature and grace."[54] The pope did not directly answer this objection but considered that the legitimate tradition of the Latin Church itself provides a sufficient response. In like manner, he made no judgment of the historical origins of the Eastern customs, that is, whether they were of apostolic origin or of a later development.

Third, Paul VI provided for the possibility of allowing in certain cases married non-Catholic ministers to be ordained to the ministerial priesthood: "A study may be allowed of the particular circumstances of married sacred ministers of Churches or other Christian communities separated from the Catholic communion, and of the possibility of admitting to priestly functions those who desire to adhere to the fullness of this communion and to continue to exercise the sacred ministry. The circumstances must be such, however, as not to prejudice the existing discipline regarding celibacy."[55] The pope underlined the authority of the Church to exercise power in this matter by referring to *Lumen Gentium* 29 and the council's decision to open the possibility of ordaining married men to the diaconate. Paul VI very clearly cautioned, however, against anyone seeing his decision as signifying a relaxation of the existing law of celibacy.

In sum, Paul VI advanced the teaching of his papal predecessors of the twentieth century, such as Pius XII, who justified priestly celibacy mostly on the grounds of ritual purity, the superiority of celibacy over marriage, the liberty of spirit and body for more intense prayer, and detachment from the world. On his part, Paul VI situated his teaching on celibacy within the context of its nature as a spiritual gift for the priest in his ministry: "In the world of man, so deeply involved in earthly concerns and too often enslaved by the desires of the flesh, the precious

---

54. Ibid., n. 41.
55. Ibid., n. 42.

and *almost divine gift* of perfect continence for the kingdom of heaven stands out precisely as 'a special token of the rewards of heaven.'"[56]

Paul VI moreover greatly amplified the magisterial teaching by drawing on the doctrine of Vatican II, especially by using various biblical and patristic themes in *Presbyterorum Ordinis* 16, in his formulation of the threefold dimension of priestly celibacy. This theological scheme greatly enhanced the intelligibility of celibacy by systematizing the various perspectives of the priestly discipline. Both the systematization and the content of the renewed teaching of Paul VI was a great advance over the method and content of his predecessors, principally Pius XII.

The threefold dimension is not found *as such* in the documents of Vatican II. Traces of it, though, appeared within two documents that used the three notions without explicitly tying them together, namely, in *Optatam Totius* 10 and *Presbyterorum Ordinis* 16. Although the fathers of Vatican II may not have intended to formulate a threefold scheme as such, they nonetheless, almost intuitively, grouped these three notions together. *Optatam Totius* 10, written prior to *Presbyterorum Ordinis* 16, was significantly the first evidence of an emerging magisterial teaching on priestly celibacy that is schematized, at least implicitly, according to a threefold paradigm. The council fathers formulated their teaching on priestly celibacy in a renewed fashion that was drawn in large measure from scriptural themes. Paul VI continued this renewal in *Sacerdotalis Caelibatus*, and subsequent magisterial teachings presented priestly celibacy in a systematic, clear manner through ample use of the threefold dimension.

The Second Vatican Council and Paul VI thus provided a new direction for magisterial doctrine on priestly celibacy. As will be shown, this new teaching will bear fruit through the development of arguments that are proportionate to the priesthood itself rather than those that are applicable to both priests and consecrated religious.

---

56. Ibid., n. 34; emphasis added. The internal citation is from Vatican Council II, *Perfectae Caritatis*, n. 12.

A Guide to Formation in Priestly Celibacy

FOLLOWING THE CALL of Paul VI in *Sacerdotalis Caelibatus* 16 for guidelines on the formation of priestly candidates in celibacy, the Congregation for Catholic Education in 1974 published *A Guide to Formation in Priestly Celibacy*.[57] Among other things, this document discusses the meaning of celibacy in contemporary priestly life, including an observation about the eschatological dimension of celibacy:

Every Christian has a duty to be united with the love of Christ and to bear witness to this love. Thus, every Christian life is permeated with an eschatological character, from martyrdom to the religious life, from the priesthood to the married state. Strictly speaking, celibacy does not, therefore, confer an eschatological character on the priesthood. The priest already has this himself, just as Christians in all other states and vocations possess it in themselves, in their own special way. But, priestly celibacy harmonizes with the eschatological aspect of the priesthood, and in certain ways, reinforces this aspect and enables the priest to be very fully immersed in the perfect love of the Risen Christ.[58]

This perceptive comment highlights the universal nature of the eschatological dimension of the Christian life, rooted in Baptism. Each baptized faithful witnesses the eternal love of Christ and lives as a visible sign of the future resurrection, already present here and now. The advantage of the specifically eschatological aspect of priestly celibacy, however, is that it enhances this already existing eschatological witness and enables the priest to be fully immersed in the love of the Risen Christ.

A Guide to Formation in Priestly Celibacy also provides a brief summary of the manifold reasons for ecclesiastical celibacy, as well as a reference to the ritual purity argument: "The Church has deep reasons for demanding celibacy of her priests. They are founded on the priest's imitation of Christ, on his role as representative of Christ, head and leader of the community, on his availability for service which is indispensable for the constant building of the Church. The Church is not prompted by

---

57. See Congregation for Catholic Education, "A Guide to Formation in Priestly Celibacy," *Origins* 4 (1974): 65, 67–76.

58. Ibid., n. 11.

reasons of 'ritualistic purity' nor by the concept that only through celibacy is holiness possible."[59]

The "deep reasons" for the law of celibacy cited above include two that relate to the Christological and ecclesiological dimensions of celibacy: the priest's imitation of Christ and his role as representative of Christ, "head and leader of the community." Furthermore, the last sentence in this text surprisingly stated that the Church does not see ritual purity as a valid argument for the defense of priestly celibacy. It is difficult to see the soundness of this assertion in view of the perennial use of the ritual purity argument in Catholic magisterial and theological texts from the early patristic period.

Aware that former magisterial documents have employed the ritual purity argument, *A Guide to Formation in Priestly Celibacy* anticipates objections by providing some measure of an explanation: "Among the historical reasons adduced to justify a priest's celibacy there may be some which are *no longer valid* with the passing of time, but this should not cause the rejection of the connection between celibacy and the priesthood. This connection is a living reality in the Church. It is an experience that is linked not so much to this or that argument as to the fundamental fact and reality of Christianity itself, which is the person of Jesus Christ, at the same time virgin and priest."[60]

It seems clear from the above context that *A Guide to Formation in Priestly Celibacy* includes ritual purity among those arguments that no longer hold validity. However, it does not claim that the former arguments are erroneous, but that they are "no longer valid with the passing of time." *A Guide to Formation in Priestly Celibacy* unfortunately does not specify the conditions that have contributed to the alleged invalidity of these arguments, for example, developments in theological anthropology and sacramental theology. Any critique of the ritual purity argument should be balanced by considering its long-standing use within Catholic theological tradition, such as providing an insight into the connection between priestly celibacy and service at the altar.

59. Ibid., n. 13. Stated as such, the teaching that "only through celibacy is holiness possible" has never been an authentic magisterial doctrine.

60. Ibid., n. 13; emphasis added.

Inter Insigniores

ALMOST TEN YEARS after *Sacerdotalis Caelibatus*, the Congregation for the Doctrine of the Faith released a document on the admission of women to the ministerial priesthood, *Inter Insigniores* (1976). Within it are discussed the reasons why the Catholic Church does not admit women to the ministerial priesthood.[61] This document contains a relevant section for priestly celibacy from an ecclesiological perspective.

In section 5, titled "The Ministerial Priesthood in the Light of the Mystery of Christ," *Inter Insigniores* explores the nature of the ministerial priesthood and provides theological justification for allowing only men to receive priestly ordination. The argument refers to the sacramental-representative role of the priest or bishop: "The Church's constant teaching, which she has declared anew and more profusely is ... that the bishop or the priest in the exercise of his ministry, does not act in his own name, *in persona propria*: he represents Christ, who acts through him: 'the priest truly acts in the place of Christ,' as St. Cyprian already wrote in the third century."[62] The supreme expression of this representation occurs in the celebration of the Eucharist, the sacrificial offering in which the people of God are associated in the sacrifice of Christ. The priest acts not only through the effective power conferred on him by Christ but "*in persona Christi*, taking the role of Christ, to the point of being his very image, when he pronounces the words of consecration."[63]

Inter Insigniores also includes a teaching on the visible, sacramental nature of the ministerial priesthood; that is, the priest is a perceptible sign that the faithful recognize with ease. The same natural resemblance is required for persons as for things: "When Christ's role in the Eucharist is to be expressed sacramentally, there would not be this 'natural resemblance' which must exist between Christ and his minister if the role of Christ were not taken by a man: in such a case it would be difficult to see

---

61. See Congregation for the Doctrine of the Faith, *Inter Insigniores*, in *From "Inter Insigniores" to "Ordinatio Sacerdotalis"* (Washington, D.C.: United States Catholic Conference, 1996), 20–52; *Acta Apostolicae Sedis* 69 (1977): 98–116.

62. Congregation for the Doctrine of the Faith, *Inter Insigniores*, n. 5.

63. Ibid.; emphasis only in the translation and not in the Latin text. In the texts of Vatican II, only *Presbyterorum Ordinis* 2 contains the fuller formula *in persona Christi capitis*.

in the minister the image of Christ. For Christ himself was and remains a man."[64] The priest is thus not only an *instrument* of Christ, but he is also a *sign* of Christ. The declaration argues that the priest himself functions as a sign and that his masculinity has a role in this signification. The same natural resemblance is required for persons as for things. Thus, the visible sign that represents Christ is the ordained male.[65]

The text then focuses on the nuptial-ecclesiological aspect of the priesthood by summarizing the nuptial covenant established by the Lord God with the chosen people, his spouse, and by describing the manner in which the Son of God became the Bridegroom of the Church by means of the Incarnation. According to *Inter Insigniores*, scriptural language reveals to the believer the mystery of God and Christ through symbols, which affect man and woman in their intimate identity. It must be a man therefore who performs those sacramental actions in which Christ himself is represented as Bridegroom and Head of the Church.[66]

Although priestly celibacy is not treated explicitly in *Inter Insigniores*, certain principles contained in the document have played a significant role in the subsequent development of the theology of priestly celibacy. Two of these mentioned earlier are the fuller development of the notion of the priest acting *in persona Christi*, especially as Bridegroom and Head of the Church, as well as the necessity of the "natural resemblance" that must exist between Christ and the male minister. These two principles in particular will be employed by Pope John Paul II in his development of the nuptial-ecclesiological dimension of the celibate priesthood, as will be seen in the next section.

John Paul II

POPE SAINT JOHN PAUL II has left to the Catholic Church a massive body of pontifical teaching, some of which has yet to be studied in depth. One area that has not garnered much attention is his teaching on the ministerial priesthood, which the pope presented through several channels, such as the weekly catechesis at the Wednesday audiences

---

64. Congregation for the Doctrine of the Faith, *Inter Insigniores*, n. 5.
65. See Sara Butler, *The Catholic Priesthood and Women* (Chicago: Hillenbrand, 2006), 81.
66. See Congregation for the Doctrine of the Faith, *Inter Insigniores*, n. 5.

and the annual Holy Thursday letter to priests.[67] John Paul II's most significant teaching on the priesthood, however, is found in *Pastores Dabo Vobis*, his 1992 postsynodal apostolic exhortation on the formation of priests.

Theology of the Body

John Paul II first systematically treated celibacy in his Wednesday audiences on the subject known as the *Theology of the Body* (1979–1984).[68] In his discourses, the pope developed a theology of the human body that breaks new ground in Catholic tradition by placing *nuptiality* at the center of Christian anthropology.[69] He emphasized that the truth of the human person is expressed through the body, which itself reveals the human person and is essentially ordered to a nuptial relationship. Along these lines, John Paul II wrote with regard to matrimony: "As ministers of a sacrament that is constituted through consent and perfected by conjugal union, man and woman are called *to express* the mysterious *'language' of their bodies in all the truth that properly belongs to it*. Through gestures and reactions, through the whole reciprocally conditioned dynamism of tension and enjoyment—whose direct source is the body in its masculinity and femininity, the body in its action and interaction—through all this *man*, the person, 'speaks.'"[70] At the core of his understanding of nuptiality stands the notion of the human body as gift.

In order to establish the notion of the "language of the body," John Paul II gave a reflective commentary on Genesis 2–4, to which he dedicated his first twenty-three catecheses. The pope taught that Adam and Eve were aware, through their consciousness, of the "nuptial meaning" of the human body; that is, the body is intrinsically ordained toward

---

67. The twenty-one Wednesday audiences on the priesthood, which John Paul II gave in 1993, are available in *Priesthood in the Third Millennium* (Chicago: Midwest Theological Forum, 1994). For his Holy Thursday letters to priests, see John Paul II, *Letters to My Brother Priests: Complete Collection of Holy Thursday Letters (1979–2005)*, ed. James Socias (Woodbridge, Ill.: Midwest Theological Forum, 2006).

68. See John Paul II, *Man and Woman He Created Them: A Theology of the Body*, trans. Michael Waldstein (Boston: Pauline, 2006), 412–57.

69. See Fergus Kerr, *Twentieth-Century Catholic Theologians: From Neoscholasticism to Nuptial Mysticism* (Malden, Mass.: Blackwell, 2007), 175.

70. John Paul II, *Man and Woman He Created Them*, n. 123:4.

marital union and is a sign of the gift of the man as person to the woman as person, and vice versa. The nuptial meaning of the body showed them that the fulfillment of a person occurs only in the mutual self-giving of the act of love.[71] Furthermore, the nakedness of the human body expressed its full meaning as a gift ordered to the communion of persons: "The human body was from the beginning a faithful witness and a perceptible verification of man's original 'solitude' in the world, while becoming at the same time, through masculinity and femininity, a transparent component of reciprocal giving in the communion of persons."[72]

Original sin, however, broke the nuptial unity that united Adam and Eve in the state of innocence. Concupiscence darkened the nuptial meaning of the human body and "original nakedness" was replaced by shame regarding the body after the Fall. Jesus Christ, however, restored this nuptial unity through his sacrifice on the Cross, which created a bond between himself, the New Adam, and his Church, the New Eve. Using Ephesians 5:21–33 as a primary text, the pope underlines the beauty of spousal love in marriage, with a creative emphasis on the physical and psychological dimensions of marital love.[73]

Because the subject of marriage was the primary focus of the Wednesday audiences, John Paul II devoted most of his talks to the nature of the sacrament of Matrimony. The pope, however, did give thirteen catecheses on celibacy in general as it applies to men and women.[74] Although he did not deal specifically with priestly celibacy, the pope provided principles that are applicable to the celibate priesthood, as will be seen from his subsequent argumentation in *Pastores Dabo Vobis*.

John Paul II invoked the threefold dimension of celibacy and first focused on the eschatological: the celibate male and female foreshadow the afterlife. Celibacy "for the Kingdom of heaven" is the prism through which Christians understand the primary meaning and purpose of the celibate vocation:

---

71. Ibid., n. 15:1; see also Kerr, *Twentieth-Century Catholic Theologians*, 178.
72. John Paul II, *Man and Woman He Created Them*, n. 27:3.
73. Ibid., nn. 87–102.
74. Ibid., nn. 73–85.

This way of existing as a human being (male and female) points out the eschato-logical "virginity" of the risen man, in which, I would say, the absolute and eter-nal spousal meaning of the glorified body will be revealed in union with God himself, by seeing him "face to face," glorified moreover through the union of a perfect intersubjectivity that will unite all the "sharers in the other world," men and women, in the mystery of the communion of saints. Earthly continence "for the kingdom of God" is without doubt a sign that *indicates* this truth and this real-ity. It is a sign that the body, whose end is not death, tends toward glorification; already by this very fact it is, I would say, a testimony among men that antici-pates the future resurrection.[75]

Celibacy for the Kingdom of heaven bears above all the character-istic of likeness to Christ, who himself made this choice for the sake of the Kingdom of heaven.[76] It is in this context that John Paul II briefly touched on the Christological dimension of celibacy. When Christ spoke of those who "made themselves eunuchs for the Kingdom of heaven" (Mt 19:12), his disciples would have understood this only on the basis of his own personal example. Such continence must have impressed itself on their consciousness as a specific trait of likeness to Christ, who had himself remained celibate for the Kingdom of heaven.[77]

In his exegesis of Ephesians 5:21–33, John Paul II suggested a nuptial-ecclesiological dimension of celibacy that draws from the Pauline nup-tial imagery: "The Pauline image of the 'great mystery' of Christ and the Church indirectly speaks also about 'continence for the kingdom of heav-en,' in which both dimensions of love, the spousal and the redemptive, are united with each other in a way that differs from that of marriage, in accord with different proportions. *Is* not the spousal *love with which Christ 'loved the Church,'* his Bride, 'and gave himself for her' equally the fullest *incarnation* of the ideal of '*continence for the kingdom of God'* (see Mt 19:12)?"[78]

John Paul II here gave a unique interpretation of Ephesians 5:21–33 insofar as he used this text, which was traditionally used in the Catho-lic theological tradition to illumine Christian matrimony in light of the nuptial relationship between Christ and the Church, to show how it

---

75. Ibid., n. 75:1. In these discourses, the pope often used "continence" as a synonym for "celibacy."

76. Ibid.

77. Ibid., n. 75:4.

78. Ibid., n. 102:6.

also can illustrate the nuptial quality of continence for the Kingdom of heaven. The pope, however, admitted that Ephesians 5 does not speak about continence for the Kingdom of heaven explicitly. On the other hand, this continence can be inferred from Ephesians 5:21–33 insofar as the redemptive-spousal love of Christ embraces every human being. Christian men and women who live this eschatological dimension of celibacy are able to link the spousal dimension of love with the redemptive dimension according to the model of Christ himself. John Paul II explained more fully: "[Celibate men and women] desire to confirm with their lives that the spousal meaning of the body—of its masculinity and femininity—a meaning deeply inscribed in the essential structure of the human person has been opened in a new way by Christ and with the example of his life to the hope united with the redemption of the body."[79] The grace of the mystery of redemption bears fruit in a particular way, according to the pope, with the vocation to continence "for the Kingdom of heaven."

In his *Theology of the Body*, John Paul treated celibacy in a broad manner that is applicable to all Christians, celibate and married. Consequently, the pope did not develop at any length the threefold dimension of *priestly* celibacy, but rather, he concentrated on "continence for the Kingdom of heaven" and on divine love as its motivating factor: "[Continence for the Kingdom of heaven] has become in the experience of the disciples and followers of Christ the act of *a particular response to the love* of the Divine Bridegroom, and therefore *acquired the meaning of an act of spousal love*, that is, of a spousal gift of self with the end of answering in a particular way the Redeemer's spousal love; a gift of self understood as a *renunciation*, but realized above all *out of love*."[80]

Mulieris Dignitatem

In his encyclical letter *Mulieris Dignitatem* (1988), which deals with the dignity and vocation of women, John Paul II briefly considered consecrated virginity.[81] The pope emphasized the spousal quality of con-

---

79. Ibid.

80. Ibid., n. 79:9.

81. See John Paul II, *Apostolic Letter on the Dignity and Vocation of Women, Mulieris Dignitatem* (1988), nn. 20–22, in John Paul II, *Theology of the Body: Human Love in the Divine Plan* (Boston: Pauline, 1997), 443–92.

secrated virginity, placing it within the context of Ephesians 5:21–32, which illustrates the relationship between Christ and the Church according to a marital bond. By means of the head/body image and the citation of Gen 2:24 ("for this reason a man will leave his father and mother"), this text in Ephesians shows how the close union of man and wife in human marriage is a great *mystery* (μυστήριον) that points to the nuptial relationship of Christ and his bride.

In a section on "Virginity for the Sake of the Kingdom," the pope taught that the bridal notion as such, seen under its feminine or receptive mode, is proper to the woman because of the "naturally spousal predisposition of the feminine personality."[82] Thus, the female virgin, seen in her physical, emotional, and psychological dimensions, better signifies the gift of self to the male Christ under the spousal imagery, because the love of Christ is symbolized as masculine in relation to the traditional symbolism of the Church as feminine. However, although the consecrated woman is a more fitting symbol of this receptive love of the bride, the consecrated man also shares in this receptivity. Therefore, the Church's bridal quality affects all of its members, both male and female: "In the Church every human being—male and female—is the 'Bride,' in that he or she accepts the love of Christ the Redeemer, and seeks to respond to it with the gift of his or her own person."[83]

Moreover, masculinity plays a significant factor in the sacramental life of the Church through the ministerial priesthood. The divine Bridegroom, the Son consubstantial with the Father, became the son of Mary; he became the "Son of Man," a male. The symbol of the bridegroom is masculine, which represents the human aspect of the divine love that God has for the Church.[84] It is fitting, and even necessary, therefore, that the ministerial priest be a man, so that he can image Christ the Head and Bridegroom in the Church, and particularly when he celebrates the Eucharist:

Since Christ, in instituting the Eucharist, linked it in such an explicit way to the priestly service of the apostles, it is legitimate to conclude that he thereby wished to express the relationship between man and woman, between what is "femi-

82. Ibid., n. 20.
84. Ibid., n. 25.

83. Ibid., n. 25.

nine" and what is "masculine." It is a relationship willed by God both in the mystery of creation and in the mystery of redemption. It is *the Eucharist* above all that expresses *the redemptive act of Christ the Bridegroom towards the Church the Bride.* This is clear and unambiguous when the sacramental ministry of the Eucharist, in which the priest *acts "in persona Christi,"* is performed by a man.[85]

What is significant in this passage is the manner in which John Paul II linked the male priest with the celebration of the Eucharist, wherein the priest acts in the person of Christ, the Bridegroom of the Church. Through this nuptial-eucharistic theology, the pope advanced a particular understanding of the priest's role in the eucharistic celebration wherein the liturgical ministry, rooted in sacramental ordination, is essentially tied to a marital covenant as expressed in Ephesians 5:21–32.

Thus, in *Mulieris Dignitatem*, John Paul II taught that the ordained priest, in virtue of his being able to act in the person of Christ, the Head and Bridegroom of Church, becomes an icon of Christ's divine and exclusive love. As will be shown, in *Pastores Dabo Vobis*, John Paul II argued that priestly celibacy most fittingly allows this iconic expression of Christ's love to shine in and through the priest.

Pastores Dabo Vobis

The 1992 postsynodal apostolic exhortation of John Paul II, *Pastores Dabo Vobis*, addressed the formation of seminarians and the ongoing formation of priests.[86] John Paul II incorporated into the document select propositions from the final report of the 1990 Eighth Ordinary General Assembly of the Synod of Bishops. The subject matter for this synod was the formation of priests in the circumstances of the present day.

John Paul II stated that *Pastores Dabo Vobis* was inspired by the bishops at the synod, who were particularly concerned with the increase of priestly vocations and the formation of seminarians in an attempt to help them to know and follow Jesus Christ, the Head and Shepherd, the Servant and Spouse of the Church.[87]

The Christological dimension of priestly ministry is the foundation-

---

85. Ibid., n. 26.

86. See John Paul II, *Post-Synodal Apostolic Exhortation: I Will Give You Shepherds, Pastores Dabo Vobis* (Boston: Pauline, 1992).

87. Ibid., n. 3.

al element in seminary formation since it is the primary point of reference for priestly identity. Seminarians are to be motivated and formed so that they desire to understand and imitate Christ himself. Through sacerdotal ordination these future priests will be configured to Christ in his relationship to his Body, the Church, and thus will participate in the ecclesiological perspective of priestly ministry. John Paul II employed four biblical images to convey the ecclesiological notion: (1) Jesus Christ is *Head* of the Church: "Christ is the head of the Church, his body, and is himself its savior,"[88] (2) Jesus Christ is *Servant*: "The authority of Jesus Christ as head coincides then with his service, with his gift, with his total, humble and loving dedication on behalf of the Church. All this he did in perfect obedience to the Father; he is the one true Suffering Servant of God, both priest and victim,"[89] (3) Jesus Christ as *Shepherd*: "By virtue of their consecration, priests are configured to Jesus the good shepherd and are called to imitate and to live out his own *pastoral charity*,"[90] and (4) Jesus Christ is the true *Bridegroom*, or *Spouse*: "Inasmuch as he represents Christ, the head, shepherd and spouse of the Church, the priest is placed not only in the Church but also in the forefront of the Church."[91]

As is indicated, the ministerial priest imitates and participates in Christ's own pastoral charity, which is the internal principle that animates and guides the priest in his ministry inasmuch as he is configured to Christ, particularly in the image of Shepherd. The essence of pastoral charity is a gift of self to the Church after the example of Christ himself. Insofar as pastoral charity is directed toward the Church, it has an intrinsic ecclesiological dynamism. Moreover, it is rooted in and expressed through the Eucharist: "The Eucharist represents, makes once again present, the sacrifice of the cross, the full gift of Christ to the Church, the gift of his body given and his blood shed, as the supreme witness of the fact that he is head and shepherd, servant and spouse of the Church. Precisely because of this, the priest's pastoral charity not only flows from the Eucharist but finds in the celebration of the Eu-

---

88. Ibid., n. 22, citing Eph 5:23.
89. Ibid., n. 21; see Mt 20:28 and Jn 13:1–20.
90. Ibid., n. 22; emphasis added; see Jn 10:11, 14.
91. Ibid., n. 22; see Eph 5:23–29.

charist its highest realization—just as it is from the Eucharist that he receives the grace and obligation to give his whole life a 'sacrificial' dimension."[92] Underlying this pastoral charity is the mystery of trinitarian communion, which is the font of this charity and the root of the relationship between Christ and the Church, and hence between the priest and the Church.[93] At the heart of the priest's relationship to Christ and the Church is the mystery of the communion of the Holy Trinity.

Continuing this theme of participation in the priesthood of Christ, John Paul II listed two primary images of the priest's relationship, in Christ, to the Church:

The priest's fundamental relationship is to Jesus Christ, *head* and *shepherd*. Indeed, the priest participates in a specific and authoritative way in the "consecration/anointing" and in the "mission" of Christ (cf. Lk 4:18–19). But intimately linked to this relationship is the priest's relationship with the Church. It is not a question of "relations" which are merely juxtaposed, but rather of ones which are interiorly united in a kind of mutual immanence. The priest's relation to the Church is inscribed in the very relation which the priest has to Christ, such that the "sacramental representation" to Christ serves as the basis and inspiration for the relation of the priest to the Church.[94]

The relation of the priest to Jesus Christ, Head and Shepherd, constitutes the *Christological* dimension of priestly ministry; the relation of the priest in Christ, Head and Shepherd, to his Church constitutes the *ecclesiological* dimension. Both relations are rooted in the priest's sacramental consecration. The priest discovers the truth of his identity in his participation in the priesthood of Christ, to whom the priest is primarily referred. Through ordination the priest becomes a living image of Christ the priest; from his union with Christ, the priest is related to the Church.

John Paul II then turned his attention to priestly celibacy and continued the prior theme of the priest's relationship to Christ and the Church. In the section on celibacy, the pope employed principles that

92. Ibid., n. 23.
93. Ibid., n. 12. See Richard Malone, "On John Paul II's *Pastores Dabo Vobis*," *Communio* 20 (1993): 569–71.
94. John Paul II, *Post-Synodal Apostolic Exhortation*, n. 16; emphasis added.

appeared in his *Theology of the Body*, such as the nuptial meaning of the body and the eschatological dimension of "celibacy for the Kingdom," in order to illustrate the nuptial meaning of celibacy: "In virginity and celibacy, chastity retains its original meaning, i.e., of human sexuality lived as a genuine sign of and precious service to the love of communion and gift of self to others. This meaning is fully found in virginity which makes evident, even in the renunciation of marriage, the 'nuptial meaning' of the body through a communion and a personal gift to Jesus Christ and his Church which prefigures and anticipates the perfect and final communion and self-giving of the world to come."[95] John Paul II maintained the focus on celibacy as a *personal gift*, as a precious service to Christ and to his Church. The pope's portrayal of celibacy-as-gift was a positive contribution to a more positive attitude that the Magisterium has adopted with regard to its teaching on celibacy and marriage.

John Paul II also appealed to the *sensus fidelium* as a touchstone of the need to retain the tradition of mandatory celibacy in the Latin Church. In perhaps his most profound statement on priestly celibacy in *Pastores Dabo Vobis*, the pope wrote:

It is especially important that the priest understand the theological motivation of the Church's law on celibacy. Inasmuch as it is a law, it expresses the Church's will, even before the will of the subject expressed by his readiness. But the will of the Church finds its ultimate motivation in the link between celibacy and sacred ordination, which configures the priest to Jesus Christ the head and spouse of the Church. The Church, as spouse of Jesus Christ, wishes to be loved by the priest in the total and exclusive manner in which Jesus Christ her head and spouse loved her. Priestly celibacy, then, is the gift of self *in* and *with* Christ *to* his Church and expresses the priest's service to the Church in and with the Lord.[96]

In this passage, two elements of the threefold dimension are evident: priestly celibacy unites the priest to Jesus Christ (the Christological dimension) and consequently orients him toward ministerial service to the Church (the ecclesiological dimension).

What is particularly significant in *Pastores Dabo Vobis* 29 is the claim of John Paul II that the Church, as Spouse of Jesus Christ, desires to be

---

95. Ibid., n. 29.

96. Ibid.; emphasis in the translation but not in the Latin text.

loved and served by a celibate priest. Just as Christ and ordained priests have an exclusive, nuptial relationship to the Church, so, too, the Church has an exclusive, nuptial relationship to the priest. Thus, the priest's exclusive relationship with the Church suggests the incongruity of his having a human, nuptial relationship. In the mind of John Paul II, the manifestation of the *sensus fidelium* on this matter is a significant argument in favor of priestly celibacy.

Finally, the pope commented on the status of priestly celibacy in the Latin Church, saying that is should not be considered simply as a legal norm or an external condition for admission to ordination. Rather, it is a value that is connected with ordination "whereby a man takes on the likeness of Jesus Christ, the good shepherd and spouse of the Church, and therefore as a choice of a greater and undivided love for Christ and his Church as a full and joyful availability in his heart for the pastoral ministry."[97]

Priestly celibacy, therefore, is more than mere ecclesiastical law; it is a *gift* for the ministerial priesthood. Celibacy flows from the priest's sacramental configuration to Christ (the Christological dimension) and thus gives to the celibate priest, united through ordination to Christ the Shepherd and Spouse, a dynamic orientation toward the Church (the ecclesiological dimension). The centrality of *pastoral charity* in the ministry and life of the priest is also underlined by reference to a "full and joyful availability in his heart for the pastoral ministry." Interestingly, John Paul II made reference to a "profound" connection between priestly celibacy and ordination. That is, through sacerdotal ordination the priest is called by God to give himself totally in pastoral ministry. Celibacy enables the priest to answer this divine call for him to give himself to Christ and his Church with an undivided heart.

In sum, John Paul II provided in *Pastores Dabo Vobis* a rich development of the teaching of Vatican II on priestly celibacy. In particular, the pope expanded the theological analogies that are commonly used to describe priestly ministry. *Lumen Gentium* 28, for example, teaches that the ministerial priest is the sacramental representative of Christ the Head in relation to his Body and of Christ the Shepherd in relation to

97. Ibid., n. 50.

his Flock. These biblical analogies convey a relationship but not an interpersonal relationship. To the familiar pairs of Head–Body, Shepherd–Flock, the pope in *Pastores Dabo Vobis* 22 added Servant and Bridegroom. The four images, Head, Servant, Shepherd, and Bridegroom, say something about Christ's relationship to the Church, which he served in a total gift of self. Likewise, the priest is to imitate Jesus Christ in this total gift of self through pastoral charity. In the teaching of John Paul II, the priest both represents Christ, at the head of the community, standing "before" God the Father on its behalf, but he also represents Christ standing "before" the Church as her Bridegroom.[98]

According to John Paul II, celibacy helps the priest most effectively to portray in his life this exclusive love of Christ. In virtue of his Baptism, the priest is *in the Church* as a member of the royal priesthood. However, in virtue of his ordination, the priest is also *in relation to the Church*: the priest is configured to Christ the Head and Spouse of the Church, which gives the priest an intrinsic relationship to the Body of Christ. Expressed in another manner, one can say therefore that the celibate priest participates in the role both of the Bridegroom and of the Bride in the mystery of grace: (1) of the "Bridegroom," in that the priest acts in the person of Christ, Head and Spouse, thus reflecting the eternal, sacrificial love that Christ has for his Church, and (2) of the "Bride," in that the priest, in virtue of being a member of the baptized faithful through baptism, enjoys a personal relationship to Christ his Head and Spouse.[99]

As an icon of Jesus Christ the Head, Shepherd, Servant, and Bridegroom of the Church, the priest "faces" the rest of the baptized.[100] Of all of these images, John Paul II favored the *spousal* image to describe the priest's relationship to the Church: "The priest is called to be a living image of Jesus Christ, the spouse of the Church.... In virtue of his configuration to Christ, the head and shepherd, the priest stands in this spousal relationship with regard to the community."[101] Thus, the priest is called

---

98. Ibid., n. 22; Butler, *The Catholic Priesthood and Women*, 99.

99. See Thomas J. McGovern, "The Spousal Dimension of the Priesthood," *The National Catholic Bioethics Quarterly* (Spring 2003): 95–110, at 102; Donald Keefe, "'In Persona Christi': Authority in the Church and the Maleness of the Priesthood," *Faith* 34 (2002): 15–24.

100. See Butler, *The Catholic Priesthood and Women*, 89.

101. John Paul II, *Post-Synodal Apostolic Exhortation*, n. 22.

to live Christ's spousal love toward the bridal Church, which requires that he be a witness to this divine marital love in full, constant, faithful, and exclusive dedication. The faithful themselves, as members of the bridal Church, recognize the need to be loved with such an exclusive love, and thus recognize the worth of the celibate priesthood.

1983 *Code of Canon Law*

AS STATED IN CHAPTER 1, the 1917 *Code of Canon Law* legislated that major clerics—bishops, priests, deacons, and subdeacons—were bound to perfect and perpetual continence. Canon 132, §1 stated in part that "[c]lerics constituted in major orders are prohibited from marriage and are bound by the obligation of observing chastity, so that those sinning against this are sacrilegious."[102] *Chastity* in this context referred to perfect and perpetual continence, and hence celibacy, because major clerics under the 1917 *Code* were almost always celibate, unless a married man received a special papal dispensation for ordination.

The legislation of canon 132, §1 of the 1917 *Code* was reaffirmed in the 1983 *Code of Canon Law*. The canons on celibacy of the 1983 *Code of Canon Law*, however, contain some important variations: (1) the introduction of the permanent diaconate, with the possibility of accepting married men, led to the creation of two categories: celibate and married deacons;[103] (2) because of the abolition of tonsure and minor orders, one now enters the clerical state by reception of the diaconate;[104] and (3) all those admitted to the presbyterate and unmarried candidates for the permanent diaconate are required to make the promise of celibacy publicly before God and the Church prior to diaconal ordination.[105]

Among the canons in the 1983 *Code* dealing with celibacy-continence,

---

102. Peters, *Pio-Benedictine Code*, 68.

103. See *Code of Canon Law Annotated: Latin-English Edition* (Montreal: Wilson & Lafleur Limitée, 1993), canon 236. Translations from the 1983 Code are taken from this work.

104. Ibid., canon 266.

105. Ibid., canon 1037. See Giuseppe Versaldi, "Priestly Celibacy from the Canonical and Psychological Points of View," in *Vatican II: Assessment and Perspectives. Twenty-Five Years After (1962–1987)*, vol. III, ed. René Latourelle, 131–56, at 138–39 (New York: Paulist, 1989); Roman Cholij, "*Observaciones críticas acerca de los cánones que tratan sobre el celibato en el Código de Derecho Canónico de 1983*," *Ius Canonicum* XXXI (1991): 291–305.

however, the most significant is canon 277. Situated among the provisions on the rights and obligations of clerics, canon 277 is divided into three parts: §1 binds all major clerics of the Latin Church to the obligation of continence and therefore to celibacy, §2 exhorts clerics to behave with prudence toward persons whose company can endanger their obligation to "continence" or give scandal to the faithful, and §3 authorizes the bishop to issue norms in support of these obligations.

Paragraph §1 gives the clearest indication of an underlying theology of clerical celibacy-continence. Drawn from *Presbyterorum Ordinis* 16, one can discern therein elements of the threefold dimension, which are indicated in brackets: "Clerics are obliged to observe perfect and perpetual continence for the sake of the kingdom of heaven [the eschatological dimension] and therefore are bound to celibacy, which is a special gift of God by which sacred ministers can more easily adhere to Christ with an undivided heart [the Christological dimension] and can dedicate themselves more freely to the service of God and man [the ecclesiological dimension]."[106] This canon first obliges clerics to a life of "perfect and perpetual continence," which in the next phrase is specified as "celibacy." The former reflects the more general meaning (abstinence from conjugal intercourse for married and nonmarried clerics) whereas the latter refers to the manner in which this abstinence is lived in the Latin Church (nonmarriage). Clerical celibacy is thus presented in the law as a secondary good that, while valued in its own right as "a special gift of God," is nevertheless ordered to the protection and support of a more fundamental good, that is, that of "perfect and perpetual continence for the sake of the Kingdom of heaven."[107] Celibacy is therefore a legal protection for continence and is a consequence of the obligation of Latin clergy to be continent.

Presbyterorum Ordinis 16—which forms the doctrinal content of canon 277, §1—refers to celibacy as being required of all who were to be promoted to sacred orders: "This sacred Council approves and confirms this legislation so far as it concerns those destined for the priesthood, and feels confident in the Spirit that the *gift* of celibacy, so appropri-

---

106. Canon 277, §1.

107. See Peters, "Canonical Considerations on Diaconal Continence," 140–50.

ate to the priesthood of the New Testament, is liberally granted by the Father, provided those who share Christ's priesthood through the sacrament of Order, and indeed the whole Church, ask for that *gift* humbly and earnestly."[108] This notion of celibacy as a *gift* is found in the first part of canon 277, §1: "Clerics are obliged to observe perfect and perpetual continence for the sake of the kingdom of heaven and therefore are bound to celibacy, which is a *special gift of God* ..." The inclusion of the notion of *gift*—which was not part of canon 132, §1 in the 1917 *Code*—points out that clerical celibacy is first and foremost a charism given by God to the ordained cleric in the Latin Church who is called to live perfect and perpetual continence.

Additionally, the canon preserves the perennial Catholic notion that continence and celibacy are integral to the ministerial priesthood. Even though *Presbyterorum Ordinis* 16 has taught that celibacy is not *essential* to the ministerial priesthood, it nevertheless can be described as *integral*, that is, there is an essential connection between the priesthood and celibacy. Levada has articulated well this connection: "If we may say that Christ's virginal celibacy was an essential part of his salvific mission, may we not also say that priestly celibacy is 'essential' to our priesthood? Perhaps the distinction used by the American Jesuit Donald Keefe could be helpful here. He would say that being a priest and being celibate belong together 'essentially,' i.e., their bond is not extrinsic, incidental, accidental, or artificial. They are not held together simply by an act of the arbitrary will of authority. Rather, they complement each other. They form an integral whole in which the one reinforces and perfects the other."[109] Celibacy is integral, and is essentially related, to the priestly life. It is spiritual gift for the priest that conforms him closely to Jesus Christ, and is consequently a gift for the people whom the priest serves.

---

108. Vatican Council II, *Presbyterorum Ordinis*, n. 16; emphasis added.

109. Levada, "Celibacy and the Priesthood," *http://www.doctrinafidei.va/documents/* rc_con_cfaith_doc_20111121_levada-celibacy-priesthood_en.html.

Directory for the Ministry and Life of Priests

IN 1994 THE CONGREGATION FOR THE CLERGY issued the *Directory for the Ministry and Life of Priests*.[110] This document was directed, through the bishops, to all the priests of the Latin Church, in particular the diocesan clergy. The text contains a section on priestly celibacy, which deals principally with the theological and pastoral motives that uphold the relationship between celibacy and the priesthood.[111] Although the three-fold scheme is not explicitly stated as such in the text, each dimension is nonetheless present. Rather than following the customary sequence, the presentation of the three dimensions in the *Directory* follows a reverse order: eschatological, ecclesiological, and Christological.

The *Directory* presents briefly the eschatological dimension in its description of celibacy as a way to freedom for the celibate priest from earthly concerns: "Like any evangelical virtue, consecrated celibacy should be seen as that liberating novelty which the world, especially today, demands as a radical testimony that following Christ is a sign of the eschatological reality."[112] This passage is followed by a citation from Matthew 19:10–12, which refers to those who make themselves eunuchs for the Kingdom of heaven. Interestingly, the *Directory* compares celibacy with the evangelical virtues—rather than simply being described as a chosen state of life—and says that it shares with poverty, chastity, and obedience the same fruit: liberation from the constraints of this world so as to bear witness to the Kingdom of God.

Second, the *Directory* contains a statement that reflects the content of *Pastores Dabo Vobis* 29 regarding the nuptial-ecclesiological dimension of priestly celibacy. The text states that the ecclesiastical discipline of celibacy manifests the will of the Church and finds its ultimate reason in the intimate bond that celibacy has with priestly ordination, which shapes the priest to Jesus Christ, Head and Spouse of the Church. The *Directory* then states that "[t]he letter to the Ephesians (cf. 5:25–27) shows a strict rapport between the priestly oblation of Christ (cf. 5:25)

---

110. Congregation for the Clergy, *Directory for the Ministry and Life of Priests* (Vatican City: Libreria Editrice Vaticana, 1994).

111. Ibid., nn. 57–60.

112. Ibid., n. 58.

and the sanctification of the church (cf. 5:26), loved with a spousal love. Sacramentally inserted into this priesthood of exclusive love of Christ for the Church, his faithful Spouse, the priest expresses this love with his obligation of celibacy, which also becomes a fruitful source of pastoral effectiveness."[113]

The *Directory* further teaches that the priest assumes a "specific juridical bond" through his promise of celibacy. This bond is the source of two blessings for the priest: (1) it is a sign of the "spousal reality present in sacramental ordination," and (2) through it the priest "acquires that true and real spiritual paternity that has universal dimensions."[114] This spiritual paternity is specified, in a particular way, in the rapport with the community to which he has been entrusted. The priest not only has a spousal relationship with the community, but he also is a father to his community.

Finally, the *Directory* describes the Christological dimension, largely paraphrasing key passages from *Presbyterorum Ordinis* 16. The principal idea in this section is the imitation of Christ: "It would be entirely immature to see celibacy as 'a tribute to be paid to the Lord' in order to receive Holy Orders rather than 'a gift received through his mercy', as a free and welcomed choice of a particular vocation of love for God and others. The example is Christ, who in going against what could be considered the dominant culture of his time, freely chose to live celibacy. In following him the disciples left 'everything' to fulfill the mission entrusted to them (Lk 18:28–30)."[115] The *gift* notion of celibacy is clearly present here. Moreover, the motive of following Christ, however, is not isolated but is linked to the motive of service for the Church; in this way the Christological and ecclesiological dimensions are interlinked. Indeed, celibacy is a "gift of self 'in' and 'with' Christ to his Church and expresses the service of the priest to the Church 'in' and 'with' the Lord."[116]

The *Directory* moreover contains a passage on the historical roots

113. Ibid.

114. Ibid.

115. Ibid., n. 59. According to the footnote to this citation, the internal quotations come from Congregation for Catholic Education, *A Guide to Formation in Priestly Celibacy*, n. 16.

116. Congregation for the Clergy, *Directory for the Ministry and Life of Priests*, n. 59. The *Directory* here is directly quoting John Paul II, *Post-Synodal Apostolic Exhortation*, n. 29.

of clerical continence and celibacy: "In following [Christ] the disciples left 'everything' to fulfill the mission entrusted to them (Lk 18:28–30). For this reason the Church, *from apostolic times*, has wished to conserve the gift of *perpetual continence* of the clergy and choose the candidates for Holy Orders from among the *celibate faithful*."[117] Each disciple was required to leave "everything," including "wife" according to the Lucan text cited, and the *Directory* implies that here is found the origin of ecclesiastical continence and celibacy. The document goes on to present several scriptural texts in support of the position that, from the earliest times, perpetual continence was practiced by the clergy.[118]

With regard to these biblical citations offered in defense of *perpetual continence* from apostolic times, the first refers to apostolic tradition itself: "So then, brothers and sisters, stand firm and hold fast to the traditions that you were taught by us, either by word of mouth or by our letter" (2 Thess 2:15). The apostle Paul is giving a broad exhortation to his hearers to follow apostolic tradition. The text itself does not prove the existence of perpetual continence among clerics in the apostolic Church, but it indicates the fundamental importance of apostolic tradition, of which perpetual continence for clerics forms a part.

The *Directory* next cites 1 Corinthians 7:5 in order to link continence to the priestly charism. Paul advises the suitability of temporary continence for married couples as a means of growing more deeply in prayer: "Do not deprive one another except perhaps by agreement for a set time, to devote yourselves to prayer, and then come together again, so that Satan may not tempt you because of your lack of self-control" (1 Cor 7:5). Although this passage does not refer explicitly to clerical continence, it does provide evidence that voluntary sexual continence existed in the early Church among married couples who wished to set aside more time for prayer.

The *Directory* then refers to 1 Corinthians 9:5, which deals with the *sister-woman* who accompanied the apostles: "Do we not have the right to be accompanied by a believing wife (ἀδελφὴν γυναῖκα) as do the other apostles and the brothers of the Lord and Cephas?" (1 Cor 9:5). *New Revised Standard Version* renders ἀδελφὴν γυναῖκα as *believing*

---

117. Ibid., n. 59; emphasis added.
118. See 2 Thess 2:15; 1 Cor 7:5, 9:5; 1 Tim 3:2–12, 5:9; Ti 1:6–8.

wife, although literally it means *sister-woman*. This phrase most probably refers to a female disciple who served the material needs of the Jesus and the apostles (see Mt 27:55, Lk 8:3). Because Paul was celibate when he wrote this passage (see 1 Cor 7:7), his relationship with such a *sister-woman* obviously would entail no conjugal activity. The *Directory* apparently uses 1 Corinthians 9:5, as interpreted by writings of some of the Church fathers, as a witness to the perpetual continence of the apostles and of their successors.

The remaining biblical citations in the aforementioned passage from the *Directory* deal with the requirement that the bishop (see 1 Tm 3:2), the presbyter (see Ti 1:6), and the deacon (see 1 Tim 3:12) be a *man of one wife*. The footnote attached to the bracket containing the scriptural references lists a series of early councils, several papal decrees of Siricius, Innocent I, and Leo the Great, and some works of Eusebius of Caesarea and Epiphanius of Salamis.[119] These sources can shed light on the meaning of the expression "perpetual continence" that is used in the *Directory*. As was mentioned in chapter 1, some Church fathers interpreted the injunction in the Pastoral Epistles—that a candidate for ordained ministry must be a *man of one wife*—to mean that absolute monogamy is the minimum guarantee that a married man could live in marital abstinence once he received the laying on of hands. The entrance into a second marriage was regarded as a sign of the inability of the man, if he were later to be made a deacon, a presbyter, or a bishop, to live the discipline of the Church, that is, future perfect and perpetual continence. These fathers argued that this Pauline formula indicated the law of perfect and perpetual continence required of clerics from apostolic times.[120]

---

119. Fn. 188: "Cf. Council of Elvira (a. 300–305) cann. 27; 33: Bruns Herm., *Canones Apostolorum et Conciliorum saec.* IV–VII, II, 5–6; Council of Neocesarea (a. 314), can. 1; Ecum. Council of Nicea I (a. 325), can. 3: *Conc. Oecum. Decree* 6; Roman Synod (a. 386): *Concilia Africae* a. 345–525, *CCL* 149 (in Council of Telepte), 58–63; Council of Carthage (a. 390): *ibid* 13. 133 ff.; Council of Trullano (a. 691), cann. 3, 6, 12, 13, 26, 30, 48: *Pont. Commissio ad redigendum CIC Orientalis* IX I/1 125–186; Siricio, decretals *Directa* (a. 386): *Patrologia Latina* 13, 1131–47; Innocent I, lett. *Dominus inter* (a. 405): Bruns, cit. 274–77. S. Leo the Great, lett. *a Rusticus* (a. 456): *Patrologia Latina* 54, 1191; Eusebius of Cesarea, *Demonstratio Evangelica* 1 9: *Patrologia Graeca* 22, 82 (78–83); Epiphanio of Salamina, *Panarion Patrologia Graeca* 41, 868, 1024; *Expositio Fidei Patrologia Graeca* 42, 822–826."

120. Cholij writes concerning this citation from the *Directory*: "The very texts used in *Presbyterorum ordinis* to support the early tradition of a married clergy have now been used to

The history of clerical continence-celibacy, however, is not the focus of the teaching of the *Directory* on celibacy. Rather, it is primarily concerned to show that priestly celibacy is intimately connected with priestly ministry in its twofold relation to Christ and the Church, rather than being an extrinsic quality added to the priesthood by ecclesiastical law.

In sum, the *Directory for the Ministry and Life of Priests*, while mostly paraphrasing key thoughts from *Presbyterorum Ordinis* 16, amplified the *ecclesiological* dimension through the use of spousal imagery: the celibate priest has a nuptial relationship to the community entrusted to him. The emphasis on nuptiality that is contained within the ecclesiological dimension is indicative of its richness and potential in the development of an integral theology of priestly celibacy.

Summary

WITH *SACERDOTALIS CAELIBATUS*, Paul VI continued the renewal of Catholic teaching, or doctrine, on priestly celibacy initiated by Vatican II. The pope presented a clear doctrine that was positive, rather than merely polemical or defensive, and which described priestly celibacy as a *gift* from God for the Church. His use of the threefold dimension has helped to present this renewed teaching in a systematic manner and proved to be an effective pedagogical tool that has influenced subsequent magisterial teaching and, as a consequence, has helped to set the framework for contemporary theological study on priestly celibacy.

It is noteworthy that Paul VI used nuptial imagery to describe the celibate priest's relation to the Church. This nuptial formulation contained the first explicit use of spousal imagery by a pope, at least in the twentieth century, to defend priestly celibacy. In speaking of the celibate priest as an icon of Christ, the Bridegroom of the Church, Paul VI went beyond the symbolism of the father of the bride in *Presbyterorum Ordinis* 16.[121]

Since the time of Paul VI, there have been many notable teachings

---

support the tradition of perpetual continence." See Roman Cholij, "Celibacy, Married Clergy, and the Oriental Code," *Eastern Churches Journal* 3, no. 3 (1996): 91–117, at 111.

121. See Paul VI, *Sacerdotalis Caelibatus*, n. 26; Vatican Council II, *Presbyterorum Ordinis*, n. 16.

on *priestly* celibacy, such as those contained in the 1983 *Code of Canon Law* and the *Directory for the Ministry and Life of Priests*. During this period, however, it was John Paul II who most thoroughly developed the threefold dimension of priestly celibacy, particularly in *Pastores Dabo Vobis*. For John Paul II, the ecclesiological dimension of priestly celibacy is rooted in the Christological dimension: the celibate priest's relationship to the Church is rooted in his relationship with Jesus Christ. Both the Christological and ecclesiological dimensions, moreover, are connected to the eschatological in the sense that the priest's union with Christ in service to the Church is ultimately a sign of the Kingdom of God to come.

In addition, John Paul II significantly developed the ecclesiological dimension of priestly celibacy. He taught that celibacy and the priesthood are intimately connected because Christ is both Head and Bridegroom of the Church. Because the priest is configured to Christ, he can have only one Spouse, namely, the Church. Thus, the priest's nuptial love for the Church has to be exclusive and permanent, and from this spousal commitment he derives his spiritual paternity. Moreover, John Paul II taught that the "Church, as spouse of Jesus Christ, wishes to be loved by the priest in the total and exclusive manner in which Jesus Christ her head and spouse loved her."[122] He thus applied the nuptial-ecclesiological dimension directly to the relationship between the priest and faithful, stressing that the priest, in being identified with Christ the Bridegroom through priestly ordination, enjoys an exclusive marital relationship with the Church, and that the Church likewise enjoys exclusive nuptial rights with regard to him. This exclusive and spousal love between the priest and the Church implies the incongruity of the priest having a human, spousal relationship.

Magisterial teaching of the Roman Catholic Church since the Second Vatican Council thus has amply used the threefold dimension, enriching and expanding the traditional doctrine on priestly celibacy. The consistency with which this scheme has been incorporated into magisterial documents is a sign of its theological and pastoral fruitfulness and value.

---

122. John Paul II, *Post-Synodal Apostolic Exhortation*, n. 29.

This renewed magisterial teaching on priestly celibacy also implicitly emphasized the dignity of the married state, by using the nuptial theme as a means of illustrating the intrinsic worth of priestly celibacy. John Paul II, in particular, has described the difference of the sexes in terms of the complementarity of man and woman in the reciprocal capacity for the personal gift of self, rather than in terms of a hierarchically structured relationship. A result of this integral teaching was that the beauty and importance of ecclesiastical celibacy was clearly noted without neglecting the dignity of sacramental marriage.

Following this review of the use of the threefold dimension in magisterial documents in recent decades, various questions arise: What is its theological value? What issues does it resolve? What questions remain? The next chapter seeks to answer these questions regarding the threefold dimension by summarizing the latter's biblical foundations and considering its effectiveness in addressing some related issues.

3

The Threefold Dimension as a
Source of Renewal of the Theology
of Priestly Celibacy

CATHOLIC THEOLOGY throughout the centuries has sought to explain the suitability of celibacy for major clerics, particularly for priests. Although the reasons offered have varied with different mentalities and situations, as Paul VI said, they "were always inspired by specifically Christian considerations, and after they have been thoroughly examined one can arrive at the underlying reasons."[1]

The process of discerning the "underlying reasons" of celibacy is part of the ongoing development of Catholic doctrine and life, constituting what Vatican II described as "a growth in insight into the realities and words that are being passed on."[2] The growth of understanding with regard to one of those "realities and words that are being passed on," namely, priestly celibacy, has come about in all three ways listed in *Dei Verbum* 8: (1) through the contemplation and study of the faithful, (2) from a spiritual experience of these realities, and (3) from the teaching of the Magisterium. Paul VI described this growth of understanding of Catholic teaching on priestly celibacy: "These [reasons given for celibacy] can be brought into clearer light only under the influence of the Holy Spirit, promised by Christ to His followers for the knowledge of things to come (cf. Jn 16:13) and to enable the people of God to increase

1. Paul VI, *Sacerdotalis Caelibatus*, n. 18.
2. Vatican Council II, *Dei Verbum*, n. 8.

in the understanding of the mystery of Christ and of the Church. In this process the experience gained through the ages from a deeper penetration of spiritual things also has its part."[3]

With regard to the reasons for priestly celibacy, Paul VI developed the teaching of Vatican II insofar as he employed in his encyclical an explicit formulation of the threefold dimension, which had been implicit in the conciliar documents. This new theological paradigm brought into the magisterial teaching on priestly celibacy a rich array of biblical and theological ideas.

Even though the threefold dimension of priestly celibacy has been a sustained feature of magisterial teaching since Vatican II, one should still submit it to a theological evaluation. Such an evaluation can be made at least in two ways: (1) by studying its biblical foundations, that is, its roots in divine revelation, thereby assessing the claim to be a legitimate development of doctrine rather than a mere theological construct, and (2) by analyzing its theological value as a whole. The present chapter therefore undertakes an evaluation of the threefold scheme: it evaluates each dimension in turn, considering for each one its biblical foundations, as well as its theological value and richness.

The Christological Dimension of Priestly Celibacy

THE ORDAINED MINISTER images and makes Christ present to the community. The *Catechism of the Catholic Church* teaches that "[i]n the ecclesial service of the ordained minister, it is Christ himself who is present to his Church as Head of his Body, Shepherd of his flock, high priest of the redemptive sacrifice, Teacher of Truth. This is what the Church means by saying that the priest, by virtue of the sacrament of Holy Orders, acts *in persona Christi Capitis*."[4] The minister is configured to Christ the High Priest, the source of all priesthood.[5] The *Catechism* continues: "Through the ordained ministry, especially that of bishops

---

3. Paul VI, *Sacerdotalis Caelibatus*, n. 18.
4. *Catechism of the Catholic Church*, art. 1548; the footnote to this article provides the following sources: *Lumen Gentium*, nn. 10, 28; *Sacrosanctum Concilium*, n. 33; *Christus Dominus*, n.11; *Presbyterorum Ordinis*, n. 2, 6.
5. See Aquinas, *Summa Theologiae*, III, 22, 4c.

and priests, the presence of Christ as head of the Church is made visible in the midst of the community of believers."[6] Furthermore, this ordained ministry continues the mission begun by the apostles, as the *Catechism* states: "Holy Orders is the sacrament through which the mission entrusted by Christ to his apostles continues to be exercised in the Church until the end of time: thus it is the sacrament of apostolic ministry. It includes three degrees: episcopate, presbyterate, and diaconate."[7] Christ sends his apostles and their successors, the bishops, to proclaim the faith and to establish his reign. He gives them a share in his mission, and from him they receive the power to act in his person.[8] Each bishop is the visible source and foundation of unity in his own particular church.[9] Priests and deacons assist the bishop in his mission.[10]

The focus of this section is the Christological dimension of *priestly* celibacy, that is, the celibacy of both the bishop and the priest. The Christological dimension refers to the priest's union with and configuration to Christ, which has consequences also for the ecclesiological and eschatological dimensions: the celibate priest, by uniting himself with Christ in pastoral charity, is united also with the Church (the ecclesiological dimension) for the sake of the Kingdom of heaven (the eschatological dimension). Because the Christological dimension is the most fundamental of the three dimensions, it is fitting that it be the first of the three to be studied according to its biblical foundations. In the following section, the New Testament indications of the celibacy of Christ are established, and this is followed by evidence of the celibacy of the apostles and of their successors as ministers of the Church.

New Testament Foundations of the Christological Dimension

Belief in a resurrection to eternal life, as taught by Jesus, clearly differed from earlier Jewish understandings of eternal life. The Jews lacked a clear notion of the resurrection of the body, at least according to preexilic beliefs. Hence, they believed that they would survive death and live on in

6. *Catechism of the Catholic Church*, art. 1549.
7. Ibid., art. 1536.
8. Ibid., art. 935.
9. See Vatican Council II, *Lumen Gentium*, n. 23.
10. Ibid., nn. 28–29.

some way through their children. It was considered necessary therefore for one to marry in order to survive through offspring; this was the way to "live eternally."[11]

Christian celibacy, however, points to another understanding, one of life after death: given the resurrection of Jesus, every Christian can hope for an individual resurrection (see Jn 6:40). The resurrection of Jesus itself gives the Christian the assurance of eternal life, so marriage and offspring cease to be imperative and celibacy becomes possible. A Christian in good conscience can forego marriage for the sake of eternal life in the Kingdom of heaven. Revelation 14:4 describes the reward of the 144,000, who had chosen celibacy in imitation of Christ: "It is these who have not defiled themselves with women, for they are virgins; these follow the Lamb wherever he goes. They have been redeemed from humankind as first fruits for God and the Lamb, and in their mouth no lie was found; they are blameless."[12]

Jesus's own celibacy thus can be seen as a prophetic lifestyle, linked to his resurrection, whereby he proclaims eternal life.[13] Jesus has given the Christian hope for an individual resurrection and has lifted the obligation to marry and have children. Christian celibacy is both new and prophetic and is a vocation that springs forth from the grace of Jesus Christ, who renews all things (see Rev 21:5).

From the celibacy of Jesus, one can then establish the biblical foundation for celibacy for the Church's ministers. Although Matthew 19:11–12 ("eunuchs for the sake of the Kingdom of heaven") addresses celibacy in general as an option freely available to Christians in accordance with their own gift, it does not indicate a specific connection between

11. In post-exilic Judaism, a clearer notion of individual eternal life existed (e.g. 2 Maccabees 7, Lk 20:27–40, Mt 22:23–33, and Mk 12:18–27). However, even in the time of Jesus there were continued disputes about this matter, as is seen between the Sadducees and Pharisees. See Matthew Ramage, *Dark Passages of the Bible: Engaging Scripture with Benedict XVI and St. Thomas Aquinas* (Washington, D.C.: The Catholic University of America Press, 2013), 196–97.

12. Rev 14:4. This passage speaks of voluntary celibacy, and only for males, although it is not clear whether the text refers literally to a special group of virgins in the Church or symbolically either to martyrs or to the whole Church as the Bride of Christ; see Meier, *The Roots of the Problem and the Person*, 344.

13. A summary of the biblical evidence of the celibacy of Jesus has been given in chapter 1. This section consists of a study of the consequences of the celibacy of Jesus in the apostolic ministry in the Church.

celibacy and the ordained ministers of the Church. Where, then, might one discern the value of celibacy for such ministers? One indication is found in Luke 18:28–30, which contains the most radical call to celibate discipleship, or in this context to perfect and perpetual continence for married men, insofar as it refers to one's "wife" in the list of the goods of marriage and family life given up for the sake of the Kingdom of God: "Peter said: 'Lo, we have left our homes and followed you.' And Jesus said to them, 'Truly, I say to you, there is no man who has left house or wife or brothers or parents or children, for the sake of the kingdom of God, who will not receive manifold more in this time, and in the age to come eternal life.'"[14] In comparison with Matthew 19:11–12, which refers to celibacy for Christians in general, this Lucan passage is directed to those *men* who have left their homes and human relationships in order to *follow Jesus*. Although Luke 18:28–30 does not refer explicitly to church ministry, it is implied insofar as Jesus is addressing Peter, who seems to be speaking on behalf of the Twelve (see v. 31).

Other than texts referring to Peter and Paul, there are no scriptural indications of the marital status of the apostles.[15] The majority of Church fathers held that the apostles who were married, on deciding to follow Jesus, gave up their conjugal lives, and thereafter practiced perfect continence.[16] This apostolic continence, among other things, allowed them to follow Jesus in his itinerant life. Having been formed by Jesus during his public life, the apostles made Christ present to the Church through their ministry. One manner in which the apostles accomplished this task was through their words and example: "Be imitators of me, as I am of Christ. I commend you because you remember me in everything and maintain the traditions just as I handed them on to you" (1 Cor 11:1–2). Paul states boldly to the Corinthians that Christ is present to them through his own exemplary life. This statement of Paul has affinities with the words of Christ himself to the Twelve: "Whoever welcomes you welcomes me, and whoever welcomes me welcomes the one who sent me" (Mt 10:40).

---

14. Lk 18:28–30; translation is from *Revised Standard Version, Catholic Edition*.

15. See Mt 8:14 (Peter's mother-in-law) and 1 Cor 7:7–8 (Paul's celibacy).

16. Cochini lists some Fathers who held this thesis, such as Clement of Alexandria (d. 215), Tertullian (d. 220), Jerome (d. 419), and Isidore of Pelusium (d. 425); see Cochini, *The Apostolic Origins of Priestly Celibacy*, 79–83.

Another example of the manner in which the apostolic ministry makes Christ present to the Church is through the ministry of reconciliation, which Paul describes in his second letter to the Corinthians: "All this is from God, who reconciled us to himself through Christ, and has given us the ministry of reconciliation; that is, in Christ God was reconciling the world to himself, not counting their trespasses against them, and entrusting the message of reconciliation to us. So we are ambassadors for Christ, since God is making his appeal through us; we entreat you on behalf of Christ, be reconciled to God" (2 Cor 5:18–20). In 2 Corinthians, Paul seeks to justify the apostolic ministry to the faithful of the local Church. Within this context, "ambassadors for Christ" refers to the apostolic ministry, which includes the work of reconciliation that has been entrusted to the church ministers who preach the message of reconciliation. Through this ministry of reconciliation the apostles are making Christ present to the Church.[17]

As Paul and the other apostles were sent by Christ through his Church in the service of the Gospel (see Acts 9:15–16, 10:1–33, 11:19–20), so, too, did they send their successors in order to continue the apostolic ministry. Ephesians 4:11–12 has a description of this ministry: "The gifts [Christ] gave were that some would be apostles, some prophets, some evangelists, some pastors and teachers, to equip the saints for the work of ministry, for building up the body of Christ." Within this context of an apostolic ministry understood as a representation of Christ himself, who was celibate, there are grounds to believe that celibacy or perfect continence formed part of the apostolic mission. Moreover, Paul describes this mission to the Romans as a "priestly service": "I have written to you rather boldly by way of reminder, because of the grace given me by God to be a minister of Christ Jesus to the Gentiles in the priestly service of the gospel of God, so that the offering of the Gentiles may be acceptable, sanctified by the Holy Spirit" (Rom 15:15–16). In his "priestly service," Paul was celibate and encouraged others to adopt that state because it facilitated union of mind and body in Christ so as to be busy with his concerns (see 1 Cor 7:25–40). The words of Paul concerning his own un-

17. See Jan Lambrecht, *Second Corinthians*, vol. 8 of *Sacra Pagina Series*, ed. Daniel J. Harrington (Collegeville, Minn.: Liturgical Press, 1999), 100.

divided heart can be understood as applying to his celibate life: "I wish that all were as I myself am" (1 Cor 7:7), and a fittingness of celibacy for those who will minister in the Church as priests can be discerned.

It was thus a belief in Christ's Resurrection as the cause of the resurrection of the elect that made celibacy a real option for Christians: "If the Spirit of him who raised Jesus from the dead dwells in you, he who raised Christ from the dead will give life to your mortal bodies also through his Spirit that dwells in you" (Rom 8:11). Furthermore, celibacy was particularly appropriate for those who would leave all to follow Jesus in apostolic ministry and for the succeeding generations of ministerial leaders. In continuity with the apostolic tradition, the bishop and the ministerial priest participate in the priestly office of Jesus Christ and fittingly share in his celibate way of life. This Christological significance of priestly celibacy is thus not a mere incidental added to the ministerial priesthood, but can be seen as part of the priestly life itself, as Cardinal Crescenzio Sepe described: "Christ willed, harmoniously and intimately, to combine the virginal state with his mission as eternal priest and mediator between heaven and earth. We can therefore affirm that chastity and virginity are not simply additional or secondary to Christ's priestly existence, but belong to its very essence. 'Don't you see,' St. Ambrose writes, 'that Christ *is* chastity, Christ *is* integrity?'"[18] As Christ is "the same yesterday and today and forever" (Heb 13:8), so priestly celibacy has been understood through the ages and still today as a significant aspect of participation in the ministry and life of Christ.

In sum, according to Catholic theological tradition, the Christological dimension of priestly celibacy is rooted in New Testament references to radical discipleship (see Mt 19:11–12; 1 Cor 7:25–40). Such passages refer to celibacy and continence in general but do not refer explicitly to the corresponding discipline lived by the Church's ministers. However, Luke 18:28–30 and the words of Paul noted earlier provide evidence for the existence of apostolic continence and celibacy, which in turn has been the foundation for the practice of major clerics living in perfect and perpetual continence throughout the centuries.

18. Crescenzio Sepe, "The Relevance of Priestly Celibacy Today," in *For Love Alone*, 66–82, at 69; see Ambrose, *De Virginitate*, 18, in *Patrologia Latina* 16, 271.

The Christological Dimension as an Aid to Understanding
Priestly Celibacy as a Charism and a Discipline

Since the Second Vatican Council some Catholics have questioned whether the institutional Church has the right to "legislate" celibacy.[19] The middle term in their argument is the charismatic nature of celibacy. In other words, if celibacy is a charism, it cannot be enforced *as a discipline* by church authority on men who are called to the ministerial priesthood. A charism, according to Vatican II, is a special grace that the Holy Spirit distributes among all the faithful: "It is not only through the sacraments and the ministrations of the Church that the Holy Spirit makes holy the People, leads them and enriches them with his virtues. Allotting his gifts according as he will (cf. 1 Cor 12:11), he also distributes special graces among the faithful of every rank.... Whether these charisms be very remarkable or more simple and widely diffused, they are to be received with thanksgiving and consolation, since they are fitting and useful for the needs of the Church."[20] A charism is thus a gift of divine grace given to the faithful to make them fit and ready to undertake the many tasks and offices for the renewal and building up of the Church. Of its nature, a charism is not imposed by church authority but is freely given by the Holy Spirit to an individual. Celibacy is one such charism, a *divine gift*, given to those who are called to it (see Mt 19:12).

Since celibacy is required of all candidates for the priesthood in the Latin Church, it also belongs to the category of *discipline*. The distinction between charism and discipline thus raises the question as to how Church authority can require the charism of celibacy for candidates to the priesthood through a disciplinary decree in canon law. For example, canon 1037 mandates that a candidate for the permanent diaconate who is not married, and likewise a candidate for the priesthood, is not to be admitted to the order of diaconate unless he has, in the prescribed rite, undertaken the obligation of celibacy, or unless he has taken perpetual vows in a religious institute.[21]

---

19. For example, see John McIntyre, "Married Priests: A Research Report," *CLSA Proceedings* 56 (1994): 130–52, at 143, and Richard Sipe, *A Secret World: Sexuality and the Search for Celibacy* (New York: Brunner/Mazel, 1990), 56.

20. Vatican Council II, *Lumen Gentium*, n. 12.

21. See 1983 *Code of Canon Law*, c. 1037.

The question, then, concerns the nature of the relationship between ecclesiastical law and clerical celibacy as charism and discipline. Some of the Fathers of Vatican II did not hesitate to raise this question. For example, João Batista da Mota y Albuquerque, archbishop of Vitoria-Espirito Santo, Brazil, asked the following in a written intervention: "An answer needs to be found in particular to the following problem: total continence is a charism. Why then is a charism imposed as a universal obligation upon Latin priests? Is it perhaps that the West has reserved the ministerial function for charismatics? In what sense?"[22]

Heinz-Jürgen Vogels continued this line of thought by noting how in the Eastern Churches the candidate for the priesthood "chooses" celibacy, while in the Latin Church it is "imposed." Vogels pointed out that "[t]he obligation inherent in the law as *lex coercens* can be interpreted in two ways: Either the law seeks to force God to grant to all candidates for priesthood and ordained priests the gift of celibacy; or, it demands from all candidates and those ordained that they wrest the gift from God."[23] According to this argument, church authority cannot demand from candidates for the priesthood, who feel the call to serve in the ordained ministry, a charism that it cannot bestow. Stickler, referring to medieval canonists who debated this issue, wrote that "[i]n seeking to explain the reasons for such a prohibition, they are at times contradictory. Some referred to a *votum*, either *expressum* or *tacitum*, or *ordini adnexum*, *solemnizatum*, that is, annexed to the order or solemnized by legitimate authority."[24] Stickler refers to part of the larger question that has persisted throughout the centuries: How can the church authority require a charism to be present in candidates for ordination, particularly when it has no control over the distribution of charismatic gifts?

In 1970 the International Theological Commission addressed the connection between priestly ministry and celibacy. In its document on priestly ministry, the commission stated:

When the hierarchy links virginity and ministry, it does not alter the nature of the charism but rather emphasizes its communitarian reference and intent, as

22. Vatican Council II, *Acta Synodalia Sacrosancti Concilii Oecumenici Vatican II*, vol. IV/V (Vatican City: Typis Polyglottis Vaticanis, 1970–1988), 275–94, at 286; translation mine.

23. Heinz-Jürgen Vogels, *Celibacy: Gift or Law?* trans. G. A. Kon (Kansas City, Mo.: Sheed & Ward, 1993), 62; see Heid, *Celibacy in the Early Church*, 333.

24. Stickler, *The Case for Clerical Celibacy*, 48.

belongs essentially to every charism. The fact that the Church requires a charismatic gift in those who exercise the ministry witnesses to the transforming power of the sacrament (word and Spirit), which confers the ministry and animates the apostle throughout his life. A radical separation between charism and law ignores the specific character that the Church derives from the Incarnation. By the Incarnation God submits himself to place and time; he receives the human nature from Mary; he depends on a few apostles and on a Church as the witnesses of his life and his words.[25]

The commission argued that one should not drive a wedge between charism and ecclesiastical law. While charisms such as celibacy are by definition *gifts*, within the ecclesial context they need to be affirmed by church authority, to which Christ has given the authority to rule the people of God.[26] Thus, in a broader theological view the authority to judge and regulate charisms has been given to the hierarchical Church.

Moreover, Paul VI wrote in *Sacerdotalis Caelibatus* that "the gift of a priestly vocation" is distinct from that which leads a person to choose celibacy in the consecrated life. But the priestly vocation, although inspired by God, is not confirmed and operative without having been tested and accepted by those in the Church who have the authority and bear the responsibility for the ordained ministry.[27]

In answer to the question, therefore, as to whether the Church has the right to impose the vow of celibacy, the International Theological Commission and Paul VI taught that church authority has a divine mandate to test and accept candidates according to their suitability for orders, and has the competence to determine criteria for suitability, such as, for instance, that those to be ordained must have the charism of celibacy and live it with an appropriate discipline. In other words, church authority chooses candidates for the priesthood in the Latin Church from among those discerned as having the charism of celibacy, and every charism, or gift, requires discipline in order to live it faithfully.

In addition to attention to the legitimate role of church authority

25. International Theological Commission, "The Priestly Ministry" [1970], in *Texts and Documents 1969–1985*, ed. Michael Sharkey (San Francisco: Ignatius, 1989), 3–87, at 73.

26. See *Catechism of the Catholic Church*, arts. 874–87, 894–96.

27. See Paul VI, *Sacerdotalis Caelibatus*, n. 15. Paul VI describes priestly celibacy as both a *gift* and a *discipline* in nn. 7 and 16.

in setting requirements for priestly ordination, what other perspective may help to resolve the tension between charism and discipline? One possible principle is the *Christological* dimension of priestly celibacy, which proposes the notion of the celibate priest as an icon of Jesus Christ. In this perspective, celibacy enables the priest to imitate Christ more perfectly and to be configured to him more closely in his own priestly life.

As surprising as it may sound, many contemporary discussions on priestly celibacy do not take into serious account the ministry and life of Jesus Christ but, rather, tend to focus on the ecclesiastical aspect of the question: How can the Church impose a charism? However, when theology focuses on the ministry and life of Christ as the exemplar of the priestly life, then celibacy is more clearly seen as a charism suitable for the priest so that he may live more freely in union with Christ, rather than being seen as simply a discipline imposed by church authority that has little or nothing to do with the priest's vocation.

The celibate priest looks directly to Christ as his model in the apostolic ministry. Paul VI stated with regard to the Christological dimension of priestly celibacy: "The Christian priesthood, being of a new order, can be understood only in the light of the newness of Christ, the Supreme Pontiff and eternal Priest, who instituted the priesthood of the ministry as a real participation in His own unique priesthood. The minister of Christ and dispenser of the mysteries of God, therefore, looks up to Him directly as his model and supreme ideal."[28] In a footnote to the final sentence, Paul VI referred to 1 Corinthians 11:1: "Be imitators of me, as I am of Christ." By citing 1 Corinthians 11:1 the pope seemed to be stating that the apostle Paul was conscious of the role that celibacy played in his own imitation of Christ.

Christ, the mediator between heaven and earth by virtue of the Incarnation, lived his life in the state of celibacy, which witnesses to his total dedication to the service of God and humankind. It is fitting, therefore, that the ministerial priest, who is called by Christ to follow him wherever he goes (see Lk 9:57), should be celibate and should live his priesthood with a heart full of pastoral charity. The celibate priest un-

28. Paul VI, *Sacerdotalis Caelibatus* n. 19.

derstands in a special way the mission and life of Christ and has the opportunity to be a coworker with him in evangelization, with a heart undivided by the cares of the world and of family (see 1 Cor 7:33–34). In every aspect of his life, the celibate priest strives to imitate the life of Christ, as John Paul II wrote: "Reference to Christ is thus the absolutely necessary key for understanding the reality of priesthood."[29]

In brief, the debate about celibacy as a charism discipline can be put into proper perspective when celibacy is seen as an *imitation of Christ*. Whenever discussions concerning celibacy focus solely on ecclesiastical and canonical perspectives, there is a danger that the full understanding of priestly celibacy in the life of the Church is lost. The Christological dimension guides a theology of priestly celibacy to consider first and foremost the nature of priestly celibacy in its relation to Christ, the exemplar whom the celibate priest imitates. Rather than being understood as a discipline only, celibacy is primarily a charism that enables the ministerial priest to unite himself closely to Christ in service to the Church. The priest is oriented in his ministry to the Body of Christ, the Church, insofar as he is united to the Head, Jesus Christ. He is to serve selflessly the flock entrusted to him insofar as he is one with the chief Shepherd, Jesus Christ. Therefore, the celibate priest looks to the Lord Jesus as the primary motivation in his living of chaste, sacerdotal celibacy. In this respect, Cardinal Basil Hume has said: "For my part, two things are important: first, the fact that our Lord was celibate. Whatever reasons were important to him, I want to make mine. Our Lord was a virgin. That too is important. We should ponder on these truths in prayer."[30]

Episcopal Celibacy in Catholic-Orthodox Dialogue

By his ordination, the priest is configured to Christ, Head of the Church. United with Christ in his headship most perfectly is the bishop who stands amid the local church as the high priest, representing Jesus Christ.[31] He exercises most preeminently the ministerial priesthood. This

29. John Paul II, *Post-Synodal Apostolic Exhortation*, n. 12.

30. Cardinal George Basil Hume, *Searching for God* (Wilton, Conn.: Morehouse-Barlow, 1977), 52.

31. See Vatican Council II, *Sacrosanctum Concilium*, n. 41; *Lumen Gentium*, n. 21.

is not exclusively a Catholic teaching, it is also shared by the Orthodox—a fact that brings a new perspective to the divergence between Orthodox and Catholics regarding clerical celibacy.

A long-standing difference between the Catholic and Orthodox Churches with regard to clerical continence and celibacy has hampered understanding between these churches. That is, the majority of priests in the Catholic Church are celibate, whereas priests in the Orthodox Churches are normally married. The interpretation of the historical data still varies and there has been no agreement regarding the origins and nature of priestly celibacy.[32]

Similarly, there are differences concerning the origins and nature of episcopal celibacy. For example, an Orthodox theologian, Peter L'Huillier, wrote:

[On universal clerical continence], the Western Church was more radical—and more consistent—than the Eastern Church. After all, praise for virginity and sexual abstinence was widespread among Christians in the entire church, and as we have seen, some Eastern writers also held the view that this state of life was "superior" and, therefore, the most appropriate for those in sacred orders. Be that as it may, this was not the main factor at work in limiting the married episcopacy. More significant was the consideration that a married bishop might be tempted *to favor his family in distributing the church's wealth.*[33]

In view of this disparity between the two traditions, it seems appropriate to sketch our own proposal of an ecumenical theology that might help bridge the divide between the Catholic and Orthodox Churches concerning clerical celibacy. The keystone to this proposal is a focus on *episcopal* celibacy seen as the preeminent manifestation of *priestly* celibacy. Laurent Touze has pointed to episcopal celibacy as an important locus for future study and development of the theology of priestly celibacy. Comparing episcopal to priestly celibacy, Touze stated: "[Episcopal celibacy] is very different, both theologically as well as historically. What's more, with the constitution *Lumen Gentium*, Vatican II defined that the episcopate is the fullness of the sacrament of Holy Orders. It is

32. See Kevin Coyle, "Recent Views on the Origins of Clerical Celibacy: A Review of the Literature from 1980–1991," *Logos: A Journal of Eastern Christian Studies* 34 (1993): 480–531.

33. Peter L'Huillier, "The First Millennium: Marriage, Sexuality, and Priesthood," in *Vested in Grace*, 22–65, at 35.

necessary to discover the specificity of the episcopate and, hence, episcopal celibacy. And it can be demonstrated with the fact that for the celibacy or continence of a bishop an exception has never been made."[34]

How can a dialogue on this particular topic be established between the Catholic and Orthodox Churches? One starting point could be the teaching of Vatican II on the episcopacy as the fullness of the priesthood. The patristic teaching on the episcopal high priesthood was recovered by Vatican II and inserted into the description of the bishop's place within the liturgical life of the Church. *Sacrosanctum Concilium* 41 made such a reference to the bishop as high priest:

> The bishop is to be considered as the High Priest of his flock from whom the life in Christ of his faithful is in some way derived and upon whom it in some way depends. Therefore all should hold in the greatest esteem the liturgical life of the diocese centered around the bishop, especially in his cathedral church. They must be convinced that the principal manifestation of the Church consists in the full, active participation of all God's holy people in the same liturgical celebrations, especially in the same Eucharist, in one prayer, at one altar, at which the bishop presides, surrounded by his college of priests and by his ministers.[35]

While the bishop governs and teaches his flock in virtue of his episcopal munera, he exercises his most eminent role through the office of sanctifying, which is fittingly described in the biblical image of the high priesthood of Christ (see Heb 5:1–10). *Lumen Gentium* 21 describes the high priesthood of the episcopacy:

> In the person of the bishops, then, to whom the priests render assistance, the Lord Jesus Christ, supreme high priest, is present in the midst of the faithful. Though seated at the right hand of God the Father, he is not absent from the assembly of his pontiffs; on the contrary indeed, it is above all through their signal service that he preaches the Word of God to all peoples and administers without cease to the faithful the sacraments of faith; that through their paternal care (cf. 1 Cor 4:5) he incorporates by a supernatural rebirth, new members into his body; that finally through their wisdom and prudence he directs and guides the people of the New Testament on their journey towards eternal beatitude.[36]

---

34. Laurent Touze, "Married Priests Will always Be an Exception," http://www.zenit.org/en/articles/married-priests-will-always-be-an-exception.

35. Vatican Council II, *Sacrosanctum Concilium*, n. 41.

36. Vatican Council II, *Lumen Gentium*, n. 21.

This text emphasizes the threefold episcopal munera: the preaching of the Word of God (the office of teaching), the administration of the sacraments (the office of sanctifying), and the guidance of the faithful (the office of governing). In each of these ministries, the bishop exercises the high priesthood of Jesus Christ.

Lumen Gentium 21 proceeds to explain the role of the bishop in shepherding the Lord's flock as a servant of Christ and a steward of the mysteries of God (see 1 Cor 4:1). The mission entrusted to the apostles by Christ through an outpouring of the Holy Spirit (see Acts 1:8, 2:4; Jn 20:22–23) is passed on to bishops through episcopal ordination. The conciliar text highlights this ordination of the bishop and the threefold munera it imparts: "The holy synod teaches, moreover, that the fullness of the sacrament of Orders is conferred by episcopal consecration, that fullness, namely, which both in the liturgical tradition of the Church and in the language of the Fathers of the Church is called the high priesthood, the acme of the sacred ministry. Now, episcopal consecration confers, together with the office of sanctifying, the duty also of teaching and ruling.... Bishops, in a resplendent and visible manner take the place of Christ himself, teacher, shepherd and priest, and act as his representatives (*in eius persona*)."[37] The episcopacy is thus the fullness of the sacrament of Orders, or "the high priesthood." Each bishop is configured to Jesus Christ the High Priest and is "the steward of the grace of the supreme priesthood," above all in the Eucharist.[38]

There are traces of this teaching among various Orthodox theologians. For example, the international Catholic-Orthodox dialogue commission made the following statement in 1988 concerning the episcopacy: "Episcopal ordination confers on the one who receives it by the gift of the Spirit, the fullness of the priesthood."[39] Furthermore, Orthodox theologian Nicholas Afanasiev described the identity of the bishop in the early Church in terms of his liturgical authority as high priest:

37. Ibid., n. 21.

38. Ibid., n. 26.

39. Joint Commission for the Theological Dialogue between the Roman Catholic Church and the Orthodox Church, "The Sacrament of Order in the Sacramental Structure of the Church with Particular Reference to the Importance of Apostolic Succession for the Sanctification and Unity of the People of God," in *The Quest for Unity: Orthodox and Catholics in Dialogue*, ed. John Borelli and John H. Hickson, 131–42 (Crestwood, N.Y.: St. Vladimir's Press, 1996).

Now, at the eucharistic assembly only the person who had a charism of high priesthood could take the place of Christ at the Last Supper, the place taken by St. Peter in the church of Jerusalem. And so the bishop became the presider of the local church by virtue of his status as a high priest. Receiving the charism of high priesthood through a special rite of ordination, the bishop thus acquired the status of the presider in the church for which he was ordained a bishop.... A bishop can assign the celebration of the Eucharist to whomever he wishes, and still retain the high priestly status. By virtue of this fact, several eucharistic assemblies can emerge within the borders of one local church but its unity will not be broken, for the bishop remains the one single high priest at all the assemblies.[40]

From a study of the high priesthood of the bishop, one can delineate what belongs to his ministry and life in the Catholic and Orthodox Churches, both of which have developed a celibate-only episcopacy. The understanding of the bishop as high priest can serve as an effective principle of integration in the theology of celibacy between the two churches because both agree that the episcopacy contains the preeminent expression of the priesthood of Christ in the Church. This approach then prompts the question as to the precise rationale for both married and celibate priests while at the same time showing that behind the married priesthood nevertheless lies the strong witness of celibate priesthood in the bishop.

The Ecclesiological Dimension of Priestly Celibacy

IMITATION OF CHRIST as model and exemplar for the celibate priest in his ministry and life, however, is not the only source of understanding the priest's identity. The study of Christ (Christology) leads to knowledge of his Body, the Church (ecclesiology). Thus, the Christological dimension of priestly celibacy seen as an imitation of Christ is related to the ecclesiological dimension of priestly celibacy seen as an aspect of the priest's relationship with the Church, the Body of Christ. Paul VI mentioned both of these perspectives in his description of the reason for priestly celibacy: "The true, profound reason for dedicated celibacy is, as we have said, the choice of a closer and more complete relationship with the *mystery of Christ and the Church* for the good of all man-

40. Nicholas Afanasiev, *The Church of the Holy Spirit*, trans. Vitaly Permiakov (South Bend, Ind.: University of Notre Dame, 2007), 238.

kind: in this choice there is no doubt, that those highest human values are able to find their fullest expression."[41]

Following this indication of Paul VI, one can say that theology can explore the underlying reasons for priestly celibacy in at least two dimensions. First, the *Christological* dimension: celibacy is chosen for a "closer and more complete relationship with the mystery of Christ." Second, the *ecclesiological* dimension: celibacy is chosen for a "closer and more complete relationship with the mystery of … the Church," as is presented in this section.

As has been stated before, the ecclesiological dimension refers to the way in which celibacy touches upon the priest's relationship to the Church. Although the ecclesiological dimension can be associated with several images of Christ, such as Head, Spouse, Servant, and Shepherd, magisterial teaching since Vatican II has favored the spousal imagery. Therefore, the scriptural references cited below deal primarily with the spousal image as the basis for the ecclesiological dimension of celibacy.

New Testament Foundations of the Ecclesiological Dimension

The ecclesiological dimension of priestly celibacy, derived from the Christological and related to the eschatological dimensions, arises from the bond established between Christ and his Church, to which Christ is related as Head, Shepherd, Servant, and Spouse. Celibacy provides the priest with the freedom to dedicate himself totally to the affairs of Christ and his Body; he surrenders himself in service to all people.

The New Testament foundations of the ecclesiological dimension rest upon the Old Testament notion of the covenant that God established with Israel on Mount Sinai. The richness of this revealed covenantal theology can be seen most notably in its nuptial dimension.[42] The story of the chosen people is the story of God's faithfulness to the spousal covenant with the virgin Israel, despite her unfaithfulness.[43] Ignace de la Potterie wrote that

41. Paul VI, *Sacerdotalis Caelibatus*, n. 54; emphasis added.

42. See Ex 19:5, Hosea 1–2, Is 37:22, Lam 2:13 ("the virgin Zion"), and Jer 18:13, Amos 5:2, Ez 16:8–14 (the "virgin Israel"); Ignace de la Potterie, *Mary in the Mystery of the Covenant* (New York: Alba House, 1992), xxv–xxx.

43. See Is 50:1, 54:5–8, 62:4–5; Jer 2:2; Mal 2:14; Susan F. Mathews, "Called to the Wed-

[t]he fundamental idea of the entire Bible is that God wishes to draw up a covenant with humankind. From the beginning to the end, from the very first prophets up to the Book of Revelation, this covenant is described under the image of marriage. As such the union between a man and a woman enables marriage to serve as the fundamental symbol of the Covenant: God is the Groom and Israel the Bride (many times unfaithful). What is said in the Old Testament of the relation between Yahweh and Israel is found again in the messianic era for the relationship between Christ and the Church.[44]

The revelation in the Old Testament prepared the way for the coming of Jesus Christ, who established the New Covenant in his person and through his death and resurrection (see Heb 1:1, Jn 1:17, 16:14). The New Covenant is not a reality totally disconnected from the Old Covenant. Rather, the New Covenant flows from the Old in a mysterious yet organic way (see Jer 31:31–34); Jesus himself said that he did not come to abolish the Law and the prophets but to fulfill them (see Mt 5:17). He anticipated his sacrificial offering on the Cross (see Mk 14:24) at the Last Supper: "This cup that is poured out for you is the new covenant in my blood" (Lk 22:20; see 1 Cor 11:25). Scott Hahn commented on the Lucan institution narrative: "Luke alone of the Synoptic Gospels specifies the cup as the "*new* covenant in my blood" (Luke 22:20), which alters the most immediate Old Testament reference from Exodus 24:6–8 (the Sinaitic Covenant) to Jeremiah 31:31. The new covenant of Jeremiah 31:31 is explicitly said to be *unlike* the broken covenant of Sinai (Jer 31:32).... In fact, the new covenant *is not a complete novum*, it is *the renewal of the Davidic covenant*."[45] Hence, the New Covenant is built on the Old and continues God's nuptial relationship with his people, who are now those baptized faithful summoned or assembled into the Church, the Body of Christ. In virtue of the Incarnation, the God-man Jesus Christ is related to the faithful *in* and *through* the Church, as Head of the Body and as Bridegroom of the Bride.

---

ding Feast of the Lamb: Covenantal Spousal Imagery from Genesis to Revelations," in *Chaste Celibacy: Living Christ's Own Spousal Love*, ed. Edward G. Mathews Jr., 39–48, at 41 (Omaha: The Institute for Priestly Formation, 2001).

44. De la Potterie, *Mary in the Mystery of the Covenant*, xxiv.

45. Scott W. Hahn, *Kinship by Covenant: A Canonical Approach to the Fulfillment of God's Saving Promises* (New Haven, Conn.: Yale University Press, 2009), 226.

The first public miracle of Jesus, the wedding feast of Cana (see Jn 2:1–11), can be seen as foreshadowing the New Covenant. On the literal level, it is a Jewish nuptial banquet. On the symbolic level, the feast portrays Jesus as the Bridegroom who establishes his covenant through the miraculous transformation of the water into wine. The miracle that Jesus performed was a sign wherein he made himself known as the divine Bridegroom of the new people of God, with whom he desired to make a new and everlasting covenant.[46]

At Cana, Jesus manifests himself as the messianic Bridegroom who signifies the establishment of the New Covenant with his espoused messianic people.[47] Furthermore, the superabundance of this wine signifies the realized eschatology of Jesus the Messiah, as Rudolf Schnackenburg wrote: "As a gift of Jesus, however the wine also is significant; it is given at the end, and it is so precious and copious that it is the eschatological gift of the Messiah. In the Old Testament (Amos 9:13; Hos 2:24; Joel 4:18; Is 29:17; Jer 31:5) and in late Judaism ... wine in abundance (along with oil or milk) is a sign of the age of salvation; in the ancient blessing of Jacob it is a characteristic of the Messiah from Judah (Gen 49:11ff)."[48] Jesus thus ushers in the age of salvation and fulfilled the Old Covenant with the New and everlasting Covenant.

Mary, on her part, can be seen as a symbol of the people of God, who, through her response "Do whatever he tells you" (Jn 2:5), invites all potential disciples to enter into the New Covenant. The substance of Mary's words hearkens back to Israel's promise of obedience to God in response to his offering of the covenant: "Everything that the Lord has spoken we will do."[49] In her urging to the complete obedience she herself had shown (see Lk 1:38), Mary personifies the new Israel, the Church of Christ.[50] Thus, the wedding feast at Cana is a sign whereby Jesus manifests himself as the Divine Bridegroom of the Church with whom he

---

46. See de la Potterie, *Mary in the Mystery of the Covenant*, 200.

47. See André Feuillet, *Etudes johanniques* (Paris: Desclée de Brouwer, 1962), 19.

48. Rudolf Schnackenburg, *Introduction and Commentary on Chapters 1–4*, vol. 1 of *The Gospel According to St. John* (New York: Seabury Press, 1980), 338.

49. Ex 19:8. The people of Israel continually renewed this promise, for example, Josh 24:24 and Neh 5:12.

50. See de la Potterie, *Mary in the Mystery of the Covenant*, 189–90.

establishes a New Covenant. The scriptural references to the Church as the Bride of Christ clearly imply that Christ was regarded as the heavenly Bridegroom.[51]

Another text that contributes to a greater understanding of New Testament nuptial ecclesiology is 2 Corinthians 11:2, in which Paul describes the church in Corinth as a woman whom he has prepared for Christ: "I feel a divine jealousy for you, for I promised you in marriage to one husband, to present you as a chaste virgin to Christ." Paul speaks of his "divine" jealousy toward the Christians of Corinth, using the Old Testament image of the jealousy of God for his Bride, the people of Israel.[52] He exhorts the Corinthians to remember that they are espoused to Christ, to whom they must be faithful. As their father, Paul's role was to "betroth" the faithful of the church of Corinth, married and unmarried alike, to Christ in virginal integrity and purity of faith. Here Paul does not image Christ himself but, rather, works on behalf of Christ.

While 2 Corinthians 11:2 describes Paul as betrothing the local church of Corinth to Christ, Ephesians 5:21–32 points out that it is Christ who takes the whole church to himself.[53] The Ephesians text uses the image of husband and wife to illustrate the relationship between Christ and his Church. Ephesians 5:23 states this succinctly: "For the husband is the head of the wife just as Christ is the head of the Church, the body of which he is the Savior." Although Ephesians 5 does not contain the term *bridegroom*, it nevertheless establishes the union of Christ with his Church as the archetype and example of the love of husband and wife.[54] Ephesians 5:25–27 describes the goal of Christ's self-sacrifice for the Church: "Husbands, love your wives, just as Christ loved the church and gave himself up for her, in order to make her holy by cleansing her with the washing of water by the word, so as to present the church to himself in splendor, without a spot or wrinkle or anything of the kind—yes, so that she may be holy and without blemish." The "washing of water by

51. See 2 Cor 11:2; Eph 5:25; Rev 19:7, 21:9; John F. McHugh, *A Critical and Exegetical Commentary on John 1–4*, ed. Graham N. Stanton (London: T & T Clark, 2009), 193.

52. See Is 50, 54; Jer 3; Hosea 1–3; Frank J. Matera, *II Corinthians: A Commentary* (Louisville, Ky.: Westminster John Knox Press, 2003), 173.

53. See Lambrecht, *Second Corinthians*, 242.

54. John P. Meier, *Mentor, Message, and Miracles*, vol. 2 of *A Marginal Jew: Rethinking the Historical Jesus* (New York: Doubleday, 1994), 943.

the word" can be understood as a reference to baptism. The word of the Gospel empowers those who hear it to believe and be baptized.[55]

The final verse, 5:32, speaks of a *mystery*. It describes the close union of man and wife in human marriage and relates it to the heavenly marriage covenant between Christ and the Church: "This is a great mystery, and I am applying it to Christ and the Church." Within this spousal relationship, Christ loves the Church and gives himself up for her in a self-giving love, and the Church in turn offers him a reciprocal love. Christ brought about this new relationship through the Incarnational "marriage." The *Catechism of the Catholic Church* states that "[t]he nuptial covenant between God and his people Israel had prepared the way for the new and everlasting covenant in which the Son of God, by becoming incarnate and giving his life, has united to himself in a certain way all mankind saved by him, thus preparing for 'the wedding-feast of the Lamb.'"[56] The Incarnation thus effects an everlasting and intimate union between the Word and humanity. Ephesians 5:21–32 refers to Christ in his role as Head and Bridegroom of the Church, not directly to priestly continence and celibacy. This passage, however, does underline Christ's spiritual marriage to the Church, a concept from which the nuptial-ecclesiological dimension of clerical celibacy would later be drawn.

With regard to indications of the nuptial-ecclesiological dimension of clerical celibacy in the New Testament, the Pastoral Letters contain references to it through the phrase "man of one wife" as applied to the episkopos (see 1 Tm 3:2), presbyteros (see Ti 1:6), and diakonos (see 1 Tm 3:12). As stated earlier, this biblical phrase was understood by some fathers such as Ephrem, Siricius, and Leo the Great as requiring that the married candidate for the ordained ministry be bound by perfect and perpetual continence.[57] This particular reading of the phrase was often accompanied by a spiritual interpretation: by virtue of his ordination

---

55. See John Paul Heil, *Ephesians: Empowerment to Walk in Love for the Unity of All in Christ* (Atlanta: Society of Biblical Literature, 2007), 246.

56. *Catechism of the Catholic Church*, art. 1612. *Gaudium et Spes* 22 states: "For by His incarnation the Son of God has united Himself in some fashion with every man."

57. See Epiphanius, *Advers. Haer. Panar.*, 59, 4, in *Patrologia Graeca* 41, 1024; Siricius *Ep. Ad Himerium Tarraconensem episcopum* 7, in *Patrologia Latina* 13, 1139; Leo the Great , *Epistula XII. Ad episcopos Mauritaniae* 3, in *Patrologia Latina* 54, 648.

the minister was bound to one spouse, the Church. In this sense, the celibate bishop or priest himself is a "man of one wife."[58]

Finally, the book of Revelation contains an abundance of nuptial language that describes the relationship between Christ and the glorified, bridal Church: "I saw the holy city, the new Jerusalem, coming down out of heaven from God, prepared as a bride adorned for her husband" (Rev 21:2). The eternal bond of God with his people in the Kingdom of heaven is here described in terms of a marriage. The heavenly Jerusalem, the Bride of Christ, symbolizes the faithful people of the New Covenant. This passage is a representative of others also in Revelation that use spousal-covenantal language (see 19:7, 22:17).

This brief review of New Testament biblical passages highlights the spousal-covenantal relationship between Christ and the Church. Although no New Testament references mention either celibacy or continence for ordained ministers in the early Church—with the possible exception of the phrase "man of one wife" in the Pastoral Letters—the Church fathers and subsequent theologians nevertheless drew on these texts to develop the nuptial-ecclesiological dimension of priestly celibacy.[59] In recent times, the Magisterium began to incorporate elements of the nuptial-ecclesiological dimension into its teaching on priestly celibacy. It can thus be seen that, although not explicit in scripture, the ecclesiological dimension of priestly celibacy has scriptural roots and can be considered as a legitimate development of scriptural doctrine.

The following passage from John Paul II is a clear example of the way in which magisterial teaching has built upon the scriptural foundation indicated above. Although the pope dealt here with the ecclesiological dimension of *priestly ministry*, one can nonetheless see the manner in which priestly celibacy harmonizes with the priest's relationship to the Church as described here:

---

58. For example, Augustine applied the phrase "man of one wife" to the bishop in *De bono coniugali*, 18, 21, in *Patrologia Latina* 40, 387–88.

59. See Epiphanius, *Advers. Haer. Panar.*, 59, 4, in *Patrologia Graeca* 41, 1024; Siricius *Ep. Ad Himerium Tarraconensem episcopum* 7, in *Patrologia Latina* 13, 1139; Aquinas, *In I ad Tim.*, c. III. lect. 1, in *Opera Omnia*, vol. *XIII* (New York: Musurgia), 1949; and Bonaventure, *Liber II Sententiarum*, d 16, a 2, q 2, in *Opera Omnia*, vol. II (Quaracchi-Firenze: Collegii S. Bonaventurae, 1889).

The priest is called to be the living image of Jesus Christ, the spouse of the Church. Of course, he will always remain a member of the community as a believer alongside his other brothers and sisters who have been called by the Spirit, but in virtue of his configuration to Christ, the head and shepherd, the priest stands in this spousal relationship with regard to the community. In his spiritual life, therefore, he is called to live out Christ's spousal love toward the Church, his bride. Therefore, the priest's life ought to radiate this spousal character, which demands that he be a witness to Christ's spousal love and thus be capable of loving people with a heart which is new, generous and pure, with genuine self-detachment, with full, constant and faithful dedication and at the same time with a kind of "divine jealousy" (cf. 2 Cor. 11:2) and even with a kind of maternal tenderness, capable of bearing "the pangs of birth" until "Christ be formed" in the faithful (cf. Gal. 4:19).[60]

The Celibate Priest as Bridegroom and Spiritual Father

First and foremost, the priest is related to Christ, to whom he is united and configured through ordination. The priest's relationship *as priest* to Jesus Christ is not primarily a spousal bond, meaning that his unity with Christ is not so much one of complementarity as it is of configuration. From the priest's configuration to Christ flows his relationship to the Church. Therefore, it is from the Christological dimension, the foundation of the study of priestly celibacy, that the ecclesiological dimension can be derived. Sara Butler described the ecclesiological dimension as being contained in some manner within the Christological dimension: "According to John Paul II [in *Pastores Dabo Vobis* 16], the priest's fundamental relationship is to Jesus Christ [the Christological dimension], but inscribed within this is a relationship to the Church [the ecclesiological dimension]. This means that the priest not only represents Christ, at the head of the community, 'facing' God the Father on its behalf; he also represents Christ 'facing the Church as her Bridegroom.'"[61] The priest's relationship to the Church has such richness that several images are needed in order to express its fullness, for example, Head, Shepherd, Servant, and Bridegroom. Among these, the Bridegroom image has gained popularity in contemporary magisterial teaching, particularly in *Pastores Dabo Vobis* 29 of John Paul II.

60. John Paul II, *Post-Synodal Apostolic Exhortation*, n. 22.
61. Butler, *The Catholic Priesthood and Women*, 89.

Christ the Bridegroom   The notion of the priest as acting in the person
of Christ the Bridegroom has its limitations. For example, the bridegroom imagery cannot express the entire nature of priestly ministry
because it does not explicitly include the notion of spiritual fatherhood.
One can further deliberate whether a celibate priest is primarily related
to the people he serves under the notion of a bridegroom or, rather, as
a father or even as a spiritual guardian. In view of this query, the following section reviews the patristic foundations of the nuptial imagery in order to illumine its strengths and weaknesses in the theology of
priestly celibacy.

Several Church fathers saw the bishop both as an image of Christ,
the Head of his Body, the Church, and an icon of the Christ, Bridegroom
of the Church.[62] The bishop symbolized Christ, Head and Spouse, in his
spiritual marriage with the Church. Leo the Great included celibacy
within this nuptial paradigm: a bishop was celibate because he had one
spouse, the Church.[63]

An aspect of the notion of episcopal celibacy can be seen in the use
of rings, which some bishops possessed as early as the third century.
In the eighth and ninth centuries, manuscripts of the Gregorian Sacra-
mentary and a few early Pontificals contain formulae that refer to the
episcopal ring as signifying the marital bond of the bishop with his people.[64] The bishop, having been espoused to his diocese, the local church,
did not enter into sacramental marriage.

In the second half of the sixth century, penitential books contained
penalties for a married priest or deacon who after ordination resumed
conjugal relations with his spouse. For a man to do so was comparable
to committing adultery against the Church.[65] Such a penalty for a lawfully wedded man would only make sense if an unwritten principle

---

62. Ephrem the Syrian applied the notion of Christ the Bridegroom to bishops in his letter to Bishop Abraham of Nisibis: "Thou hast no wife, as Abraham had Sarah; behold, thy
flock is thy wife. Bring up her children in thy faithfulness," cited in Robert Murray, *Symbols of
Church and Kingdom: A Study in Early Syriac Tradition* (London: Cambridge University Press,
1975), 151.

63. See Leo the Great, *Epistula XII. Ad Episcopos Mauritaniae* 3, in *Patrologia Latina* 54, 648.

64. See Herbert Thurston, "Rings," in *New Catholic Encyclopedia*, 1st ed., 59–60.

65. See Alphons Stickler, "Le célibat en occident au Moyen Âge," in Coppens, ed., *Sacerdoce et célibat: Etudes historiques et théologiques*, 381–82.

were well known, namely, that the cleric, on ordination, was considered to be living in a spousal relationship with the Church, which would preclude sexual relations with his spouse by mutual consent with regard to his earlier, sacramental marriage. Heid explained the spousal agreement to live in perfect and perpetual continence: "This was because, in the case of spouses, the continence of the one put the chastity of the other at some risk. And therefore they were allowed to practice permanent continence only by mutual agreement. This was in keeping with the pastoral rule that no ascetically minded lay person could force the spouse against his or her will to promise to renounce marital relations."[66]

In the scholastic era, theologians in the West began to stress the connection between the ordained priesthood and the spousal significance of celibacy. Saint Thomas Aquinas (1225–1274) taught that the bishop, mentioned in 1 Timothy 3:2 (*man of one wife*), should have been married only once so that he might integrally symbolize Christ in his nuptial relationship to the Church.[67] For Aquinas, Christ was incarnated as a man (male) because he was the Head of the Church in a way analogous to a husband being the "head" of the woman in marriage (see Eph 5:23). Saint Bonaventure (1221–1274) described the sacramental symbolism of the bishop imaging Christ the Head.[68] Referring to the ordination of bishops, Bonaventure wrote that "[t]he other orders prepare for the episcopate, if one conducts himself well in them; but the bishop is the Bridegroom of the Church: therefore, since a woman is not able to be advanced to the episcopate, but only a man, since she would not be the Bridegroom of the Church, therefore it belongs only to men to be advanced to the preceding orders."[69]

Bonaventure saw the reservation of orders to men alone as a requirement rooted in the order of creation. He not only stated that the bishop is a spouse of the Church but also extended this symbolism to the preparatory ordinations as well, including the presbyters, deacons,

66. Heid, *Celibacy in the Early Church*, 331–32; see Peters, "Canonical Considerations of Diaconal Continence," 153–55, on the canonical perspectives of uxorial consent.

67. Aquinas, *In I ad Tim., c. III, lect. 1*, 598.

68. See Bonaventure, *Liber II Sententiarum*, 403.

69. Bonaventure, *Liber IV Sententiarum*, d 25, a 2, q 1, d 25 in *Opera Theologica Selecta* (Quarrachi-Firenze: Collegii S. Bonaventurae, 1941), 638; translation mine.

and those in minor orders. Bonaventure linked nuptial imagery and the ministries below the episcopate. This specific theology of the spousal dimension of the priesthood and the lower ministerial orders, as distinguished from the nuptial imagery applied by the Church fathers to bishops alone, was a relatively late theological development.[70]

This perspective of the nuptial-ecclesiological dimension of priestly celibacy remained constant, with few modifications, until the Second Vatican Council where it was proposed by several council fathers as a fitting description of the celibate priest. None of the conciliar documents, however, directly employed the image of the Christ the Bridegroom in describing the celibate priest in his relationship with the Church. It was only later with *Sacerdotalis Caelibatus* of Paul VI that the bridegroom image began to be incorporated clearly into magisterial documents: "The consecrated celibacy of the sacred ministers actually manifests the virginal love of Christ for the Church, and the virginal and supernatural fecundity of this marriage, by which the children of God are born but not of flesh and blood."[71]

Although the bridegroom image is a valuable aid in illustrating the priest's relationship to the Church and in justifying his celibacy, other images are needed in order to complement the nuptial analogy within the ambit of the ecclesiological dimension. For example, the head-body image avoids the danger of "hypostasizing" the Church in distinction from Christ, which some theologians argue is a defect of the bridegroom analogy.[72] Other perspectives can provide a balance to the bridegroom image, for example, the friend of the Bridegroom and the spiritual father.

Friend of the Bridegroom   The patristic notion of the bishop as friend of the Bridegroom places restrictions on the bridegroom analogy insofar as it prevents the bishop from appropriating to himself the spousal character of Christ. Because the celibate bishop acts for Christ the

70. See Manfred Hauke, *Die Problematik um das Frauenpriestertum vor dem Hintergrund der Schöfungs-und Erlösungsordnung* (Paderborn: Verlag Bonifatius-Druckerei, 1982), 447–48.

71. Paul VI, *Sacerdotalis Caelibatus*, n. 26; see Jn 1:13.

72. See Paul McPartlan, "Who Is the Church? Zizioulas and von Balthasar on the Church's Identity," *Ecclesiology* 4 (2008): 271–88, at 277–86.

Bridegroom but is not the Bridegroom, he is to be understood as the friend who stands *with* or *in the place of* the Bridegroom.

Among the Church fathers, Augustine in particular developed this image. He saw the bishop as the friend of the Bridegroom and drew his reflections from a meditation on the person and mission of John the Baptist in his role of the friend or "best man" of Jesus (see Jn 1:27). Augustine taught that the bishop did not have the right to take to himself the bride of Christ and therefore could not be called the Bridegroom. In his dispute with the Donatists, Augustine saw the bishop rather as the *friend* of the Bridegroom, whose role is described in the Gospel: "He who has the bride is the Bridegroom; the friend of the Bridegroom, who stands and hears him, rejoices greatly at the Bridegroom's voice" (Jn 3:29). Augustine wrote, "All good pastors are in one and are one. They tend the flock and Christ tends the flock. For the friends of the Bridegroom do not say that they rejoice in their own voice, rather, they rejoice on account of the voice of the Bridegroom. It is Christ himself, therefore, who tends the flock when they are tending it. He says, 'I tend it,' because his voice is in theirs, and in them is his love."[73]

The authentic pastor listens to Christ and is able to speak with Christ's own voice. He finds joy in his efforts to preserve and strengthen the bond between the Bride and the Bridegroom so that the bridal Church may belong only and wholly to Christ. Accordingly Augustine argued that the bishop himself is not the Bridegroom but the latter's best friend, who is able to facilitate the coming together of the Bridegroom and the Bride; that is, the bishop acts in an intermediary role between Christ and the Church, rather than in the role of Christ himself.[74] Augustine was careful to avoid saying that the bishop was the Bridegroom in order to preserve Christ's unique spousal role in relation to the Church.[75]

The analogy of the friend of the Bridegroom has been helpful in de-

73. Augustine, *Sermon 46*, in *Patrologia Latina* 38, 287.

74. See Michael Sherwin, "'The Friend of the Bridegroom Stands and Listens': An Analysis of the Term *Amicus Sponsi* in Augustine's Account of Divine Friendship and the Ministry of Bishops," *Augustinianum* 38 (1998): 197–214, at 210–12.

75. See Augustine, *Sermo Dobeau 26* [Sermo 198 augmented], in *Works of Saint Augustine: A Translation for the 21st Century*, ed. John E. Rotelle and Boniface Ramsey, part II, vol. 11 of *Newly Discovered Sermons* (Hyde Park, N.Y.: New City Press, 1998), 452.

fining the role the bishop has toward the Church, and it preserves Christ's unique and irreplaceable role in the economy of salvation. However, what bearing does this imagery have on clerical celibacy? Although John the Baptist, the scriptural *friend of the Bridegroom*, was indeed celibate, the imagery does not seem to necessitate that the bishop be celibate. Marriage in itself does not negate the fulfillment of the essential role of being the best friend, which is to stand by Christ the Bridegroom and to guard the bridal Church. While this may be true, celibacy nevertheless accentuates better the single-heartedness and devotion of the friend toward the person and interests of the Bridegroom.

Presbyterorum Ordinis 16 at first glance seems to refer to this imagery of the best friend: "By means of celibacy, then, priests profess before men their willingness to be dedicated with undivided loyalty to the task entrusted to them, namely that of espousing the faithful to one husband and presenting them as a chaste virgin to Christ (cf. 2 Cor 11:2). They recall that mystical marriage, established by God and destined to be fully revealed in the future, by which the Church holds Christ as her only spouse."[76] This task of espousing and presenting the bride to Christ in 2 Corinthians 11:2, however, is generally interpreted as referring to a task of the father of the bride rather than of the best friend. Thus, this passage from *Presbyterorum Ordinis* 16 is rather oblique concerning the nuptial perspective of celibacy.

The analogy of the friend of the Bridegroom is useful in providing a necessary boundary to the nuptial image: it prevents any tendency for the bishop to attribute to himself the role of Bridegroom of the Church and instead reminds him of his servant role: "Whoever would be great among you must be your servant" (Mt 20:26). Moreover, it underlines the responsibility of the bishop, and the priest as his assistant, *to assist* Christ the Bridegroom in guarding the integrity of the bridal Church. This task of derived guardianship, entrusted to the bishop through ordination, can be seen as related to the meaning of *episkopos* ("overseer").

Spiritual Father   The idea of the priest as a spiritual father has not been treated extensively in this book because in magisterial teaching

76. Vatican Council II, *Presbyterorum Ordinis*, n. 16.

the ecclesiological dimension tends to be interpreted in terms of nuptial imagery. Nevertheless, the perspective of spiritual fatherhood is an important element of the theology of the priesthood and has been part of contemporary magisterial teaching. Some scriptural indications and theological notes will be given in this section to provide a background to this perspective on priesthood.

The texts of the Old Testament describe the role of the "father" in various ways: founder, ancestor, originator, or prototype (see Jabel in Gn 4:20ff; Phinehas in 1 Mc 2:54); chief minister or high-ranking administrator (see Joseph in Gn 45:8; Eliakim in Is 22:21); one who is highly respected (see Naaman in 2 Kgs 5:13; Job in Job 29:16); priest (see Jgs 17:10, 18:19); prophet (see 2 Kgs 2:12, 6:21); and teacher of wisdom (see Prv 4:1; Sir 3:1). The head of the household functions as a priest at the Passover meal (see Ex 12:1–14, 21–28).[77] The patriarchs are fathers of God's people in both the biological and spiritual sense but especially the latter insofar as they passed on a spiritual inheritance. Thus, Abraham is described as the father of all believers (see Rom 4:11).

With regard to the New Testament, Jesus never refers to himself as "father" and instructed his disciples to call no man "father" (see Mt 23:9) in order to emphasize that all fatherhood comes from God.[78] Nevertheless Jesus manifests his own fatherhood in the way in which he sometimes addressed his disciples: "Children, how hard it is to enter the kingdom of God! (Mk 10:24); "Little children, yet a little while I am with you" (Jn 13:33)"; and "My son, your sins are forgiven" (Mk 2:5).

The apostles speak of their ministry as one of paternity. For example, John calls his disciples his "little children" seven times in his first epistle (see 1 Jn 2:1, 12, 28; 3:7, 18; 4:4 and 5:21) and Peter calls Mark "my son" (see 1 Pt 5:13). Paul writes to the Corinthians: "For though you have countless guides in Christ, you do not have many fathers. For I

77. See Fernando Benicio Felices Sánchez, *La Paternidad Espiritual del Sacerdote* (San Juan, P.R.: S.N, 2006), 23–25; and Felix Donahue, "The Spiritual Father in the Scriptures," in *Abba: Guides to Wholeness and Holiness East and West*, Cistercian Studies Series 38, ed. John R. Sommerfeldt, 3–36, at 3–5 (Kalamazoo, Mich.: Cistercian Publications, 1982).

78. See Carter Harrell Griffin, "Supernatural Fatherhood through Priestly Celibacy: Fulfillment in Masculinity: A Thomistic Study" (STD diss., Pontificia Università della Santa Croce, Rome, 2010); "Supernatural Fatherhood." I have drawn from Griffin's dissertation in this section on spiritual fatherhood.

became your father in Christ Jesus, through the Gospel" (1 Cor 4:15).
Paul also calls himself the father of Onesimus (see Phlm 1:10), describes
his ministry to the Thessalonians as that of a father with his children
(see 1 Thess 2:11), names Timothy his "true child of faith" (see 1 Tm 1:2)
and "beloved son" (see 2 Tm 1:2) and refers to Titus as his "true child in
a common faith" (see Ti 1:4). Paul clearly uses words that describe his
fatherly relationship with those whom he has begotten in Christ.

In the patristic era, the idea of spiritual paternity was applied first to
the desert monks, who fathered others through their charity, instruction,
and mercy.[79] Among others, the writings of Saint Ignatius of Antioch
and the *Didascalia Apostolorum* contain references to the supernatural
paternity of bishops and presbyters.[80] Attributing spiritual fatherhood
to bishops and priests also occurs in some later patristic writings, especially those of Saints Ambrose, Ephrem, Athanasius, Gregory of Nyssa,
Augustine, and Gregory the Great.[81] In the medieval period, Aquinas
referred to priestly fatherhood in his discussion on the virtue of piety
in the *Summa Theologiae*.[82] After the scholastic era several theologians
wrote about the spiritual fatherhood of priests, such as Saints John of
Avila and Alphonsus Liguori.[83]

The use of the title "father" for bishops and priests has been part
of the Catholic tradition, particularly in the Latin Church. Beginning in
the fourth century the title "father" began to be reserved for metropoli-
tans in Rome, Alexandria, and Carthage. By 400, the Council of Toledo
used the title "papa" only for the bishop of Rome, although sporadically
it was still used for other bishops as well.[84] In the thirteenth century,
the title was used regularly again for members of the mendicant Orders,

79. See André Louf, "Spiritual Fatherhood in the Literature of the Desert," in *Abba: Guides
to Wholeness and Holiness East and West*, ed. John R. Sommerfeldt, 7–63, and Sánchez, *La Paternidad Espiritual del Sacerdote*, 42–46.

80. See Ignatius of Antioch, *Ephes* 2, 3, 6, 7; *Trall* 3.1, *Magn* 6 .1; *Didascalia Apostolorum* 5, 8, 9.

81. See Sánchez, *La Paternidad Espiritual del Sacerdote*, 46–59, for a summary of the teaching of the fathers on spiritual fatherhood; Henri de Lubac, *The Motherhood of the Church: Followed by Particular Churches in the Universal Church and an Interview Conducted by Gwendoline
Jarczyk*, trans. Sergia Englund (San Francisco: Ignatius, 1982), 85–91.

82. See Aquinas, *Summa Theologiae*, II–II, 102, 1.

83. See Sánchez, *La Paternidad Espiritual del Sacerdote*, 62–78.

84. Ibid., 41.

and in recent times the Anglo-Saxon world has used the title for both secular and religious priests.[85]

Magisterial teaching in the twentieth century increasingly emphasized the spiritual fatherhood of priests, beginning with *Lumen Gentium*, *Christus Dominus*, and *Presbyterorum Ordinis* of Vatican II.[86] More recently, Paul VI, John Paul II, and Benedict XVI have underlined the significance of the spiritual fatherhood of priests.[87]

Although priests are those who usually are considered spiritual fathers, the stronger witness of fatherhood actually belongs to bishops. Cardinal Henri de Lubac wrote, "For it is through them, successors of the first apostles, that the divine life continues to be transmitted, and it is they who have the responsibility of seeing to it that the 'virginity' of the faith is preserved both intact and fruitful.... The bishops joined together in council are called 'the Fathers.' The same holds true for those whose line extends from the beginning, assuring not only the authentic transmission of a doctrine but also the propagation of a life."[88] Therefore, whatever is attributed to priests with regard to spiritual fatherhood, can also be said in a more fundamental sense of bishops.

Theological reflection on spiritual fatherhood can complement the nuptial imagery with regard to priestly ministry and celibacy. As an image of Christ the Bridegroom, the priest is in relation to the Church itself, that is, to *the whole community of believers*. Sara Butler wrote about this broader relationship: "Only if this is true [that the ministerial priesthood differs in kind and not only in degree from the common priesthood] does the ordained priest take the part of the Bridegroom vis-à-vis the Bride, and the other baptized, exercising their common priesthood, take that of the Bride vis-à-vis the Bridegroom."[89]

85. See Jerome Rono Nyathi, "Priesthood Today and the Crisis of Fatherhood: Fatherlessness in Africa with Special Reference to Zimbabwe" (STD diss., Pontifical University of St. Thomas, Rome, 2002), 49–50.

86. See Vatican Council II, *Lumen Gentium*, nn. 6, 28, 37; *Presbyterorum Ordinis*, nn. 9, 16; *Christus Dominus*, nn. 16, 28.

87. See Paul VI, *Sacerdotalis Caelibatus*, nn. 26, 31, 56, 96; John Paul II, *Familiaris Consortio*, n. 11, 13, 16, 28, 36; *Post-Synodal Apostolic Exhortation*, nn. 12, 15, 16, 18, 21–23, 29; *Pastores Gregis*, nn. 7, 37, 43.

88. De Lubac, *Motherhood of the Church*, 85–86.

89. Butler, *The Catholic Priesthood and Women*, 91.

On the other hand, the idea of spiritual father better describes the priest's relationship with each *individual* member of the Church.[90] It seems to be the experience of priests that they see themselves primarily as spiritual fathers of the people rather than as a bridegroom. Spiritual fatherhood implies an engendering of spiritual life in the faithful whom they beget in Christ through the ministries of preaching, sanctifying and shepherding.

Celibacy accentuates and aids spiritual fatherhood insofar as the celibate priest renounces fatherhood according to the flesh in order to exercise in the fullest possible manner fatherhood according to the spirit.[91] The priest accomplishes this fatherhood principally through preaching the word of God and administering the sacraments, whereby he builds the members of the Body of Christ (see Acts 6:4).

Vatican II recognized the close link between spiritual fatherhood and priestly celibacy when it said with regard to celibacy: "[Priests] are less encumbered in their service of his kingdom and of the task of heavenly regeneration. In this way they become better fitted for a broader acceptance of fatherhood in Christ."[92]

Evaluation of the Bridegroom Image   With regard to the manner of expressing the priest's relationship to the Church, no one image or analogy fully articulates the ecclesiological dimension in all its richness. The bridegroom image needs to be complemented by others, such as those of best friend and spiritual father. Rather than being a comprehensive summary, each image is related to others and can be likened to a tessera in the theological mosaic. For example, John Paul II in *Pastores Dabo Vobis* enlarged the theological analogies of *Lumen Gentium* 28, which portrayed the ministerial priest as the sacramental representative of Christ the Head in relation to his Body and of Christ the Shepherd in relation to his flock. These images refer to relationships but not to interpersonal relationships. In *Pastores Dabo Vobis* 21–23, which is titled

90. The celibate priest can also relate to the whole community as a father after the example of Jesus in Mk 2:5, 10:24, and Jn 13:33.

91. "St. Joseph became a father in an extraordinary way, without begetting his son in the flesh. Isn't this, perhaps, an example of the type of fatherhood that is proposed to us, priests and bishops, as a model?" John Paul II, *Rise, Let Us Be On Our Way* (New York: Warner, 2004), 141.

92. Vatican Council II, *Presbyterorum Ordinis*, n. 16.

"Configuration to Christ, Head and Shepherd, and Pastoral Charity," John Paul II added the personal images of Servant and Bridegroom to the Head-Body and Shepherd-Flock pairs. Butler commented on *Pastores Dabo Vobis* 22: "The Head-body comparison suggests the organic unity of a single person, and the Shepherd-flock comparison uses a corporate, but non-personal image to portray the Church. *Pastores Dabo Vobis* augments these biblical analogies, expanding 'Head' to include 'Servant,' and 'Shepherd' to include 'Bridegroom.' Being 'Head' implies having an authority over others, but Jesus exercised his headship in the manner of the Suffering Servant of God.... So also, the Good Shepherd lays down his life for his sheep (Jn 10:11), and the Bridegroom loves and gives up his life for his Bride (Eph 5:25)."[93] These four images—Head, Servant, Shepherd, and Bridegroom—all relate some particular aspect of *Christ's* relationship to the Church, which the priest serves in imitation of Christ. Furthermore, these images can be complemented with others, such as Father of the Bride, Best Friend, and Spiritual Father.

The predominance of the image of the priest as Bridegroom in recent magisterial teaching may have been prompted by the movement for women's ordination, which moved the Magisterium to elaborate on the nature of maleness vis-à-vis the ministerial priesthood. Reflections on the maleness of the ordained priesthood led to consideration of the priest's spousal link with the Church. Magisterial texts subsequently began to defend the male-only priesthood through use of the nuptial image of the priesthood.[94] John Paul II likewise employed the bridegroom-bride analogy in his defense of priestly celibacy, particularly in *Pastores Dabo Vobis*.[95]

While the bridegroom image does not summarize the fullness of the ecclesiological dimension, it is still a valid image for expressing the interpersonal bond of Christ and his Church. In addition, it seems to be specifically apt for Christians in a contemporary culture in which awareness of and regard for marriage and marital love—and, conse-

93. Butler, *The Catholic Priesthood and Women*, 88.

94. Particularly in *Inter Insigniores*, n. 5.

95. "In virtue of his configuration to Christ, the head and shepherd, the priest stands in this spousal relationship with regard to the community," John Paul II, *Post-Synodal Apostolic Exhortation*, n. 22.

quently, celibacy and celibate love—has weakened. For this reason, John Paul II in his *Theology of the Body* and *Pastores Dabo Vobis* sought to strengthen both marriage and the celibate priesthood through the use of the nuptial image rooted in Ephesians 5. Although the teaching of John Paul II has emphasized the nuptial aspect of the ecclesiological dimension, his teaching on this aspect nevertheless dovetails well with the broader magisterial presentation on priestly celibacy. There are indeed other images that are needed for an integral presentation of the ecclesiological dimension of the priest's ministry, such as those of best friend and spiritual father. However, a good argument can be made for priestly celibacy in those cases also.

The Nuptial-Ecclesiological Dimension and Ritual Purity

In *Sacerdotalis Caelibatus*, Paul VI listed among the objections to mandatory priestly celibacy in the Latin Church the resistance to the idea of the need for the priest to maintain ritual purity: "The reasons justifying the perfect chastity of the Church's ministers seem often to be based on an overly pessimistic view of man's earthly condition or on a certain notion of the purity necessary for contact with sacred things."[96] Although the pope did not directly respond to this criticism, he seemed to allude to it in a subsequent passage: "Consideration of the 'manifold suitability' (cf. *Presbyterorum Ordinis* 16) of celibacy for God's ministers is not something recent. Even if the explicit reasons [in favor of celibacy] have differed with different mentalities and different situations, they were always inspired by specifically Christian considerations; and after they have been thoroughly examined one can arrive at the underlying reasons."[97] The appeal to ritual purity seems to belong to those considerations that have pertained to "different mentalities and different situations" but that "were always inspired by specifically Christian considerations."

The assertion that ritual purity was inspired by Christian considerations would strike some as erroneous, such as Joseph Komonchak, who maintained that Paul VI did not utilize the ritual purity argument because of its inadequacy to address the relationship between celibacy and human sexuality: "It is not surprising that Pope Paul's encyclical

96. Paul VI, *Sacerdotalis Caelibatus*, n. 6.
97. Ibid., n. 18.

does not mention ritual purity as a motive, since his own teaching on sexuality and marriage in *Humanae Vitae* represents a substantial development (not to say correction) of the view of sexuality often reflected when that motive was invoked in the past."[98] Whatever may have been his opinion on the theological value of the ritual purity argument, Paul VI underlined that priestly celibacy derives from other, more fundamental motives. His decision to omit the use of the ritual purity argument in *Sacerdotalis Caelibatus*, however, does not necessarily imply that he judged it to be an erroneous justification for celibacy. Rather, the ritual purity argument—with its long-standing use in patristic, theological, and magisterial teaching—has been part of the Catholic Church's perennial defense and explanation of clerical continence and celibacy.

The following section outlines the Jewish understanding of ritual purity, which served as a background for the Catholic understanding of the relationship between human sexuality and the liturgy. This short study provides a foundation for understanding the ecclesiological dimension of priestly celibacy in its nuptial perspective.

Ritual Purity in the Judaic Law   The "purity laws" are those laws in the Pentateuch that qualify certain actions, states of being, persons, or things as *tahor* (clean, pure) or *tame* (unclean, impure). There are several types of purity laws: ritual, moral, genealogical and dietary. Among these regulations, *ritual* purity refers primarily to one's ability to participate in the cultic acts in the temple. Underlying the notion of ritual purity was the understanding that everything to do with the weakness and mortality of humans must be kept separate from the holiness of the Lord God and from the holy space that is God's temple. Separation is the concrete, visible expression of the exalted holiness of God, and the ritual purity laws maintained this protective system of separation.[99]

On the other hand, ritual *impurity* signifies a usually temporary condition resulting from the normal cycle of human life: birth, disease, sexual activity and death. The elements of this cycle of human life are necessary and unavoidable for any person living in society. John Meier wrote, "There was nothing morally evil or sinful about these processes,

98. Komonchak, "Celibacy and Tradition," 13.
99. See Meier, *Law and Love*, 343–50.

if they were handled properly. However, these key activities of human existence involve major transitions from one human condition to another. They betoken a certain crossing of a threshold (hence the designation "liminal" experiences) and often unleash mysterious and powerful fluids connected with the conferral or diminution of life."[100]

All who had come into contact with these bodily fluids were considered to be ritually impure until they had undergone certain purification rites. These bodily fluids were believed to possess some aspect of life, and thus were the objects that served as vehicles for transmitting ritual impurity. Blood in particular was seen as imbued with divine life, and semen was understood to be a form of blood. To come into contact with blood was to come into contact with the divine and thus one contracted a ritual impurity, "a holy contamination," rather than a moral impurity. Through activities such as war and hunting, sexual activity, and the touching of a corpse, a person came into contact with blood outside of their normal place.[101] A person who was "contaminated" in this way had to undergo a process that would lead him from impurity to purity, which then would allow him to enter the temple or to handle sacred things like sacrificial food. For example, after childbirth a woman had to offer a holocaust and a sin offering (see Lv 12:1–8). Because the Jewish people considered marriage as something holy and childbirth as the greatest blessing, the new mother was not rendered morally impure by giving birth, but rather, having "touched" the creative power of the Lord God, she had to be ritually purified before she could resume normal, day-to-day activities.[102]

In the Mosaic Law, there were particularly stringent rules regulating worship in the temple. The Levites and priests were required to practice ritual continence during their time of service in the temple (see Ex 19:15; Lv 15). A priest became ritually impure through sexual activity outside specified times (see 1 Sm 21:5; 2 Sm 11:11) and was required

100. Ibid., 344.

101. See Jacob Neusner, "Purity and the Priesthood in the Hebrew Scriptures and Rabbinic Tradition," in *For Love Alone*, 129–36; and Jacob Neusner, *The Idea of Purity in Ancient Judaism* (Leiden: Brill, 1973), 108.

102. See Raymond E. Brown, Joseph A. Fitzmyer, and Roland E. Murphy, eds., *The New Jerome Biblical Commentary* (Englewood Cliffs, N.J.: Prentice-Hall, 1990), 726.

to undergo certain purification rites before he could participate again in the liturgy (see Lv 15:16–18). In certain rabbinic texts, the liturgical objects themselves were understood to "pollute," for example, the handling of a sacred scroll would *soil* the hands of the rabbi, and he was required to wash his hands *after* reading it.[103] An overemphasis on this exterior purity, however, eventually led to a type of formalism against which the prophets preached; they strove to teach the people to recognize the importance of an interior purity of mind and heart (see Hos 6:6; Am 4:1–5; Is 6:5; Jer 13:27).

Ritual Purity in the Patristic Tradition   Although the Catholic Church grew from this Jewish tradition, it did not accept all of the laws concerning ritual purity. Cochini described the Church's adaptation of Old Testament purity laws to the ministerial priesthood: "If we first go back to the Old Testament's prescriptions concerning the sanctity of priests, we cannot help but be struck by the fact that only the sexual interdictions survived the deep mutations that put a definitive end to the rules on purity and impurity. Neither the defilement incurred by contact with a corpse; nor bodily infirmities, leprosy, or the prohibitions against certain categories of food; nor any irregularities of the old Judaic Code were retained in the law of patristic times—abolished, just like circumcision, those imperfect practices of a past Covenant!"[104] Indeed, almost all of the requirements for attaining ritual purity were dropped, such as bathing. Hence, ritual purity in the early Church was limited to the rules dealing with sexual behavior in relation to either participating in or celebrating the Eucharist.

Early evidence of sexual continence in relation to prayer is found in 1 Corinthians 7:5–7, in which the apostle Paul described the close relationship between prayer and the abstention from conjugal intercourse: "Do not deprive one another except perhaps by agreement for a set time to devote yourselves to prayer, and then come together again, so that Satan may not tempt you because of your lack of self-control. This I say

103. See *Mishnah Yadaim*, 3:2, as cited in *New Jerome Biblical Commentary*, 522. Even today, the liturgical vessels used at Mass are said to be *purified* when elements of the sacred species are removed.

104. Cochini, *The Apostolic Origins of Priestly Celibacy*, 429.

by way of concession, not of command. I wish that all were as I myself am. But each has a particular gift from God, one having one kind and another a different kind" (1 Cor 7:5–7). Paul saw this abstention from sexual relations as a condition for intimacy with God through prayer. The patristic meditation upon 1 Corinthians 7 consequently linked efficacy in prayer, particularly in the intercessory prayer of the priest, to *purity*, the Latin of which is *pudicitia*.[105] According to the fathers, a violation of this purity occurred when a married priest had conjugal relations with his wife.[106] The purpose of Christian ritual purity therefore was not for the sake of physical cleanness but for the dedication of one's life to prayer to God and to the service of the Church. Perpetual priestly continence and celibacy were considered a precondition for the unceasing prayer required of the priest if he were to fulfill well his intercessory role.[107]

However, it can be affirmed that the concept of ritual purity in some cases had become a vehicle for expressing tendencies that are hostile to human sexuality. Some fathers used language in the context of ritual purity that cast doubts upon the integral goodness of human sexuality and marriage.[108] Peter Brown described the reaction to Jerome's view of marriage in the latter's *Against Jovinian*: "Roman Christians were shocked by Jerome's assertion that even first marriages were regrettable, if pardonable, capitulations to the flesh, and that second marriages were only one step away from the brothel. He went on to suggest that priests were holy only in so far as they possessed the purity of virgins. The married clergy were mere raw recruits in the army of the church, brought in because of a temporary shortage of battle-hardened veterans of lifelong celibacy."[109]

Despite such excesses, many of the fathers and subsequent theologians gave a more positive evaluation of human sexuality and of the holiness of the conjugal act. Clement of Alexandria, for example, promoted

105. See J. Francis Stafford, "Eucharistic Foundation of Sacerdotal Celibacy," *Origins* 23 (1993): 211–16, at 212.

106. See Ambrose, *De Officiis* III, in *Patrologia Latina* 104b–5a, 247–48.

107. See Origen, *Hom. 6, 6 in Lev.*, in *Grieschische Christliche Schriftsteller Orig.* 6, 370, 2.

108. See Jerome, *Adversus Jovinianum I, in Patrologia Latina* 23, 231c–32b, 234d; Tertullian, *De Exhortatione Castitatis*, in *Patrologia Latina* 2, 913–30.

109. Brown, *The Body and Society*, 377.

a liturgical purity that was accompanied by a positive attitude toward the sexual act; sexual intercourse is holy for baptized couples, and even semen is sacred.[110] It seems that some of the contemporary misunderstanding of the patristic concept of ritual purity stems from the fathers' use of the vocabulary of levitical ritualism, even though they did not necessarily subscribe to the Jewish or even pagan beliefs that the words conveyed. The patristic language of ritual purity at times was ambiguous and did not have the distinctions that would correct and purify any anticorporeal sentiment conveyed by the vocabulary. This ambiguity frustrated the fathers' attempt to express the relationship between human sexuality and the celebration of the Eucharist. A case in point is the following statement of Siricius: "If intercourse is a defilement, then the priest ought to stand in readiness to carry out his heavenly function, [he] who is to pray for the sins of another, lest he himself be found unworthy."[111] Siricius's use of "defilement" (*pollutio*) seems to imply that sin is involved in the marital act itself. While in a few of the patristic writings this may have been the case, the majority of such expressions seem to reflect an ambiguity of language. Cochini argued along this line in his interpretation of the fathers' use of *defilement* and of similar expressions: "When 'defilement' is mentioned, it is because the sanctuary where the liturgy is celebrated is not, to the Fathers' minds, a suitable place to bring even the thought of activities whose whole value is merely earthly, and it would be difficult to find words that would express this idea in a genteel way. Both the nobility of the conjugal act and its unsuitability to be brought within the sanctuary are true things, and the Fathers believed both were true. Although they tried with all their might to explain the problem correctly, they were not always successful."[112] Special care is thus needed to avoid making the assumption that the Church fathers, when using ritual purity language, were judging the conjugal act to be per se sinful. Rather, they were aware of the need for the priest to be unified in his body and soul while offering the sacrifice of the Eucharist. In other words, licit sexual activity for the married priest would divide his

110. See Clement of Alexandria, *Stromata*, 3, 6, 46, 5, in *Griechische Christliche Schriftsteller Clem. Alex.* 2/4, 217, 23–25.

111. Siricius, *Ad Gallos Episcopos*, in *Patrologia Latina* 13, 1186.

112. Cochini, *The Apostolic Origins of Priestly Celibacy*, 252.

concentration and siphon away energy needed to make a wholly integral offering in union with Christ the High Priest.[113] Ambrosiaster articulated this paradox well: "Compared to the stars, the light of a lamp is but fog; while compared to the sun, the stars are obscure; and compared to the radiance of God, the sun is but night. Thus are the things which, in relationship to us, are licit and pure, and are as if illicit and impure with respect to the dignity of God; indeed, no matter how good they are, they are not appropriate to the person of God."[114]

The Nuptial Dimension, Pastoral Charity, and the Eucharist   Following the lead of Paul VI,[115] this section considers the principal "specific considerations" that motivate the Catholic notion of ritual purity and the relation between the ministerial priesthood and the celebration of the Eucharist. This relationship is effectively expressed through the ecclesiological dimension of priestly celibacy. That is, the patristic understanding of ritual purity, which influenced magisterial teaching on priestly celibacy for the succeeding centuries, successfully separated itself from both pagan and Jewish understandings of ritual purity because of its eucharistic focus. Concerning the difference between the Christian notion of celibacy and Jewish or pagan understandings, de Lubac pointed to the Eucharist as the distinguishing factor: "This consecration through celibacy is understood and justified only if the very idea of Christian ministry is received in faith and retained in its proper originality instead of being equated with profane pagan or Jewish models ... in short, only if we keep alive the holy reverence for the Eucharist which was evident from the beginning at the center of every Christian community and which is the very heart of the Church."[116]

The centrality of the Eucharist, rather than the moral or ascetical state of the priest, is a hermeneutical key for understanding the motiva-

---

113. The Second Council of Carthage mandated that major clerics were "to be continent in all things, so that they may obtain *in all simplicity* what they are asking from God," Second Council of Carthage, *Corpus Christianorum* 149, 13; emphasis added.

114. Ambrosiaster, *Questiones Veteris et Novi Testamenti*, 127, in *Corpus Scriptorum Ecclesiasticorum Latinorum* 50, 415; quoted in Cochini, *The Apostolic Origins of Priestly Celibacy*, 252 (fn. 248).

115. See Paul VI, *Sacerdotalis Caelibatus*, n. 18.

116. De Lubac, *Motherhood of the Church*, 132–34.

tion that underlies the concept and practice of ritual purity with regard to priestly celibacy in the Catholic tradition. Cochini affirmed this view:

It is the liturgy, and the Eucharistic liturgy in particular, that, making the Pascal mystery become a reality, leads the Christian people and, in a special and permanent role, "the servant of the altar" to an identification with Christ praying and offering himself to the Father for the salvation of the world. Christ himself is present, God-Man, associating his ministers with his person and his sacrifice, and not an impersonal or abstract divinity generating irrational taboos. There is as much difference between "ritual continence" and the celibacy-continence of the priests of Jesus Christ as there is between the pagan rituals, no matter how respectable they are, and the sacrifice of the Cross.[117]

As will be shown, the ecclesiological dimension of priestly celibacy is itself closely related to the Eucharist. It also provides a framework in which marriage, human sexuality, and celibacy can be understood in their interrelationships. The ecclesiological dimension provides the language and concepts that can help to avoid the ambiguous expressions of the patristic era that at times have been understood as promoting negative attitudes toward matrimony and human sexuality.

In order to show the link between the ecclesiological dimension of priestly celibacy and the Eucharist, this section advances a brief argument in the following manner: (1) the ecclesiological dimension qua *nuptial* expresses the priest's exclusive relationship to the bridal Church, (2) priestly celibacy and pastoral charity are intrinsically united and mutually perfect each other, and (3) both priestly celibacy and pastoral charity flow forth from and are oriented toward the Eucharist.

First, the ecclesiological dimension of priestly celibacy refers to various roles that the priest has vis-à-vis the Church, such as head, shepherd, servant, and spouse.[118] With regard to its *nuptial* perspective, the ecclesiological dimension signifies the priest's relation to the Church insofar as he stands in the person of Christ the Bridegroom. Paul VI wrote the following about the ecclesiological dimension of priestly celibacy: "'Laid hold of by Christ' (Phil 3:12) unto the complete abandonment of one's entire self to Him, the priest takes on the likeness of Christ most

117. Cochini, *The Apostolic Origins of Priestly Celibacy*, 253.
118. See John Paul II, *Post-Synodal Apostolic Exhortation*, n. 3.

perfectly, even in the love with which the eternal Priest has loved the
Church His Body and offered Himself entirely for her sake, in order to
make her a glorious, holy and immaculate Spouse."[119]

The pope underscored that the celibate priest becomes more like
Christ through the love with which "the eternal Priest has loved the
Church His Body and offered Himself entirely for her sake." The priest
participates in this same love that Christ has for his Church. The faithful
on their part reciprocate that love. John Paul II emphasized this nuptial relationship between the priest and the faithful: "The Church, as
spouse of Jesus Christ, wishes to be loved by the priest in the total and
exclusive manner in which Jesus Christ her head and spouse loved her.
Priestly celibacy, then, is the gift of self *in* and *with* Christ *to* his Church
and expresses the priest's service to the Church in and with the Lord."[120]
John Paul II taught that the Church enjoys an exclusive, "marital" claim
on Christ her Bridegroom. In other words, as Christ and ministerial
priests have an exclusive, nuptial relationship to the Church, so also the
Church has an exclusive, nuptial relationship to the priest. The priest's
exclusive relationship with the Church thus suggests the incongruity of
his having a human, nuptial relationship.

Second, an effect of this spousal relationship between Christ and his
Church is an innate desire of the faithful to be loved by the priest. In
magisterial documents, this priestly love is called *pastoral charity*, which
animates and guides the priest in his ministry.[121] The pastoral charity of
the priest is a participation in Christ's own pastoral charity and it enables
the priest to give himself totally to the Church: "The essential content of
this pastoral charity is the gift of self, the total gift of self to the Church,
following the example of Christ.... The gift of self, which is the source
and synthesis of pastoral charity, is directed toward the Church. This
was true of Christ who 'loved the Church and gave himself up for her'
(Eph 5:25), and the same must be true for the priest."[122] Pastoral charity

119. Paul VI, *Sacerdotalis Caelibatus*, n. 26.

120. John Paul II, *Post-Synodal Apostolic Exhortation*, n. 29.

121. For example, see Vatican Council II, *Presbyterorum Ordinis*, n. 14, and John Paul II, *Post-Synodal Apostolic Exhortation*, nn. 22–23. Augustine describes pastoral charity as an *amoris officium*: Augustine, *In Iohannis Evangelium Tractatus* 123, 5, in *Corpus Christianorum Latinorum* 36, 678.

122. John Paul II, *Post-Synodal Apostolic Exhortation*, n. 23.

is the primary motivation of the priest's ministry and life, and it enables the priest to imitate Christ in his service. Celibacy, which forms part of the priest's imitation of the ministry and life of Christ, becomes fruitful and efficacious to the extent that pastoral charity informs and perfects it. Following the example of Jesus, the priest should focus his charity in particular on the poor, the marginalized, and those neglected by society.

If pastoral charity animates and perfects the priest in his celibacy, then the converse is also true. Priestly celibacy facilities growth in pastoral charity, as Vatican II taught: "[Celibacy] is at the same time a sign and a stimulus for pastoral charity and a special source of spiritual fecundity in the world,"[123] and Paul VI affirmed: "The free choice of sacred celibacy has always been considered by the Church 'as a symbol of, and stimulus to, charity': it signifies a love without reservations; it stimulates to a charity which is open to all."[124] Celibacy is a both a sign of and a stimulus to pastoral charity. In the context of service to the Church, the celibate priest imitates Christ who "loved the Church and gave himself up for her" (Eph 5:25). The priest through his celibate life is in a position to place the Church and its members as his first interest, and with this concrete spirituality he becomes capable of loving the universal Church and that part entrusted to him with a deep pastoral charity. For his celibate love to become perfected, the priest first must look to Christ himself in order to receive his own pastoral charity: "The primary point of reference of the priest's charity is Jesus Christ himself. Only in loving and serving Christ the Head and Spouse will charity become a source, criterion, measure and impetus for the priest's love and service to the Church, the Body and Spouse of Christ."[125]

Third, the *Eucharist* is the wellspring of growth in priestly celibacy and *pastoral charity*. The celibate priest is most effective in his ministry to the extent that he is imbued with pastoral charity. Vatican II taught that the Eucharist is the source of pastoral charity: "This pastoral charity flows mainly from the eucharistic sacrifice, which is thus the center and root of the whole priestly life. The priestly soul strives thereby to apply to

---

123. Vatican Council II, *Presbyterorum Ordinis*, n. 16.

124. Paul VI, *Sacerdotalis Caelibatus*, n. 24; the internal citation is from Vatican Council II, *Lumen Gentium*, n. 42.

125. John Paul II, *Post-Synodal Apostolic Exhortation*, n. 23.

itself the action which takes place on the altar of sacrifice."[126] The priest's *pastoral charity* flows mainly from the celebration of the Eucharist, from which the priest receives the grace and obligation to give his whole life a sacrificial dimension.[127] Consequently, the graces given to the priest to live a fruitful and life giving *celibacy* are also drawn from the Eucharist. Vatican II stated: "The liturgy is the summit toward which the activity of the Church is directed; at the same time it is the font from which all her power flows.... From the liturgy, therefore, and especially from the Eucharist, as from a font, grace is poured forth upon us; and the sanctification of men in Christ and the glorification of God, to which all other activities of the Church are directed as toward their end, is achieved in the most efficacious possible way."[128] Here the Eucharist is described as the universal source of grace for all the faithful and the goal of all activities of the Church. Therefore, the charism of priestly celibacy, as with pastoral charity, has its source and ultimate goal in the Eucharist.

Furthermore, the priest's relationship with the faithful is realized most intimately in the celebration of the Eucharist, where the priest assumes the sacramental role of Christ the Bridegroom in virtue of acting in the person of Christ the Head and Bridegroom of the Church. John Paul II elaborated this theme in *Mulieris Dignitatem*:

We find ourselves at the very heart of the Pascal Mystery, which completely reveals the spousal love of God. Christ is the Bridegroom because "he has given himself": his body has been "given," his blood has been "poured out" (cf. Lk 22:19–20). In this way "he loved them to the end" (Jn 13:1). The "sincere gift" contained in the sacrifice of the cross gives definitive prominence to the spousal meaning of God's love. As the Redeemer of the world, Christ is the Bridegroom of the Church. *The Eucharist is the Sacrament of our redemption.* It is *the Sacrament of the Bridegroom and of the Bride.* The Eucharist makes present and realizes anew in a sacramental manner the redemptive act of Christ, who "creates" the Church, his body. Christ is united with this "body" as the bridegroom with the bride.[129]

126. Vatican Council II, *Presbyterorum Ordinis*, n. 14. John Paul II built upon this conciliar teaching by stating that Holy Orders is the *specific* source of pastoral charity: "Pastoral charity, which has its specific source in the sacrament of holy orders, finds its full expression and its supreme nourishment in the Eucharist," John Paul II, *Post-Synodal Apostolic Exhortation*, n. 23.

127. See John Paul II, *Post-Synodal Apostolic Exhortation*, n. 23.

128. Vatican Council II, *Sacrosanctum Concilium*, n. 10.

129. John Paul II, *Mulieris Dignitatem*, n. 26.

Implicit in the pope's statement is the idea that during the celebration of the Eucharist the priest stands in the person of Christ, the Bridegroom of the Church. John Paul II outlined this teaching in *Pastores Dabo Vobis*: "Christ stands 'before' the Church and 'nourishes and cherishes her' (Eph 5:29), giving his life for her. The priest is called to be the living image of Jesus Christ, the spouse of the Church.... In his spiritual life, therefore, he is called to live out Christ's spousal love toward the Church, his bride."[130] The pope moreover stated that "[i]ndeed, the Eucharist represents, makes once again present, the sacrifice of the cross, the full gift of Christ to the Church, the gift of his body given and his blood shed, as the supreme witness of the fact that he is head and shepherd, servant and spouse of the Church."[131] Hence, the nuptial-ecclesiological dimension of celibacy denotes the priest's exclusive, marital relationship to the bridal Church. Priestly celibacy and pastoral charity are bound together and mutually perfect each other. Furthermore, both priestly celibacy and pastoral charity flow forth from and are oriented toward the Eucharist, which is the very celebration of the act that seals the nuptial relationship between Christ and the Church, namely, his sacrifice on the Cross.

Thus, ritual purity, as seen through the lens of the nuptial-ecclesiological dimension of priestly celibacy, considers the wider demands of the relationship expressed between Christ and the Church when the Eucharist is celebrated. The question then is not so much whether the priest is ritually pure insofar as he has abstained from sexual contact— although this remains an important point when understood in a Catholic sense—but whether he has given himself fully to the bridal Church in sacrificial, pastoral charity. Standing in the person of Christ, the Head and Bridegroom of the Church, the celibate priest is called to give his whole body and soul, in service to the people of God.

Consequently, the *purity* required with regard to the ecclesiological dimension of priestly celibacy is the purity of the priest's *pastoral charity in service to the Church*, which culminates in his self-offering in the Eucharist. The priest's effort at his own growth in holiness is aided through the centering of his life, including his celibacy, on the celebration of the Eucharist, in which the whole spiritual good of the Church is

---

130. John Paul II, *Post-Synodal Apostolic Exhortation*, n. 22.
131. Ibid., n. 23.

contained.[132] Acting in the person of Christ the Head, the priest unites himself with the offering and places on the altar his entire life.[133]

In sum, there is a purity related to the Eucharist that is required of the priest. The ecclesiological dimension highlights it as a purity of nuptial love for the Church rather than simply as a purity from personal sexual defilement. The ecclesiological dimension of priestly celibacy complements and augments the traditional ritual purity argument.

Is the latter now to be considered theologically obsolete? For Benedict XVI it did not appear to be so. On June 16, 2009, the pope published a letter commemorating the 150th anniversary of the birth of Saint John Vianney in which he also proclaimed a *Year for Priests*.[134] Within the letter the pope described the three evangelical counsels—poverty, chastity, and obedience—as providing a sure road for priests to attain the desired goal of Christian perfection. In his treatment of chastity, the virtue that animates priestly celibacy, Benedict XVI said of the Curé of Ars: "It could be said that it was a chastity suited to one who must daily touch the Eucharist, who contemplates it blissfully and with that same bliss offers it to his flock. It was said of him that 'he radiated chastity;' the faithful would see this when he turned and gazed at the tabernacle with loving eyes."[135] It is noteworthy that *chastity*, or celibacy lived according the virtue of chastity, is described here by Benedict XVI in language that has affinities with the ritual purity notion of celibacy: the pope described John Vianney as having a resplendent chastity fitting for "one who must daily touch the Eucharist."[136] This is rather remarkable insofar as no pope or magisterial document had used ritual purity language since Pius XII.[137]

If the traditional ritual purity argument is retrieved in future magis-

132. See Vatican Council II, *Presbyterorum Ordinis*, n. 5.

133. See Paul VI, *Sacerdotalis Caelibatus*, n. 29.

134. See Benedict XVI, "Letter of His Holiness Pope Benedict XVI Proclaiming a Year for Priests on the 150th Anniversary of the 'Dies Natalis' of the Curé of Ars," *Origins* 39 (2009): 116–21.

135. Ibid., 119.

136. Benedict XVI's concern with the sacred liturgy is particularly expressed in Joseph Ratzinger, *The Feast of Faith: Approaches to a Theology of the Liturgy*, trans. Graham Harrison (San Francisco: Ignatius, 1986), and *The Spirit of the Liturgy*, trans. John Saward (San Francisco: Ignatius, 2000).

137. See Pius XII, *Sacra Virginitas*, nn. 23–24.

terial teaching, then the nuptial-ecclesiological dimension can enhance it with its own proper theological insights, particularly through its focus on pastoral charity. Theologians on their part have the opportunity to help to develop an integral presentation of ritual purity that can meld the best of the patristic insights with the nuptial understanding of priestly celibacy.

The Eschatological Dimension of Priestly Celibacy

THE TERM *ESCHATOLOGY* signifies the ensemble of doctrines about the "last things,"[138] that is, the end of the existing world and the ultimate destiny of each human person. The Bible itself refers to a future time when the course of history will be changed to such an extent that one can speak of an entirely new state of reality.[139] In his Second Letter, Peter looks forward to "new heavens and new earth" (2 Pt 3:13), and in the Acts of the Apostles he explains the outpouring of the Spirit at Pentecost as already the gift of the "last days," fulfilling the prophecy of Joel (see Acts 2:16–17; Jl 3:1–5).

The eschatological dimension of priestly celibacy refers to the prophetic witness of the celibate priest to the end times, to the Kingdom of God and the heavenly realities that will never pass away. Vatican II stated in *Presbyterorum Ordinis* 16 that "[m]oreover [celibate priests] are made a living sign of that world to come, already present through faith and charity, a world in which the children of the resurrection shall neither marry, nor be given in marriage (cf. Lk 20:35–36)."[140] Priestly celibacy impacts the faithful in three significant ways: (1) it reminds them that the final stages of salvation have already begun here on earth (see 1 Cor 7:29–31); (2) it points to the final, heavenly goal of their earthly pilgrimage;[141] and (3) it serves as a warning of the danger of overinvolvement with earthly concerns, enslavement to the desires of the flesh, and of inordinate attachment to created goods, even to marriage. Celibacy lived authentically

---

138. ἔσχατοα, from ἔσχατον, which generally means "end times." See "Eschatology in Early Judaism," in Katharine Doob Sakenfeld, ed., *The New Interpreter's Dictionary of the Bible*, 1st ed.

139. "Eschatology," in David Freedman, ed., *Anchor Bible Dictionary*, 1st ed.

140. Vatican Council II, *Presbyterorum Ordinis*, n. 16.

141. See Paul VI, *Sacerdotalis Caelibatus*, n. 34.

directs a person's focus to heaven and to what is necessary on the journey to attain that end. Since Vatican II, the Magisterium has attributed such an eschatological significance to the celibacy of priests, both diocesan and religious.[142] In contrast, *Perfectae Caritatis* 12—summarizing traditional Catholic teaching—attributes an eschatological witness to women and men religious, who through their vow of chastity become signs of the age to come.[143]

New Testament Foundations of the Eschatological Dimension

The scriptural passage most commonly used for establishing the eschatological significance of celibacy is Matthew 22:30, where Jesus states that in the Resurrection "they [men and woman] neither marry nor are given in marriage, but are like angels in heaven."[144] Jesus teaches here that marriage will give way to a new form of life in heaven. Life in heaven will be of a different order, modeled on the angelic life.

With the resurrection of Jesus, Christians could believe in and hope for their own resurrection. Because Jesus rose from the dead and would bring to life those who died believing in him (see Jn 6:40; Rom 8:11), the Christian now had the option of forgoing marriage for the sake of eternal life in the Kingdom of heaven. Jesus's own celibacy functions as a prophecy of the new and eternal life of heaven, fundamentally linked to his resurrection.

The apostle Paul continues the teaching of Jesus on the transitory nature of the created world and the perduring reality of the Kingdom of heaven. His epistles contain various eschatological references that indicate the Kingdom of heaven as the final destiny of those who believe in Jesus. Paul encourages the faithful, whether married or celibate, to focus their eyes on the eternal, lasting things above, "where Christ is, seated at the right hand of God" (Col 3:1). He further exhorts them to anticipate the coming reign of God in the end times, when all will be raised from the dead (see 1 Thess 4:14–17).

142. For a detailed theological study on the eschatological dimension of priestly celibacy after Vatican II, see Joseph Höffner, "Pour le royaume des cieux: dix thèses sur le célibat des prêtres," in *Sacerdoce et célibat: Etudes historiques et théologiques*, ed. Joseph Coppens, 573–83 (Gembloux: Duculot, 1971).

143. See Vatican Council II, *Perfectae Caritatis*, n. 12.

144. Mk 12:24–25 and Lk 20:34–36 can also be cited in this regard.

In order to serve better the Lord and to focus on heavenly realities, Paul counsels men and women to live celibately, for "the present form of this world is passing away" (1 Cor 7:31). In 1 Corinthians 7, Paul teaches that devotion to the Lord's affairs is the motivation for celibacy, the celibate man is freer to please the Lord (see 1 Cor 7:32). This rationale seems different from that given by Jesus, who proposed the *Kingdom of heaven/God as the goal* (see Mt 19:27–30; Mk 10:28–31; Lk 18:28–30). Paul's motivation seems more subjective and centered on the individual in the service of Christ, rather than just the Kingdom of God. On this matter, Raniero Cantalamessa wrote: "There is one difference between the two texts (Jesus' and Paul's) and it is important to note it. According to Jesus, a person may remain unmarried 'for the sake of the Kingdom of Heaven,' that is, for a *cause*; according to Paul, marriage is renounced "for the sake of the Lord," i.e. for a *person*."[145] Cantalamessa argued that this represents an advancement of the Christian understanding of celibacy, one due not to Paul but to Jesus, who became "the Lord" by his death and resurrection.[146] Thus, the fundamental motivation for Christian celibacy is devotion to the person of the Lord Jesus.

The scriptural texts cited speak of an eschatological dimension of celibacy *in general* but do not indicate one that is particular to *ordained ministers* as such. However, Luke 18:28–30 implies the eschatological significance of ministerial celibacy, when Peter speaks, seemingly on behalf of the Twelve: "'Lo, we have left our homes and followed you.' And Jesus said to them, 'Truly, I say to you, there is no man who has left house or wife or brothers or parents or children, for the sake of the kingdom of God, who will not receive manifold more in this time, and *in the age to come eternal life.'*"[147] In the Lucan text, the Twelve are not only leaving the goods of this earth, but they are also journeying toward something beyond this life. The rewards they could expect for making the sacrifice of leaving everything for the sake of the Kingdom of God, even wife and children, will be manifold in this life and even greater in the age to come.

145. Raniero Cantalamessa, *Virginity: A Positive Approach to Celibacy for the Sake of the Kingdom of Heaven*, trans. Charles Serignat (Staten Island, N.Y.: Alba House, 1995), 21.

146. Ibid., 21.

147. Lk 18:28–30; translation from *Revised Standard Version, Catholic Edition*; cf. Mt 19:27–30 and Mk 10:28–31.

Other than Luke 18:28–30, the scriptural texts that are the foundation for the eschatological dimension of *priestly* celibacy refer to celibacy *in general* as a sign of the eschaton. In this respect, the eschatological dimension of apostolic, ministerial celibacy is not strongly present in scripture but is implicitly contained in the texts already mentioned. In sum, the eschatological significance of priestly celibacy reflects the preeminence of the Kingdom of God, which is already present already on earth in mystery but which will reach its perfection only with the final coming of the Lord Jesus (see Rev 22:17, 21).

The Eschatological Dimension as a Theo-Centric and Liturgical Characteristic of Celibacy

Mandatory priestly celibacy in the Latin Church, despite contemporary disagreement among some Catholics concerning its suitability, provides a practical advantage for priests by allowing the priest greater freedom and flexibility in fulfilling his pastoral work. In *Sacerdotalis Caelibatus*, Pope Paul VI underlined some of the practical benefits of priestly celibacy lived in the spirit of pastoral charity: "[Celibacy] gives to the priest, even in the practical field, the maximum efficiency and the best disposition of mind, psychologically and affectively, for the continuous exercise of a perfect charity. This charity will permit him to spend himself wholly for the welfare of all, in a fuller and more concrete way."[148] In addition to facilitating the sacerdotal mission by freeing the priest from the duties of marriage and family in order to serve more freely the people of God, celibacy helps the priest to grow in pastoral charity, thus orienting his ministerial activity to a supernatural purpose.[149]

Although being free from the demands of domestic life can benefit the priest from a practical standpoint, this freedom is not the primary motivation for priestly celibacy—rather it is the *priest's union with Christ through liturgical and intercessory prayer*. The practical benefits of celibacy, such as providing the priest with more time and energy to devote to pastoral ministry and to be seen by the faithful as being free for them, are secondary in relation to this primary motivation.

---

148. Paul VI, *Sacerdotalis Caelibatus*, n. 32.

149. See Vatican Council II, *Presbyterorum Ordinis*, n. 16; and Paul VI, *Sacerdotalis Caelibatus*, n. 24.

Priestly celibacy first and foremost is *theocentric*. Pope Benedict XVI, in his 2006 Christmas address to the Roman Curia, highlighted the priest's total dedication to God by quoting the psalm verse: "The Lord is my chosen portion and my cup, you hold my lot" (Ps 16:5). The pope then commented on the psalm:

The priest praying in this Psalm interprets his life on the basis of the distribution of territory as established in Deuteronomy (cf. 10: 9). After taking possession of the Land, every tribe obtained by the drawing of lots his portion of the Holy Land and with this took part in the gift promised to the forefather Abraham. The tribe of Levi alone received no land: its land was God himself. This affirmation certainly had an entirely practical significance. Priests did not live like the other tribes by cultivating the earth, but on offerings. However, the affirmation goes deeper. The true foundation of the priest's life, the ground of his existence, the ground of his life, is God himself.[150]

Benedict XVI went on to explain that the Catholic Church, in this Old Testament interpretation of priestly life, sees helpful indications for the meaning of its own priesthood. The priest of today can make his own what the Levite said in ancient times: "The Lord is my chosen portion and my cup"; that is, God himself is the priest's portion of land, the external and internal foundation of his existence. The pope emphasized that the "theocentricity" of priestly existence is a necessary anchor in an entirely function-oriented world based on calculable and ascertainable performance. The priest must know God intimately in order to be an effective apostle to humanity. If the priest fails to focus on God in his ministry, his priestly zeal quickly diminishes.[151]

Benedict XVI then related the theocentric notion of priestly ministry—the "land" on which the priest builds his ministry—to priestly celibacy: "The true foundation of celibacy can be contained in the phrase: *Dominus pars*—You are my land. It can only be theocentric. It cannot mean being deprived of love, but must mean letting oneself be consumed by passion for God and subsequently, thanks to a more intimate way of being with him, to serve men and women, too. Celibacy must be a witness to faith: faith in God materializes in that form of life which

150. See Benedict XVI, "Address to the Roman Curia," *L'Osservatore Romano* (January 3, 2007): 5–7, at 6.
151. Ibid., 6.

only has meaning if it is based on God."[152] The pope thus made it clear that the primary motivation for the celibacy of the priest must be divine and not human or practical. A desire for being free from human ties in order be available to others in fact could develop easily into a self-centered lifestyle that spares the priest from the sacrifices demanded by matrimony, into an egoism which could lead to spiritual poverty and to a hardening of the heart.[153] The authentic spirituality of priestly celibacy, on the other hand, opens the priest to a life of selfless service that is motivated by a desire for divine intimacy.

For Benedict, celibacy means to "be consumed by passion for God" and to enjoy a more intimate union with him. As a result of this prayerful union, the priest is better able "to serve men and women." This priority of intimate union with God in prayer naturally leads the priest to service to the faithful in pastoral charity. Benedict XVI concluded his reflection by stating that the world needs celibacy as a divine witness that is based upon the decision to welcome God as the "land" where one finds one's own existence. The pope implies that the celibate priest's surrender of himself to God as his only possession is to be nurtured and sustained by his life of prayer and sacramental ministry.

In this 2006 Christmas address, Benedict taught that priestly celibacy is not purely for practical benefit in this world, for example, giving the priest more time for ministry, but is rather a *means* by which the priest gives himself fully to God and thence more fully to service in the world. The pope's teaching is drawn from an Old Testament text— Psalms 16:5—that centers on the election of the Levites as a priestly people. His use of this psalm verse enriches the scriptural roots of the magisterial teaching on celibacy. Benedict XVI provided a theocentric motivation for priestly celibacy, which foremost consists of a prayerful union with God. This account, however, is incomplete insofar as it does not address liturgical prayer, which is the most eminent *priestly* prayer. The priest's total dedication to God and to the Church in *liturgical worship* is a way in which the eschatological dimension of *priestly* celibacy can be understood more fully.

One way of entering into such a liturgical understanding of priestly celibacy is through Paul VI's description of the eschatological dimension:

---

152. Ibid.   153. Ibid.

Our Lord and Master has said that "in the resurrection they neither marry nor are given in marriage, but are like angels in heaven" (Mt 22:30). In the world of man, so deeply involved in earthly concerns and too often enslaved by the desires of the flesh, the precious divine gift of perfect continence for the kingdom of heaven stands out precisely as "a singular sign of the blessings of heaven" (*PC*, n. 12), it proclaims the presence on earth of the final stages of salvation (cf. 1 Cor 7:29–31) with the arrival of a new world, and in a way it anticipates the fulfillment of the kingdom as it sets forth its supreme values which will one day shine forth in all the children of God.[154]

Although an eschatological witness can also be attributed to consecrated religious,[155] Paul VI applied it here to the ministerial priest, whose celibacy "anticipates the fulfillment of the kingdom as it sets forth its supreme values," which will one day shine forth in all the blessed in heaven.

How, then, is this eschatological witness specifically applied to the celibate priest? Insofar as the eucharistic liturgy states that "we await the blessed hope and the coming of our Savior, Jesus Christ,"[156] the priest's celibacy harmonizes well with the eschatological nature of the liturgy over which he presides, which is a foretaste of the heavenly life that is a liturgy of praise and adoration (see Rev 5:6–14, 7:9–12). Even though an unceasing life of prayer is not literally possible in this earthly life, priests still are able to approach it by dedicating themselves to a life of prayer and intercession through their sacerdotal celibacy, thus being "like the angels in heaven." Such an understanding of the primary motivation of priestly celibacy deepens and corrects a purely practical view of the charism.

This extension of Paul VI's teaching into a specifically liturgical understanding of the eschatological dimension, however, may seem to be somewhat forced. Nonetheless, support for this connection can be found in Catholic theological tradition. Origen (d. 254), for example, provided two homilies that can serve as an avenue for arriving at a liturgical understanding of the eschatological dimension. In his twenty-third homily on the book of Numbers, Origen described the various liturgical feast days, and he speaks of a metaphorical "feast of feasts"

154. Paul VI, *Sacerdotalis Caelibatus*, n. 34.

155. See Vatican Council II, *Perfectae Caritatis*, n. 12; and *Lumen Gentium*, n. 42.

156. United States Conference of Catholic Bishops, *The Roman Missal* (Totowa, N.J.: Catholic Book Publishing, 2011), 517; cf. Ti 2:13.

that has no interruption: the feast of unceasing prayer.[157] Mindful of the periodic continence observed by lay people before attending the Eucharist, Origen wrote about the necessity of unceasing prayer (see 1 Thess 5:17) and refers to Paul's counsel that married couples should agree to remain continent for a period of time in order to pray (see 1 Cor 7:5).[158] Christ, however, commanded believers to pray always (see Lk 18:1). Does it not follow then that believers should practice perpetual continence? Origen answered: "[Because Paul recommends temporary continence for married people] it is certain that the perpetual sacrifice is impeded in those who serve conjugal needs. This is why it seems to me that the offering of a perpetual sacrifice belongs to that one alone who has pledged himself to perpetual and continual chastity. But there are other feast days for those who perhaps are not able to offer the sacrifices of chastity perpetually."[159] These "other feast days" indicate that marriage and conjugal union are not obstacles to prayer as such; the prayer life of married couples, however, is not "perpetual" because of conjugal union. Those who are perpetually continent or celibate, on the other hand, are able to approach more closely a life of unceasing prayer because their prayer is not interrupted by satisfying conjugal needs, which includes sexual union.

Who are these Christians who live a celibate or perfectly continent life for the sake of unceasing prayer and as a sign of the Kingdom of heaven? Origen provided the answer in his sixth homily on Leviticus, where he focused on priests and their intercessory prayer.[160] Origen saw Moses as a prototype of the celibate priest of the New Testament. Just as the success of the Exodus depended on Moses's intercession, the successful mission of the Church depends on the mediation of the priest of Jesus Christ: "[Moses] does not rush to battle; he does not fight against

157. See Origen, *Homilies on Numbers*, trans. Thomas P. Scheck, Ancient Christian Texts, ed. Christopher A. Hall (Downers Grove, Ill.: IVP Academic, 2009) 139–47; *Hom. 23, 3 in Num*, in *Griechische Christliche Schriftsteller Orig.* 7, 215, 11–16.

158. See Origen, *Homilies on Numbers*, 141–42.

159. Ibid., 142.

160. See Origen, *Homilies on Leviticus 1–16*, trans. Gary Wayne Barkley, The Fathers of the Church, A New Translation (Patristic Series) 83, ed. Thomas P. Halton, 116–28 (Washington, D.C.: The Catholic University of America Press, 1990); *Hom. 6, 6 in Lev*, in *Griechische Christliche Schriftsteller Orig.* 6, 370, 2.

enemies. But what does he do? He prays and as long as he prays his people prevail. If 'he should relax and lower his hands' (Ex 17:11), his people are defeated and are put to flight. Thus let the priest of the Church also pray unceasingly that the people who are under him may defeat the invisible Amalachite hosts who are the demons that assail those 'who want to live piously in Christ (2 Tm 3:12).'"[161] As Moses could not let his arms of intercession drop, so too the priest of the New Covenant cannot afford to let his arms weaken. His perseverance in prayer is a guarantee of the salvation of the faithful. For Origen the theology of priestly intercession is governed by this principle, and the obligation to celibacy and perfect continence derives from it.[162] It follows that, being always in the presence of God in intercession—especially in liturgical ministry—the priest does not have the leisure needed for married life.[163]

Origen's witness to the connection between celibacy and priestly-liturgical prayer was affirmed at the Second Council of Carthage (390), which promulgated laws regulating clerical continence in relation to the offering of the sacraments:

Bishop Genethlius says: "As was previously said, it is fitting that the holy bishops and priests of God as well as the Levites, i.e., those who are *in the service of the divine sacraments*, observe perfect continence, so that they may obtain in all simplicity what they are asking from God; what the apostles taught and what antiquity itself observed, let us also endeavor to keep."

The bishops declared unanimously: "It pleases us all that bishop, priest, and deacon, guardians of purity, abstain from [conjugal intercourse] with their wives, so that *those who serve at the altar* may keep perfect chastity.[164]

Perfect continence was to be observed for the sake of prayer "so as to obtain in all simplicity what they are asking from God" (*quo possint simpliciter quod a Deo postulant impetrare*). The council's reference to those who are "in the service of the divine sacraments" and "who serve at the

161. Origen, *Homilies on Leviticus 1–16*, 128.

162. See Cochini, *The Apostolic Origins of Priestly Celibacy*, 251, upon which I have relied for this synthesis of Origen's thought on priestly intercession and celibacy.

163. Jerome wrote: "If a layperson, or any believer, is not able to pray unless he abstains from conjugal intercourse, the priest, who must always offer sacrifices for the people, must always pray. If he must always pray, he therefore must always abstain from the use of marriage," Jerome, *Adversus Jovinianum* I, in *Patrologia Latina* 23, 257a.

164. Second Council of Carthage, *Corpus Christianorum* 149, 13; emphasis added.

altar" affirms the priestly-cultic nature of this motivation. However, the service of the sacraments need not refer only to the celebration of the Eucharist, as Ambrosiaster stated: "Is all that is allowed in the presence of others also allowed in the presence of the Emperor? So much the more is it so in the affairs of God. That is the reason why God's priests must be purer than others; indeed he appears as his personal representative, and he is effectively his vicar; so that what is permitted to others is not permitted to him. It is necessary that he take the place of Christ every day; whether by praying for the people or by offering the Sacrifice or administering Baptism."[165] The prayer of the priest includes the Eucharist but also encompasses the celebration of the other sacraments, prayer in general, and other exercises of the *munus sanctificandi*. For example, Ambrosiaster also wrote, "[Priests and deacons] have to be present at the church every day.... They have to offer the sacrifice every week for the local population, and even if not every day for strangers, it's at least twice a week for the local populations. And furthermore, there is no shortage of sick people to baptize nearly every day.... If [the apostle] orders laymen to abstain temporarily [from conjugal relations] in order to attend to prayer, how much more [incumbent is it] on deacons and priests, they who have to pray day and night for the people entrusted to them."[166] The pastoral activity of the priest thus includes more than the simple celebration of the Eucharist: it embraces the wide range of priestly ministry. Nonetheless, the priest's prayerful intercession is most excellently accomplished in the Eucharist, which is the high point of priestly ministry.

Throughout the centuries Catholic theology has noted that celibacy facilitates priestly prayer. For example, Saint Raymond of Peñafort singled out priestly prayer as a key motivation for celibacy when he wrote that "[t]he reason [for priestly celibacy] is twofold: sacerdotal purity, in order that they may obtain in all sincerity that which with their prayers they ask from God ... ; the second reason is that they may pray unhindered (1 Cor 7:5) and exercise their office. They cannot do both things

165. Ambrosiaster, *Quaestiones Veteris et Novi Testamenti*, in *Corpus Scriptorum Ecclesiasticorum Latinorum* 50, 414–15; translation from Cholij, *Clerical Celibacy in East and West*, 167.

166. Ambrosiaster, *In Epistolam B. Pauli ad Timotheum primam*, III, 12–13, in *Patrologia Latina* 17, 470b–71b; translation from Cholij, *Clerical Celibacy in East and West*, 166.

together: that is, to serve their wife and the Church."[167] Raymond of Pe-ñafort, drawing from the patristic tradition, underlined various motivations that can be advanced in favor of priestly celibacy and not just that of purity. He actually listed three such motivations, because his second reason includes two parts: (1) ritual purity ("sacerdotal purity") and (2) unhindered prayer ("that they may pray unhindered") and (3) priestly ministry in general ("exercise their office"). Only the third reason would include "practical" aspects of priestly ministry; the other two relate to the priest's prayer life, which includes his liturgical prayer. The practical fruits of sacerdotal celibacy are placed within the richer and deeper context of those related to the priest's dedication to God in prayer. In sum, because the prayer that is most characteristic of the priest, namely, the liturgical prayer over which he presides, is intrinsically eschatological,[168] it can be said that the eschatological dimension of celibacy has a particular relevance for the priest, who proclaims the presence on earth of the final stages of salvation with the arrival of the new world and ultimately anchors his practical service of men and women.[169] The celibate priest in his liturgical prayer is thus able to pray efficaciously in adoration of God and in prayerful intercession for the Church and the world. He participates in the "here and now" of the Kingdom of God already present on earth. In his prophetic witness of the Kingdom of heaven, the celibate priest points to God as the source and goal of all human life in this age.

Moreover, the liturgical motivation for priestly celibacy that has often in the past been interpreted solely in terms of ritual purity (i.e., the priest must be pure in order to exercise his liturgical ministry) can now be interpreted also in eschatological terms (i.e., it is appropriate for the priest to be celibate because that is the life of the Kingdom and the liturgy over which he presides is its foretaste). The eschatological dimension therefore serves not only as a corrective to a pragmatic view, but it also enhances and completes the ritual purity view of priestly celibacy.

The celibate priest is helped in his eschatological witness by other members of the people of God, who contribute in their own ways to

---

167. Raymond of Peñafort, *Summa Iuris Canonici*, ed. J. Rius Serra (Barcelona: Universidad de Barcelona, 1945), 59; translation from Stickler, *The Case for Clerical Celibacy*, 50.

168. See Vatican Council II, *Sacrosanctum Concilium*, n. 8.

169. See Paul VI, *Sacerdotalis Caelibatus*, n. 34.

proclaiming the coming Kingdom of heaven.[170] However, that which distinguishes the celibate priest from the consecrated religious or lay faithful as a witness to the Kingdom of heaven is the manner in which he accomplishes this task of witness *as a priest*, that is, by the giving himself over to divine worship and priestly intercession, primarily through the celebration of the Eucharist.

Celibacy witnesses to eternal values and constitutes an invitation to look beyond the ephemeral and to realize that there is more to life than simply the present moment. Perhaps an implicit sense of this significance may be a reason why the world has been uneasy about religious celibacy. At the vigil of the end of the Year for Priests (June 10, 2010) Benedict XVI commented on the witness of priestly celibacy: "One great problem of Christianity in today's world is that it does not think anymore of the future of God. The present of this world alone seems sufficient. We want to have only this world, to live only in this world. So we close the doors to the true greatness of our existence. The meaning of celibacy as an anticipation of the future is to open these doors, to make the world greater, to show the reality of the future that should be lived by us already as present."[171]

The eschatological dimension of priestly celibacy invites the people of God to a deeper prayer life insofar as it signifies the eternal values of the Kingdom of heaven and calls them to a deeper participation in the liturgy, which is its foretaste. Sacerdotal celibacy is radically theocentric, and it serves as a reminder to the Church that the ministerial priesthood is a participation in the eternal priesthood of Jesus Christ, who came to glorify the Father (see Jn 17:4) and who "lives forever to make intercession" for the world (Heb 7:25).

An Integrated Theology of Priestly Celibacy

Cardinal Marc Ouellet has proposed an integration of the motives for priestly celibacy, noting that *Sacerdotalis Caelibatus* "does not manage to go beyond a juxtaposition of different motives that lack a more profound principle of integration."[172] Ouellet centered his perspective on an

---

170. See Vatican Council II, *Lumen Gentium*, nn. 48–51; and *Sacrosanctum Concilium*, n. 8.

171. Benedict XVI, "A Sacrament, a New Life to Make Room for God," *L'Osservatore Romano* (June 16, 2010), 1, 6–7, 10, at 7.

172. Marc Cardinal Ouellet, "Priestly Celibacy and the Life of the Church: Contemporary

eschatological vision of priestly ministry, which presupposes a pneumatological Christology, as well as a trinitarian and nuptial ecclesiology. He stated that the contemporary theological challenge is to integrate the justifications for celibacy in a unified perspective that highlights that which is specific to priestly ministry. The key to this integration lies in a deeper understanding of the relationship between the Eucharist and the Church, with an emphasis placed on the eschatological dimension of the Eucharist.

Several scriptural texts referring to the Eucharist (see Mt 6:29; Jn 12:32; Jn 6:54; 1 Cor 11:26; Rev 19:7) draw attention to the mystery of the Trinity and of the Church, which are manifested in the priestly offering Christ makes of himself to the Father in love, in the power of the Holy Spirit (see Heb 9:14). This sacrificial, eucharistic offering is a gift for the Church-Bride as an everlasting memorial of the New Covenant: "This eschatological and nuptial gift of Christ the Lord to his Bride passes through the hearts and hands of his ministers, who exercise not only a sacramental office but, properly speaking, an eschatological service. This is what we must seek to understand more deeply in order to unify the Christological, ecclesiological, and eschatological reasons for priestly celibacy."[173]

In order to achieve an integration of the motives for priestly celibacy, Ouellet first considered the word of God as the starting point for the doctrine of the priesthood. The priestly ministry of the word, which is exercised in various ways, attains its properly eschatological dimension within the celebration of the Eucharist. The priest, as minister of the word, represents Christ the Bridegroom as God's definitive word to humanity, and this word culminates in the Eucharist, the supreme act of sacrificial offering by Christ. Ouellet wrote, "This act of the divine Bridegroom is absolutely Trinitarian, for it implies the three divine Persons in the unity of Love that transcends time. This Love gives itself to us so that we might participate in it sacramentally, through the priest ordained for this purpose. Since he is sacramentally united to Christ the Bridegroom, the priest communicates in him not only as a member of the ecclesial community, but first as a minister of Christ himself, who

_____

Values and Challenges," in *Celibacy and the Priesthood: Divine Gift and Cultural Anomaly*, ed. Arthur Kennedy (Boston: Saint Botolph Press, 2012), 1–39, at 15.

173. Ibid., 20.

gives himself bodily and virginally to his Bride the Church."[174] In virtue of the ministerial service of the Paschal mystery, which makes the Kingdom of God present "even now," priestly celibacy appears in its proper perspective. Thus, the perfect and perpetual continence of the priest can be viewed as an eschatological state of life in perfect harmony with the Eucharistic mystery: "In other words, it is the irruption of the eschatological Kingdom in the Eucharistic mystery, nuptially uniting Christ and the Church, which fundamentally justifies the requirement of the Latin Church with respect to its ministers and the pertinence of its two-thousand-year tradition."[175] Rather than being seen as simply an ecclesiastical discipline, priestly celibacy is the priest's participation in the Kingdom of God that is already present, which gives reason for the call to live and love as Christ the Bridegroom.

Ouellet, moreover, grounded his vision of ecclesiastical celibacy in the Trinitarian foundation and communitarian dimension of priestly ministry, particularly in the ministry and life of the bishop, who through episcopal ordination becomes part of the college of bishops.[176] The ministerial priest, on his part, becomes a cooperator of the bishop and a member of a college of priests. Bishops thus exercise their ministry in an "affective and effective" solidarity that testifies to their hierarchical communion and the membership in the college of bishops. The hierarchical and communitarian witness of the episcopacy is essential to the life of the Church. It forms a supporting structure rooted in the communion of the Trinity inasmuch as bishops, with priests as their collaborators, incarnate the eschatological ministry of Christ and are ordained by the Holy Spirit for the service of the common priesthood of the faithful. Ouellet then stated that "[i]n this collegial context of the fullness of the priesthood, ecclesiastical celibacy, maintained by the Church in both East and West, shows itself to be in perfect harmony with the spiritual fatherhood of the Bishop, who points simultaneously to his Trinitarian origin and to the Eucharistic fruitfulness of the risen Christ. Ultimately, this fatherhood reveals the mystery of the Father, of whom the Bishop

174. Ibid., 21.

175. Ibid.

176. See Vatican Council II, *Lumen Gentium*, n. 28; *Christus Dominus*, n. 4; *Presbyterorum Ordinis*, n. 8.

is a privileged image, according to St. Ignatius of Antioch."[177] The father-hood of the bishop gives to celibacy a dimension of fruitfulness that goes beyond reason of pastoral availability. Furthermore, for both bishop and priest, spiritual fatherhood witnesses to sacramental fraternity, which testifies to the triune love that "gives itself to be shared."

Ouellet concluded his reflection by focusing on pastoral charity as the ideal of priestly perfection, which flows above all from the Eucha-ristic sacrifice.[178] This priestly love stands at the root and center of the whole life of the priest and is both merciful and spousal. Thus, by begin-ning with the ministry of the word and culminating in the Eucharist as the source of pastoral charity, Ouellet has given a coherent synthesis of priestly celibacy that not only is based in an eschatological dimension of priestly celibacy but also includes the Christological and ecclesiologi-cal dimensions: "With the support of a theology of the Covenant rooted in biblical symbolism of the wedding feast, and relying on a Christolog-ical renewal of eschatology, we envisaged priestly ministry and celibacy as an eschatological service of the Word of God that extends to the sac-ramental proclamation of the Paschal mystery. That is to say, this ser-vice extends to the holy Eucharist, the nuptial mystery par excellence of Christ and the Church."[179]

Summary

THIS CHAPTER has presented in a systematic manner the threefold di-mension as a way of contributing to the development of the theology of priestly celibacy. The biblical foundations of the three dimensions have been explored, followed by an elaboration of their respective theologi-cal value and fruitfulness.

The principal contributions of the threefold scheme of priestly celi-bacy as outlined in this chapter are as follows. First, Christological di-mension can promote a deeper understanding of priestly celibacy as both a charism and a discipline. This distinction underlines the funda-mental notion of celibacy as primarily a charism (gift) to aid the priest

177. Ouellet, "Priestly Celibacy and the Life of the Church," 23–24.
178. See Vatican Council II, *Presbyterorum Ordinis*, n. 14.
179. Ouellet, "Priestly Celibacy and the Life of the Church," 32.

in his growth in holiness and ministerial fruitfulness, whereas celibacy as a discipline builds on this charismatic nature of celibacy and is ordered to its protection and perfection. Moreover, the Christological dimension is useful in underscoring episcopal celibacy as a starting point for ecumenical dialogue on the subject of clerical celibacy between Orthodox Christians and Catholics.

Second, the ecclesiological dimension is beneficial in illuminating the rich images of the priest in his relation to the Church, such as spiritual father and bridegroom. It is also important in helping to enhance the traditional ritual purity argument, particularly through a focus on pastoral charity and the Eucharist. Additionally, the insights provided by the ecclesiological perspective underline the need for the priest to focus his attention and energy on those whom he serves, particularly the poor and the neglected.

Third, the eschatological dimension can help to correct an overly pragmatic understanding of priestly celibacy by underscoring its theocentric and liturgical orientation. The eschatological dimension also can be used as a principle for integrating the elements of the threefold scheme, as was articulated by Ouellet.

Indeed, the threefold dimension has proven to be a useful tool for elaborating and developing the theology of priestly celibacy. This development builds on the traditional presentations given by the fathers, the Magisterium, and theologians throughout the centuries, which emphasized the ritual purity argument and superiority of virginity over marriage. Ritual purity was one of the principal reasons historically given by Catholic teaching and theology for the suitability of priestly continence and celibacy, its primary value consisting in its highlighting a connection between priest's chaste continence and his offering of the Eucharist. Insofar as the Eucharist is the source and summit of the Christian life, including priestly life, it follows that the relationship of sacerdotal celibacy to the Eucharist should be the particular focus of the theology of priestly celibacy, such as that provided by Ouellet. In view of the richness of his synthesis, it is worthwhile to explore in the final chapter two new perspectives of priestly celibacy in its relationship with the Eucharist.

4

The Eucharist and Priestly Celibacy

P AUL VI encouraged theologians to delve more deeply into the meaning of priestly celibacy in order to discover "the inner recesses and wealth of its reality."[1] Thus, there is a need to explore the hidden riches of sacerdotal celibacy, particularly through searching for a systematic account that summarizes well its various elements.

Of the three dimension of priestly celibacy, the ecclesiological—which considers the way in which celibacy touches upon the minister's relationship to the Church—has garnered most attention from the Magisterium and theologians since Vatican II. However, the Christological dimension—which refers to the priest's union with and configuration to Christ—is the foundational aspect of priestly celibacy. In this respect, John Paul II wrote in *Pastores Dabo Vobis* 29: "The will of the Church finds its ultimate motivation in the link between celibacy and sacred ordination, *which configures the priest to Jesus Christ*, the head and spouse of the Church."[2] On this statement of John Paul II, Stickler commented: "These words can be considered the central nucleus of the theology of celibacy which has been developed in the apostolic exhortation and which has been offered as the *foundation for future development, study and consideration*."[3] Stickler recognized that the configuration of the

1. "This vision seems to us so profound and rich in truth, both speculative and practical, that we invite you, venerable brothers, and you, eager students of Christian doctrine and masters of the spiritual life, and all you priests who have gained a supernatural insight into your vocation, to persevere in the study of this vision, and to go deeply into the inner recesses and wealth of its reality," Paul VI, *Sacerdotalis Caelibatus*, n. 25.

2. John Paul II, *Post-Synodal Apostolic Exhortation*, n. 29; emphasis added.

3. Stickler, *The Case for Clerical Celibacy*, 101; emphasis added.

priest to Christ through priestly ordination is the foundational consideration of celibacy (the Christological dimension). The ministerial priest discovers his true identity through his participation in the priesthood of Christ, to whom the priest is primarily referred. From his union with Christ, the priest is related to the Church (the ecclesiological dimension). This relationship is described through a multiplicity of images, for example, Head, Servant, Shepherd, and Bridegroom. In addition, the priest's union with Christ orients him toward the Kingdom of heaven (the eschatological dimension), principally through his celebration of the Eucharist. The ecclesiological dimension thus occupies a middle position. That is, through his union with Christ (the Christological dimension), the priest serves the Church (the ecclesiological dimension). His priestly service, however, is for the sake of the Kingdom of heaven (the eschatological dimension).

The priest's active ministry is vivified by *pastoral charity*, the priest's gift of self to the Church after the example of Christ. Pastoral charity has an intrinsically ecclesial dynamism that flows from and is preeminently expressed through the Eucharist: "The Eucharist represents, makes once again present, the sacrifice of the cross, the full gift of Christ to the Church, the gift of his body given and his blood shed, as the supreme witness of the fact that he is head and shepherd, servant and spouse of the Church. Precisely because of this, the priest's pastoral charity not only flows from the Eucharist but finds in the celebration of the Eucharist its highest realization—just as it is from the Eucharist that he receives the grace and obligation to give his whole life a "sacrificial" dimension."[4] Underlying this pastoral charity is the mystery of Trinitarian communion, which is the font of all charity and the root of the relationship between Christ and the Church and, hence, between the priest and the Church.[5] This Trinitarian communion, however, is accessed in a preeminent way through the Eucharist, the source and summit of the Christian life.[6]

In view of the Eucharist being the source and summit of priestly ministry and life, this concluding chapter treats the eucharistic foundations

4. John Paul II, *Post-Synodal Apostolic Exhortation*, n. 23.

5. Ibid., n. 12.

6. See Vatican Council II, *Lumen Gentium*, n. 11.

of priestly celibacy in order to illumine—through the use of the threefold scheme to the extent that is possible—the nature of priestly celibacy.

A Eucharistic-Eschatological Theology of Priestly Celibacy

ALTHOUGH VATICAN II has taught that the ministerial priesthood is centered on the Eucharist,[7] subsequent magisterial teaching has not proposed a developed argument that explicitly ties priestly celibacy to the Eucharist. It would be thus fruitful to form a theological synthesis of priestly celibacy that is explicitly connected to the Eucharist and that would complement the traditional ritual purity argument. The previous chapter summarized Ouellet's synthesis, in which he focused on the eschatological dynamism of the Eucharist as the integrating principle of a theology of priestly celibacy. This section proposes an account that likewise is based on the eschatological dimension of the Eucharist.

Presbyterorum Ordinis 16 broke new ground when it attributed an eschatological witness to priestly celibacy, regardless of whether it was lived out by a diocesan or religious priest.[8] Nevertheless, its account of the eschatological dimension of priestly celibacy is similar to the description given in *Perfectae Caritatis* 12 of the chastity of consecrated religious insofar as both describe their respective eschatological significance as being ordered "for the sake of the Kingdom of heaven." Is there a particular distinction between priestly celibacy and religious chastity in these two instances? Cochini suggests a difference:

> The consecration of a virgin (or a continent non-priest) appears to be a total gift of self to God "for the Kingdom of God." The virgin has to please the Divine Spouse in all things, to direct all her faculties toward him, and to surrender to him without any reservations, her body and soul. The minister of Christ, on the other hand, must be continent, less in virtue of a charismatic desire to belong totally to God (though it goes without saying that such a disposition is in keeping with his state)

---

7. See Vatican Council II, *Sacrosanctum Concilium*, n. 10; *Lumen Gentium*, nn. 21, 28; *Presbyterorum Ordinis*, n. 5.

8. "[Celibate priests] are made a living sign of that world to come, already present through faith and charity, a world in which the children of the resurrection shall neither marry, nor be given in marriage," Vatican Council II, *Presbyterorum Ordinis*, n. 16.

than in order to obtain the necessary conditions for the achievement of his specific mission, or, in other words, his functions as a mediator.[9]

Priestly mediation thus constitutes a specific difference that distinguishes celibacy from consecrated chastity. In particular, priestly mediation is centered on the *Eucharist*, which provides a solid foundation for theological development of the subject of priestly celibacy.[10]

Along these lines, John Paul II provided references the Eucharist as a foundation for the whole of Christian life and mission in *Ecclesia de Eucharistia*: "The implementation of this program of a renewed impetus in Christian living passes through the Eucharist.... Every commitment to holiness, every activity aimed at carrying out the Church's mission, every work of pastoral planning, must draw the strength it needs from the Eucharistic mystery and in turn be directed to that mystery as its culmination."[11] This observation provides a general outline concerning a way to assemble a synthesis—using magisterial texts and theological reflection—of priestly celibacy centered on the Eucharist. Other more specific magisterial texts provide contours for establishing a relationship between celibacy and the Eucharist, particularly in the eschatological understanding of the Eucharist. *Sacrosanctum Concilium* 41, for example, gives an account of the eucharistic celebration of a local church around the bishop: "The principal manifestation of the Church consists in the full, active participation of all God's holy people in the same liturgical celebrations, especially in the same Eucharist, in one prayer, at one altar, at which the bishop presides, surrounded by his college of priests and by his ministers."[12] This text can be understood as describing the visible manifestation of the final eschatological assembly, which was mentioned earlier in *Sacrosanctum Concilium* 8: "In the earthly liturgy we take part in the foretaste of the heavenly liturgy which is celebrated in the holy city of Jerusalem towards which we journey as pilgrims."[13]

9. Cochini, *The Apostolic Origins of Priestly Celibacy*, 438.

10. See Vatican Council II, *Lumen Gentium*, n. 26.

11. John Paul II, *On the Eucharist: Ecclesia de Eucharistia*, n. 60 (Washington, D.C.: United States Conference of Catholic Bishops, 2003), 65.

12. Vatican Council II, *Sacrosanctum Concilium*, n. 41.

13. Ibid., n. 8; see John Zizioulas, *Being as Communion* (Crestwood, N.Y.: St. Vladimir's Press, 1985), 149, 157–58.

In addition, *Lumen Gentium* 23 states that the local churches gathered around their bishops are "constituted after the model of the universal Church." Although "universal Church" often refers to the worldwide Church, the more profound sense of the term refers to the heavenly Church according to an eschatological view (see *Lumen Gentium* 2). This heavenly assembly is richly described in the Letter to the Hebrews, in a passage that can signify the Christian community gathered for the Eucharist: "You have come to Mount Zion and to the city of the living God, the heavenly Jerusalem, and to innumerable angels in festal gathering, and to the assembly of the first-born who are enrolled in heaven, and to a judge who is God of all, and to the spirits of just men made perfect, and to Jesus, the mediator of a new covenant, and to the sprinkled blood that speaks more graciously than the blood of Abel."[14]

Every celebration of the Eucharist opens up to this assembly of the angels and saints gathered around Christ in the heavenly Jerusalem. The eschatological dimension of the liturgy is rooted in the *present* participation in the heavenly Jerusalem through the offering of the Eucharist *here and now*. Consequently the Eucharist thrusts the worshipping assembly into the *future* reality of heavenly life, as the preceding text from Hebrews seems to affirm. The liturgical assembly is taken also into the *past* through the mystery of the Eucharist, as Paul McPartlan described: "As we unpack its [the Eucharist's] manifold mystery, there are the past and the future, too, or rather there is the past *in* the future, the memorial of Calvary in the midst of the anticipation of the kingdom. Though we may appear to be looking *backward* in this celebration, by re-enacting what the Lord did at the Last Supper, it is clear that Jesus himself was looking *forward* in that sacred meal and that, therefore, in the deepest sense, so are we, as we do what he did."[15] Therefore, the Eucharist in its threefold dimension—past, present, and future—comprehends time and eternity. Each of the faithful is able to participate fully in this mystery. However, the priest who offers the Eucharist represents Christ at the center of the heavenly liturgy to come. It is highly appropriate that he be celibate both because of his imaging of the celibate

---

14. Heb 12:22–24; see Paul McPartlan, *Sacrament of Salvation: An Introduction to Eucharistic Ecclesiology* (Edinburgh: T&T Clark, 1995), 1–13, at 4–5.

15. Ibid., 12.

Christ and of the eschatological nature of this celebration that anticipates the age to come in which there will be no marrying and giving in
marriage (see Lk 20:36). The following words of Benedict XVI to priests
fits well with the eucharistic-eschatological context just described:

> This unification of his "I" with ours implies that we are "drawn" also into the real-
> ity of his Resurrection; we are going forth towards the full life of resurrection. Je-
> sus speaks of it to the Sadducees in Matthew, chapter 22. It is a "new" life in which
> we are already beyond marriage (cf. Mt 22:23–32). It is important that we always
> allow this identification of the "I" of Christ with us, this being "drawn" towards
> the world of resurrection. In this sense, celibacy is anticipation. We transcend this
> time and move on. By doing so, we "draw" ourselves and our time towards the
> world of the resurrection, towards a new and true life. Therefore, celibacy is an
> anticipation, a foretaste, made possible by the grace of the Lord, who draws us
> to himself, towards the world of the resurrection. It invites us always anew to
> transcend ourselves and the present time, to the true presence of the future that
> becomes present today.[16]

The pope stated that priestly celibacy is "an anticipation, a foretaste,
made possible by the grace of the Lord, who draws us to himself, towards
the world of the resurrection." Priestly celibacy can thus be connected
with the Eucharist insofar as both are anticipations of the second coming of Christ and the life and liturgy of the heavenly Jerusalem. The connection here is provided through an *eschatological orientation*.

The liturgical assembly with the bishop, "constituted after the model of the universal Church," (*Lumen Gentium* 23) anticipates in a preeminent way the eschatological realities to which the Eucharist is oriented.
Gathering the presbyters and deacons around him, in the presence of
the baptized faithful, the bishop offers the eucharistic sacrifice and thus
leads the worshipping faithful in the making present of the future Kingdom of God. In virtue of his celibacy, the bishop—and the priest by extension—is more apt to be drawn into the heavenly Jerusalem because
he is free from earthly cares that arise from marriage and family. Moreover, through the sacrificial offering of the Eucharist by the celibate
bishop or priest, the community is better able to *anticipate* the future
resurrection and the Kingdom of heaven through the celebration of the

---

16. Benedict XVI, "A Sacrament, a New Life to Make Room for God," 7.

Eucharist, as well as to *participate* in its present reality. These anticipatory and participatory characteristics of the eschatological dimension of priestly celibacy achieve their most sublime expression in the Eucharist.

In view of these distinctions, a particular eschatological perspective of *priestly* celibacy comes to light. Rather than being described in terms of concepts that are also applied to consecrated religious men and women, this perspective links the priest's celibacy especially with his celebration of the Eucharist. The eschatological dimension of priestly celibacy points to the world of the Resurrection and the heavenly Jerusalem, the very realities that are anticipated in the celebration of the Eucharist. Through the grace of the Lord Jesus, celibacy invites the priest, who offers the Eucharist, to transcend himself and the present world in order to ascend to the heavenly reality "to the true presence of the future that becomes present today."[17]

Priestly Celibacy, Pastoral Charity, and the Eucharist

THE POSTSYNODAL apostolic exhortation of Benedict XVI, titled *Sacramentum Caritatis*,[18] was the fruit of the Eleventh General Assembly of the Synod of Bishops (2005), which focused on the Eucharist as the source and summit of the Church's life and mission. This papal exhortation contains insights into priestly celibacy that can provide an outline for a Eucharist-centered theology of priestly celibacy.

In the section "The Eucharist and Priestly Celibacy," Benedict XVI pointed out that the synod fathers wished to emphasize the need for ministerial priests to be completely configured to Christ. Priestly celibacy facilitates this configuration by enabling the priest to dedicate his whole person to Christ in ministerial service to the people of God: "This choice [celibacy] on the part of the priest expresses in a special way the dedication which conforms him to Christ and his exclusive offering of himself for the Kingdom of God. The fact that Christ himself, the eternal priest, lived his mission even to the sacrifice of the Cross in the state

---

17. Ibid.

18. See Benedict XVI, *The Sacrament of Charity: Sacramentum Caritatis* (Washington, D.C.: United States Conference of Catholic Bishops, 2007).

of virginity constitutes *the sure point of reference* for understanding the meaning of the tradition of the Latin Church."[19]

The pope then reaffirmed the obligation of sacerdotal celibacy in the Latin Church based on the blessings that it confers on the Church and the world:

> This choice [of celibacy] has first and foremost a nuptial meaning; it is a profound identification with the heart of Christ the Bridegroom who gives his life for his Bride. In continuity with the great ecclesial tradition, with the Second Vatican Council and with my predecessors in the papacy, I reaffirm the beauty and the importance of a priestly life lived in celibacy as a sign expressing total and exclusive devotion to Christ, to the Church and to the Kingdom of God, and I therefore confirm that it remains obligatory in the Latin tradition. Priestly celibacy lived with maturity, joy and dedication is an immense blessing for the Church and for society itself.[20]

Benedict XVI reaffirmed here the sign value of priestly celibacy according to the threefold dimension: it expresses the priest's "total and exclusive devotion to Christ" (the Christological dimension), "to the Church" (the ecclesiological dimension) "and to the Kingdom of God" (the eschatological dimension).

Benedict XVI thus summarizes well contemporary magisterial teaching on priestly celibacy: (1) the Christological dimension signifies the priest's union with Christ, who is the source and motivation for priestly celibacy. This is the foundational significance of priestly celibacy: "The fact that Christ himself, the eternal priest, lived his mission even to the sacrifice of the Cross in the state of virginity constitutes the sure point of reference for understanding the meaning of the tradition of the Latin Church"; (2) the ecclesiological dimension refers to the manner in which the priest is related to the Church in his ministry and particularly highlights the nuptial meaning of priestly celibacy: "This choice has first and foremost a nuptial meaning; it is a profound identification with the heart of Christ the Bridegroom who gives his life for his Bride"; and (3) the eschatological dimension refers to the goal of priestly celibacy, the Kingdom of heaven, for which the priest sacrifices earthly marriage and fam-

---

19. Ibid.; emphasis added.
20. Ibid.

ily: "This choice on the part of the priest expresses in a special way ... his exclusive offering of himself for the Kingdom of God."

It is significant that Benedict XVI did not deal explicitly with the relationship between the Eucharist and priestly celibacy in this section titled "The Eucharist and Priestly Celibacy." Although at first glance this may seem to be a glaring oversight, it is reasonable to assume that the title indicates the heart of the matter (which may be understated if not hidden) and provides a stimulus for taking a deeper gaze into the Eucharistic foundations of priestly celibacy.

One interpretative key in the text is the nuptial meaning of celibacy, which the pope describes as a "profound identification with the Heart of Christ the Bridegroom who gives his life for his Bride." This reference to the priest's participation in the sacrificial outpouring of Christ for his bridal Church points to the nuptial-ecclesiological significance of celibacy, which is expressed preeminently in the Eucharist. As noted earlier, celibacy is a sign and stimulus for pastoral charity, which itself flows forth from the Eucharist. It is worthwhile, then, to explore briefly the connections between priestly celibacy, pastoral charity, and the Eucharist.

Celibacy, which forms part of the priest's imitation of the life of Christ, becomes fruitful to the extent that *pastoral charity* informs and perfects it. Pastoral charity itself is a participation in Christ's own pastoral charity and it enables the priest to give himself totally to the Church. As pastoral charity perfects the priest in his celibacy, so too does priestly celibacy facilitate growth in pastoral charity, as Paul VI stated: "The free choice of sacred celibacy has always been considered by the Church 'as a symbol of, and stimulus to, charity': it signifies a love without reservations; it stimulates to a charity which is open to all."[21] Celibacy is thus both a sign of and a stimulus to pastoral charity. In the context of service to the Church, the celibate priest imitates Christ who "loved the Church and gave himself up for her" (Eph 5:25). Yet pastoral charity itself is rooted in the Eucharist, as Vatican II teaches: "Pastoral charity flows mainly from the eucharistic sacrifice, which is thus the center and

---

21. Paul VI, *Sacerdotalis Caelibatus*, n. 24; the internal citation is from Vatican Council II, *Lumen Gentium*, n. 42. See John Paul II, *Post-Synodal Apostolic Exhortation*, n. 23.

root of the whole priestly life."[22] Thus, the priest's *pastoral charity* flows from the celebration of the Eucharist, from which the priest receives the grace and obligation to give his whole life a sacrificial dimension.[23]

Consequently, the graces given to the priest to live a fruitful celibacy should be understood as being drawn from the Eucharist: "The liturgy is the summit toward which the activity of the Church is directed; at the same time it is the font from which all her power flows."[24] The Eucharist is the universal source of grace for all the faithful and the goal of all the activities of the Church. Hence, the charism of priestly celibacy, as with pastoral charity, has its own source and ultimate goal in the Eucharist.

In and through the Eucharist, the priest is perfected in his relationship with Christ, whom he represents (the Christological dimension), and is more intimately related to the Church, which gathers around him at that moment (the ecclesiological dimension) and to the Kingdom of heaven of which the celebration gives a foretaste (the eschatological dimension). Thus, in his self-offering during the eucharistic celebration, the priest expresses in the fullest way the threefold dimension of priestly celibacy. It can be said that the priest's growth in priestly life and holiness is aided through centering his whole life, including his celibacy, on the celebration of the Eucharist, in which the whole spiritual good of the Church is contained.[25] Acting in the person of Christ the Head, the priest unites himself with the sacrificial offering placed on the altar.[26] Through his eucharistic offering, thanksgiving, sacrifice, and communion, the priest is enabled to serve the faithful with Christ-like pastoral charity, as he and they "await the blessed hope and the coming of our Savior, Jesus Christ."[27]

---

22. Vatican Council II, *Presbyterorum Ordinis*, n. 14; see *Lumen Gentium*, n. 28, *Presbyterorum Ordinis*, n. 2.

23. See John Paul II, *Post-Synodal Apostolic Exhortation*, n. 23.

24. Vatican Council II, *Sacrosanctum Concilium*, n. 10.

25. See Vatican Council II, *Presbyterorum Ordinis*, n. 5.

26. See Paul VI, *Sacerdotalis Caelibatus*, n. 29.

27. See United States Conference of Catholic Bishops, *The Roman Missal*, 517; Ti 2:13.

Summary

THE TWO PROPOSALS in this chapter summarize various perspectives of priestly celibacy as seen in relation to the Eucharist. The first account seeks to develop a particular *priestly* eschatological perspective of celibacy. The key notion in this formulation is the priest's celebration of the Eucharist, wherein his celibacy draws attention to the world of the Resurrection and the heavenly Jerusalem. By the grace of God, celibacy assists the priest to rise above himself and the present world in order to ascend to the heavenly realities presented during the celebration of the Eucharist. The faithful on their part are also drawn into this upward movement through their active participation in the celebration of the Eucharist, having been led and inspired by the priest as an eschatological sign.

The second proposal, which is takes its point of departure from *Sacramentum Caritatis of Benedict XVI*, considers the integral connection between celibacy, pastoral charity, and the Eucharist. In his mission and life, the priest is called by God to center his whole life, including his celibacy, on the offering of the Eucharist, wherein Christ's sacrifice on Calvary is re-presented in a sacramental manner. Acting in the person of Christ the Head, the priest unites himself with the offering placed upon the altar. Precisely through his eucharistic offering, thanksgiving, sacrifice, and communion, the priest is enabled to serve the faithful with Christ-like pastoral charity.

In addition to these two syntheses, a consideration of the *nuptial* mystery of the Eucharist provides a fitting concluding thought on the richness of gift of priestly celibacy. John Paul II has written that

[t]*he Eucharist is the Sacrament of our Redemption*. It is *the Sacrament of the Bridegroom and of the Bride.* The Eucharist makes present and realizes anew in a sacramental manner the redemptive act of Christ, who "creates" the Church, his body. Christ is united with this "body" as the bridegroom with the bride.... It is the *Eucharist* above all that expresses *the redemptive act of Christ the Bridegroom towards the Church the Bride.* This is clear and unambiguous when the sacramental ministry of the Eucharist, in which the priest acts "*in persona Christi,*" is performed by a man.[28]

28. John Paul II, *Mulieris Dignitatem*, n. 26.

By means of his sacramental configuration to Christ, Head and Shepherd, the priest stands in a spousal relationship toward the community of the faithful. In his ministry, the priest is called by God to radiate the authentic spousal love of Jesus Christ. Celibacy aids the priest to be a witness to Christ's spousal love and, moreover to love the people with a heart that is "new, generous and pure, with genuine self-detachment, with full, constant and faithful dedication and at the same time with a kind of 'divine jealousy' (cf. 2 Cor 11:2) and even with a kind of maternal tenderness."[29]

Priestly spousal love is particularly evident as the priest celebrates the Mass. The priest, acting in the person of Christ the Head and Bridegroom and in the name of the Church, offers the sacrifice of the death of and resurrection of Christ to the Father in the Holy Spirit.[30] In bringing new life to the bride in the sacraments, especially in the Eucharist, the priest acts in a *husbanding* role and as a father. In confecting and administering the Eucharist, the priest brings new life to the family of Heaven. Priestly celibacy enhances and facilitates this nuptial dimension of the eucharistic sacrifice of the Holy Mass, which is the sacramental source of the graces for holiness and salvation for the whole Mystical Body of Christ on earth.

29. John Paul II, *Post-Synodal Apostolic Exhortation*, n. 22.
30. See *Catechism of the Catholic Church*, n. 1689.

Conclusion

FOR CENTURIES, Catholic theology has developed arguments to justify the suitability of celibacy and continence for major clerics, particularly for priests. The reasons offered have varied throughout the centuries. The challenge in developing a systematic account of celibacy, however, is to pinpoint the more fundamental motives that underlie the various reasons given for clerical celibacy and continence. Related to the investigation of these fundamental Christian motives is the question of the "newness" of priestly celibacy: whether the theology underlying the discipline of celibacy and continence in the Latin Church was influenced by New Testament motivations that are essentially related to Christ and to the ordained ministry instituted in the Church, or whether it was drawn from the Old Testament and/or from other non-Christian sources. Throughout this book the former position has been argued.

For example, the New Testament indicates that the apostles and early church ministers were not obliged to marry; neither were they explicitly bound to observe the Old Testament regulations concerning ritual purity. Rather, the motivations for celibacy and continence are unique to the New Testament, that is, (1) the life of Christ and the example of the apostle Paul (celibacy), (2) the ostensible life of the married apostles after their call to ministry (perfect and perpetual continence), (3) the vocation of the eunuch "for the Kingdom of heaven," (4) the belief in Christ's resurrection as the cause of the elect's resurrection, (5) Paul's counsel that an unmarried man be free of anxiety, and (6) one particular interpretation of the Pauline formula "man of one wife." The early Church drew from these biblical themes in order to defend and explain clerical continence and celibacy.

Furthermore, it has been noted that from the patristic era, the *discipline* of clerical continence and celibacy in the Latin Church was accompanied by an underlying *teaching* that interpreted the discipline. From the fourth to the twentieth centuries, clerical continence and celibacy were explained primarily through the arguments of ritual purity, the superiority of celibacy to marriage, a greater freedom for pastoral ministry, and a life in imitation of Christ. The two most widely used arguments were those that stemmed from ritual purity and the superiority of the celibacy over marriage.

Although the ritual purity argument can be understood in a sense that is consonant with sound Catholic tradition, some interpretations tended toward the anticorporeal. Perhaps for this reason Church teaching no longer presents this argument in defense of celibacy.[1] Furthermore, the Magisterium has also avoided the Tridentine doctrine on the superiority of celibacy over marriage, apparently in sensitivity to the emphasis that Vatican II placed on the dignity and holiness of marriage.[2] However, it is important to note that the Magisterium has not explicitly repudiated these two arguments, which still provide valuable insights into the nature of clerical continence and celibacy.

The magisterial teaching on priestly celibacy before Vatican II also tended to be expressed from a negative standpoint; that is, celibacy "frees" a priest from those things that "hinder" him from love of and service to the faithful of the Church. Although this perspective provides a valid insight, the positive dimensions of priestly celibacy, such as the good of a dynamic spiritual paternity, need also to be articulated. While celibacy helps the priest to attain liberation *from* earthly responsibilities tied to marriage, it also facilitates freedom *for* attaining a closer identification with Christ.

The emergence of a threefold dimension, implicitly present in *Presbyterorum Ordinis* of Vatican II and explicitly in *Sacerdotalis Caelibatus* of Paul VI, provided a much-needed renewal of the method and content of the theology of celibacy. Among other things, it gave a positive and an other-directed emphasis to celibacy by presenting it as a charism,

---

1. The one exception being a brief comment on St. John Vianney by Benedict XVI: see "Year for Priests," 119.

2. See Vatican Council II, *Gaudium et Spes*, nn. 41, 49.

or gift, that is ordered to the sanctification of the priest and the faithful whom he serves, particularly in his service toward the poor and the forgotten in contemporary society. The renewed presentation of celibacy also avoids an overly introspective understanding of the priesthood wherein one argues for celibacy based on what is good and supportive for the priest himself. In sum, the threefold scheme has effectively formed magisterial teaching and has influenced the framework for contemporary theological study on priestly celibacy.

John Paul II is to be credited with developing the threefold dimension, particularly in *Pastores Dabo Vobis*. He had a predilection for the ecclesiological dimension and taught that the ministerial priesthood and celibacy are intimately connected because Christ is at one and the same time both the Head of the Body, the Church, and the Bridegroom. Following patristic teaching, John Paul II stated that because the priest is configured to Christ, he can have only one spouse, namely, the Church. Thus, the priest's love for the Church is necessarily exclusive and permanent, and from this spousal bond the priest is given spiritual fatherhood.

Furthermore, John Paul II wrote in *Pastores Dabo Vobis* 29 that the "Church, as spouse of Jesus Christ, wishes to be loved by the priest in the total and exclusive manner in which Jesus Christ her head and spouse loved her." The pope used here the nuptial-ecclesiological dimension in order to illumine the relationship between the priest and the faithful: the priest, insofar as he is identified with Christ the Bridegroom through the priestly ordination, enjoys an exclusive marital relationship with the Church, and the Church likewise enjoys exclusive nuptial rights with regard to him. This exclusive and spousal love between the priest and the Church implies the incongruity of the priest also having a human, spousal relationship.

The preceding summary recounts only some of the positive fruits of the renewed theology of priestly celibacy, many of which have been uncovered through the systematic use of the threefold scheme. Nevertheless, there exist still more layers of meaning pertaining to a specifically Christian view of priestly celibacy that await further investigation. What, then, are some of these areas for theological reflection?

First, through the course of this study priestly celibacy has appeared

✓ as a charism intrinsically related to the ministerial priesthood. Thus, while priestly celibacy is not *essential* to the priesthood, it is *integral* to it: the bond that unites priesthood and celibacy is not extrinsic, incidental, or artificial. Priesthood and celibacy are not bound together by an act of the will of ecclesial authority. Rather, they form an integral whole in which the one complements, reinforces, and perfects the other. Further reflection then is needed about priestly celibacy as a *charism* given by the Holy Spirit to those called to the ministerial priesthood in the Latin Church.

Not only is celibacy an integral part of the ministerial priesthood and a charism given by the Holy Spirit, it also has theological value. That is, sacerdotal celibacy forms part of the teaching of the Church, as Levada stated:

> In my view, it seems right to speak of the reasons that support the congruence or fittingness of priestly celibacy as "doctrinal." Not every doctrinal development will result in a dogmatic definition, of the type that led to definitions of the Immaculate Conception by Pope Pius IX in 1854, or of papal primacy and infallibility at the First Vatican Council in 1870. Perhaps a comparison with Catholic teaching about the ordination of women would be helpful here. In both cases there is an appeal to tradition. But in the case of the ordination of women, the tradition can be found from the time of the apostles to the present, and in both East and West; thus Pope John Paul II was able to declare that the exclusion of women from ordination represents a truth of the universal ordinary Magisterium of the Church *definitive tenenda*, that must be held as infallibly certain. Without raising an expectation of a dogmatic declaration in regard to celibacy, it seems to me that the links of celibacy to the doctrine of priesthood justify the notion of doctrinal development, thus excluding arguments about celibacy as solely a disciplinary matter.[3]

Indeed, although priestly celibacy is not *required by divine mandate for all priests*, the established reasons given for its suitability are *doctrinal* and not simply *disciplinary*. Moreover, it is a charism given by the Holy Spirit to the candidate for ordination, who in turn freely accepts the gift and lives it in his priestly ministry. Therefore, the first task for further study is for theologians to explore more in depth the riches of priestly celibacy as both a part of *Catholic doctrine* and as a *charism*.

3. See Levada, "Celibacy and the Priesthood."

Second, this present study has provided a distinct account of *priest-ly* continence and celibacy and, hence, has not investigated subject matters related to it, several of which beckon for further investigation: (1) the theology of the married priesthood; (2) the study of diaconal continence and celibacy, along with the vexing question about married permanent deacons and continence; (3) the potential application of the threefold dimension to celibate lay faithful, which can open up an understanding of the particular nature of the charism of celibacy among the laity; and (4) the mutual influence and enrichment of the married and celibate states. The study of the profound spiritual dynamism between the two vocations is particularly important in building up reciprocal respect and understanding in a world where both suffer a serious and sustained attack.

Third, there is a need to explore in more depth the connection between the priestly celibacy and the Eucharist. Celibacy facilitates the priest's union with Jesus Christ, and the Eucharist is the locus par excellence for this encounter wherein the priest is also able to unite himself intimately with the faithful in this sacramental offering. Referring to the celibate priest's sacramental offering during Mass, Jeremy Driscoll wrote that "[the Eucharist is] the place of his most intense intimacy with Jesus and of his greatest and deepest pastoral availability to his people. In the Eucharist the priest gives himself away at one and at the same time to Jesus and to the people."[4]

Sacerdotal celibacy, therefore, is not simply Christological, ecclesiological, and eschatological. It is also intrinsically *eucharistic*. Being configured to Jesus Christ, High Priest, the celibate priest finds the full meaning of his life in his offering of the eucharistic mystery, which expresses the redemptive act of the Christ the Bridegroom toward the bridal Church. This is clear and unambiguous when the sacramental ministry of the Eucharist is celebrated by a man, who acts *in persona Christi Capitis*.[5] Moreover, this symbolism is made even clearer when the man is celibate, for his celibacy, according to Archbishop Allen Vigneron, signifies the total gift of himself to the bridal Church, in imita-

4. Jeremy Driscoll, "Celibacy in the Diocesan Priesthood: A Monk's Reflection," *Origins* 42 (2012): 37–40, at 40.

5. See John Paul II, *Mulieris Dignitatem*, n. 26.

BIBLIOGRAPHY

Afanasiev, Nicholas. *The Church of the Holy Spirit*. Translated by Vitaly Permiakov. South Bend, Ind.: University of Notre Dame, 2007.

Alberigo, Giuseppe, and Joseph A. Komonchak, eds. *The Council and the Transition: The Fourth Period and the End of the Council, September 1965–December 1965*. Vol. V of *History of Vatican II*. Maryknoll, N.Y.: Orbis, 2006.

Allen, Joseph J., ed. *Vested in Grace: Priesthood and Marriage in the Christian East*. Brookline, Mass.: Holy Cross Orthodox Press, 2001.

Aquinas, Thomas. *Summa Theologiae*. In *Sancti Thomae Aquinatis opera Omnia*. Vol. X. Leonine edition. Rome: Ex Typographia Polyglotta S. C. de Propaganda Fide, 1889.

———. *Opera Omnia*. Vol. XIII. New York: Mursurgia, 1949.

Arató, Pál. *Paulus PP. VI, 1963–1978: Elenchus bibliographicus/collegit Pál Arató; denuo refudit, indicibus instruxit, Paolo Vian*. Brescia: Istituto Paolo VI, 1981.

Augustine. *The Trinity*. Translated by Stephen McKenna, C.ss.R. Washington, D.C.: The Catholic University of America Press, 1963.

———. *Works of Saint Augustine: A Translation for the 21st Century*. Edited by John E. Rotelle and Boniface Ramsey. Part II. Vol. 11 of *Newly Discovered Sermons*. Hyde Park, N.Y.: New City Press, 1998.

Austen, Jane. *Emma*. Edited by James Kinsley with an introduction by Adela Pinch. Oxford: Oxford University Press, reissued 2008.

Bergoglio, Jorge Mario, and Abraham Skorka. *On Heaven and Earth: Pope Francis on Faith, Family and the Church in the 21st Century*. New York: Random House, 2013 (English edition).

Bertram, Jerome. *The Chrodegang Rules: The Rules for the Common Life of the Secular Clergy from the Eighth and Ninth Centuries. Critical Texts with Translations and Commentary*. Aldershot: Ashgate, 2005.

Bertrams, Wilhelm. *The Celibacy of the Priest: Meaning and Basis*. Translated by Patrick Byrne. Westminster, Md.: Newman Press, 1963.

Bickell, Gustav W. "Der Cölibat eine apostolische Anordnung." *Zeitschrift für Katholische Theologie* 2 (1878): 26–64.

Bonaventure. *Opera Omnia*. Vol. II. Quarrachi-Firenze: Collegii S. Bonaventurae, 1889.

———. *Opera Theologica Selecta.* Quarrachi-Firenze: Collegii S. Bonaventurae, 1941.

Borelli, John, and John H. Erickson, eds. *The Quest for Unity: Orthodox and Catholics in Dialogue.* Crestwood, N.Y.: St. Vladimir's Press, 1996.

Bouscaren, T. Lincoln, and Adam Ellis, eds. *Canon Law: A Text and Commentary, 4th Edition.* Milwaukee: Bruce, 1966.

Brown, Peter. *The Body and Society: Men, Women, and Sexual Renunciation in Early Christianity.* New York: Columbia University Press, 1988.

Brown, Raymond E., Joseph A. Fitzmyer, and Roland E. Murphy, eds. *The New Jerome Biblical Commentary.* Englewood Cliffs, N.J.: Prentice-Hall, 1990.

Bulman, Raymond, and Frederick Parrella, eds. *From Trent to Vatican II: Historical and Theological Investigations.* Oxford: Oxford University Press, 2006.

Butler, Sara. *The Catholic Priesthood and Women.* Chicago: Hillenbrand, 2006.

Cahill, Lisa Sowle. *Sex, Gender, and Christian Ethics.* Cambridge: Cambridge University Press, 1996.

Callam, Daniel. "The Frequency of Mass in the Latin Church, ca. 400." *Theological Studies* 45 (1984): 613–50.

Cantalamessa, Raniero. *Virginity: A Positive Approach to Celibacy for the Sake of the Kingdom of Heaven.* Translated by Charles Serignat. Staten Island, N.Y.: Alba House, 1995.

Carlen, Claudia, ed. *The Papal Encyclicals 1903–1939.* Ann Arbor, Mich.: Pierian, 1990.

———, ed. *The Papal Encyclicals 1939–1958.* Ann Arbor, Mich.: Pierian, 1990.

———, ed. *The Papal Encyclicals 1958–1981.* Ann Arbor, Mich.: Pierian, 1990.

Casel, Odo. *Mysterium der Ekklesia; von der Gemeinschaft aller Erlösten in Christus Jesus. Aus Schriften und Vorträgen.* Mainz: Matthias Grünewald, 1961.

Catechism of the Catholic Church. 2nd ed. Washington, D.C.: United States Catholic Conference, 1997.

Cholij, Roman. *Clerical Celibacy in East and West.* Leominster: Fowler Wright, 1988.

———. "Observaciones críticas acerca de los cánones que tratan sobre el celibato en el Código de Derecho Canonico de 1983." *Ius Canonicum* XXXI (1991): 291–305.

———. "Priestly Celibacy in Patristics and in the History of the Church." In *For Love Alone, Reflections on Priestly Celibacy,* edited by Jose Sánchez, 31–52. Slough, U.K.: St. Pauls, 1993.

———. "Celibacy, Married Clergy, and the Oriental Code." *Eastern Churches Journal* 3, no. 3 (1996): 91–117.

Cochini, Christian. *The Apostolic Origins of Priestly Celibacy.* Translated by Nelly Marans. San Francisco: Ignatius, 1990.

Code of Canon Law Annotated: Latin-English Edition. Montreal: Wilson & Lafleur Limitée, 1993.

Code of Canons of the Eastern Churches. Washington, D.C.: Canon Law Society of America, 1992.

Commissio et Secretaria Praeparatoria Concilii Oecumenici Vaticani II, ed. *Acta et*

Documenta Concilio Oecumenico Vaticano II Apparando, Series II (Praeparatoria). Vatican City: Typis Polyglottis Vaticanis, 1964–1969.

Congar, Yves. *Mon journal du concile.* Vol. II. Paris: Cerf, 2002.

Congregation for Catholic Education. "A Guide to Formation in Priestly Celibacy." *Origins* 4 (1974): 65, 67–76.

Congregation for the Clergy. *Directory for the Ministry and Life of Priests.* Vatican City: Libreria Editrice Vaticana, 1994.

Congregation for the Doctrine of the Faith. "Inter Insigniores." *Acta Apostolicae Sedis* 69 (1977): 98–116.

———. *From "Inter Insigniores" to "Ordinatio Sacerdotalis."* Washington, D.C.: United States Catholic Conference, 1996.

Coppens, Joseph, ed. *Sacerdoce et célibat: Etudes historiques et théologiques.* Gembloux: Duculot, 1971.

Coustant, Pierre, ed. *Epistolae Romanorum Pontificum.* Farnborough: Gregg Press, 1967.

Coyle, Kevin. "Recent Views on the Origins of Clerical Celibacy: A Review of the Literature from 1980–1991." *Logos: A Journal of Eastern Christian Studies* 34 (1993): 480–531.

Donahue, Felix. "The Spiritual Father in the Scriptures." In *Abba: Guides to Wholeness and Holiness East and West,* Cistercian Studies Series 38, edited by John R. Sommerfeldt, 3–36. Kalamazoo, Mich.: Cistercian Publications, 1982.

Driscoll, Jeremy. "Celibacy in the Diocesan Priesthood: A Monk's Reflection." *Origins* 42 (2012): 37–40.

Egana, Francisco. "Religious and the New Rite for the Ordination of the Deacon." *Consecrated Life* 17, no. 2 (1992): 98–121.

Fagerbert, David W. *On Liturgical Asceticism.* Washington, D.C.: The Catholic University of America Press, 2013.

Feuillet, André. *Etudes johanniques.* Paris: Desclée de Brouwer, 1962.

Fichter, Joseph. *Wives of Convert Priests.* Kansas City, Mo.: Sheed and Ward, 1992.

Flannery, Austin, ed. *More Post Conciliar Documents.* Collegeville, Minn.: Liturgical Press, 1982.

———, ed. *Vatican Council II: The Conciliar and Post Conciliar Documents.* Northport, N.Y.: Costello, 1998.

Ford, J. Massingberd. *A Trilogy on Wisdom and Celibacy.* The Cardinal O'Hara Series: Studies and Research in Christian Theology at Notre Dame 4. Notre Dame, Ind.: Prentice-Hall, 1967.

Foucault, Michel. *Power/Knowledge: Selected Interviews and Other Writings, 1972–1977.* Edited by Colin Gordon. New York: Pantheon, 1980.

———. *Le souci de soi: histoire de la sexualité.* Volume III. Paris: Gallimard, 1984.

———. *The History of Sexuality.* Translated by R. Hurley. Volume III. New York: Pantheon, 1986.

————. *The Cambridge Companion to Foucault.* 2nd edition. Edited by Gary Gutting. Cambridge: Cambridge University Press, 2003, 2007.

Friedberg, Aemilius, ed. *Corpus Iuris Canonici.* 2 Vols. Graz: Akademische Druck— U. Verlagsanstalt, 1955.

Funk, Franz X. "Der Cölibat keine apostolische Anordnung." *Theologische Quartalschrift* 61 (1879): 208–47.

Galot, Jean. "The Priesthood and Celibacy." *Review for Religious* 24 (1965): 930–56.

————. *Theology of the Priesthood.* Translated by Robert Balducelli. San Francisco: Ignatius, 1985.

Griffin, Carter Harrell. "Supernatural Fatherhood through Priestly Celibacy: Fulfillment in Masculinity: A Thomistic Study." STD diss., Pontificia Università della Santa Croce, Rome, 2010.

Gryson, Roger. *Les origines du célibat ecclésiastique du premier au septième siècle.* Gembloux: Duculot, 1970.

Hahn, Scott W. *Kinship by Covenant: A Canonical Approach to the Fulfillment of God's Saving Promises.* New Haven, Conn.: Yale University Press, 2009.

Hauke, Manfred. *Die Problematik um das Frauenpriestertum vor dem Hintergrund der Schöpfungs-und Erlösungsordnung.* Paderborn: Verlag Bonifatius-Druckerei, 1982.

Heid, Stephan. *Celibacy in the Early Church: The Beginnings of a Discipline of Obligatory Continence for Clerics in East and West.* Translated by Michael J. Miller. San Francisco: Ignatius, 2000.

Heil, John Paul. *Ephesians: Empowerment to Walk in Love for the Unity of All in Christ.* Atlanta: Society of Biblical Literature, 2007.

Höffner, Joseph. "Pour le royaume des cieux: dix thèses sur le célibat des prêtres." In *Sacerdoce et célibat: Etudes historiques et théologiques,* edited by Joseph Coppens, 573–82. Gembloux: Duculot, 1971.

Holl, Karl, ed. *Die Griechischen christlichen Schriftsteller der ersten drei Jahrhunderte.* Leipzig: J. C. Hinrichs, 1922.

Hume, Cardinal George Basil. *Searching for God.* Wilton, Conn.: Morehouse-Barlow, 1977.

International Theological Commission. *Texts and Documents 1969–1985.* Edited by Michael Sharkey. San Francisco: Ignatius, 1989.

————. *Theology Today: Perspectives, Principles, and Criteria.* Washington, D.C.: The Catholic University of America Press, 2012.

J. M. T. *Le célibat d'aprés une loi naturelle.* Paris: Editions de Pierre-Prat, 1932.

Jaki, Stanley L. *Theology of Priestly Celibacy.* Front Royal, Va.: Christendom Press, 1997.

John of the Cross. *The Collected Works of St. John of the Cross.* Translated by Kieran Kavanaugh, OCD, and Otilio Rodriquez, OCD. Garden City: N.Y.: Doubleday, 1964.

Joint Commission for the Theological Dialogue between the Roman Catholic Church and the Orthodox Church. "The Sacrament of Order in the Sacramental Structure of the Church with Particular Reference to the Importance of Apostolic Succession for the Sanctification and Unity of the People of God." In *The Quest for Unity: Orthodox and Catholics in Dialogue*, edited by John Borelli and John H. Erickson, 131–42. Crestwood, N.Y.: St. Vladimir's Press, 1996.

Jonkers, E. J., ed. *Acta et Symbola Conciliorum Quae Saeculo Quarto Habita Sunt*. Leiden: Brill, 1954.

Keefe, Donald. "'In Persona Christi': Authority in the Church and the Maleness of the Priesthood." *Faith* 34 (2002): 15–24.

Kennedy, Arthur, ed. *Celibacy and the Priesthood: Divine Gift and Cultural Anomaly*. Boston: Saint Botolph Press, 2012.

Kerr, Fergus. *Twentieth-Century Catholic Theologians: From Neoscholasticism to Nuptial Mysticism*. Malden, Mass.: Blackwell, 2007.

Komonchak, Joseph. "Celibacy and Tradition." *Chicago Studies* 20, no. 1 (1981): 5–17.

Kowalski, Anthony P. *Married Catholic Priests: Their History, Their Journey, Their Reflections*. Mequon, Wisc.: Caritas, 2004.

Lambrecht, Jan. *Second Corinthians*. Vol. 8 of *Sacra Pagina Series*. Edited by Daniel J. Harrington. Collegeville, Minn.: Liturgical Press, 1999.

Latourelle, René, ed. *Vatican II: Assessment and Perspectives*. Vol. III of *Twenty-Five Years After (1962–1987)*. New York: Paulist, 1989.

Laurent, Vitalien. "L'oeuvre canonique du concile in Trullo (691–692), source primaire du droit de l'église orientale." *Revue des etudes byzantines* 23 (1965): 7–41.

Lecordier, Gaston. "Une récente apologie du célibat ecclésiastique." *Revue apologétique* 561 (1932): 685–700.

Lécuyer, Joseph. *What Is a Priest?* Translated by Lancelot Sheppard. New York: Hawthorn, 1959.

Legrand, Lucien. "The Prophetical Meaning of Celibacy." *Review for Religious* 20 (1961): 330–46.

Levada, William. "Celibacy and the Priesthood." http://www.vatican.va/roman_curia/congregations/cfaith/documents/rc_con_cfaith_doc_20111121_levada -celibacy-priesthood_en.html.

L'Huillier, Peter. "The First Millenium: Marriage, Sexuality, and Priesthood." In *Vested in Grace: Priesthood and Marriage in the Christian East*, edited by Joseph J. Allen, 22–65. Brookline, Mass.: Holy Cross Orthodox Press, 2001.

Lonergan, Bernard. *Verbum: Word and Idea in Aquinas*. 2nd edition. Edited by David B. Burrell, C.S.C. Notre Dame, Ind: University of Notre Dame Press, 1970.

———. *Doctrinal Pluralism*. Milwaukee: Marquette University Press, 1971.

Lorenzi, Lorenzo de, ed. *Paul de Tarse: apôtre du notre temps*. Rome: Abbaye de Saint Paul, 1979.

Louf, André. "Spiritual Fatherhood in the Literature of the Desert." In *Abba: Guides* to Wholeness and Holiness East and West. Cistercian Studies Series 38, edited by John R. Sommerfeldt, 37–63. Kalamazoo, Mich.: Cistercian Publications, 1982.

Lubac, Henri de. The Motherhood of the Church: Followed by Particular Church in the Universal Church and an Interview Conducted by Gwendoline Jarczyk. Translated by Sergia Englund. San Francisco: Ignatius, 1982.

Lynch, John E. "Marriage and Celibacy of the Clergy: The Discipline of the Western Church: An Historico-Canonical Synopsis." The Jurist 32 (1972): 14–38, 189–212.

MacIntyre, Alasdair. After Virtue. 2nd edition. Notre Dame, Ind.: University of Notre Dame Press, 1984.

Malone, Richard. "On John Paul II's Pastores Dabo Vobis." Communio 20 (1993): 569–71.

Margerie, Bertrand de. "Luzes Antigas e Novas sobre o Celibato." Revista Eclesiástica Brasileira 22 (1962): 616–37.

Matera, Frank J. II Corinthians: A Commentary. Louisville, Ky.: Westminster John Knox Press, 2003.

Mathews, Edward G. Jr., ed. Chaste Celibacy: Living Christ's Own Spousal Love. Omaha: Institute for Priestly Formation, 2001.

Mathews, Susan F. "Called to the Wedding Feast of the Lamb: Covenantal Spousal Imagery from Genesis to Revelations." In Chaste Celibacy: Living Christ's Own Spousal Love, edited by Edward G. Mathews Jr., 39–48. Omaha: The Institute for Priestly Formation, 2001.

McGovern, Thomas J. "The Spousal Dimension of the Priesthood." The National Catholic Bioethics Quarterly (Spring 2003): 95–110.

McHugh, John F. A Critical and Exegetical Commentary on John 1–4. Edited by Graham N. Stanton. London: T and T Clark, 2009.

McIntyre, John. "Married Priests: A Research Report." CLSA Proceedings 56 (1994): 130–52.

McPartlan, Paul. Sacrament of Salvation: An Introduction to Eucharistic Ecclesiology. Edinburgh: T and T Clark, 1995.

———. "Who Is the Church? Zizioulas and von Balthasar on the Church's Identity." Ecclesiology 4 (2008): 271–88.

Meier, John P. The Roots of the Problem and the Person. Vol. 1 of A Marginal Jew: Rethinking the Historical Jesus. New York: Doubleday, 1991.

———. Mentor, Message, and Miracles. Vol. 2 of A Marginal Jew: Rethinking the Historical Jesus. New York: Doubleday, 1994.

———. Law and Love. Vol. 4 of A Marginal Jew: Rethinking the Historical Jesus. New Haven, Conn.: Yale University Press, 2009.

Michael, Emil. Ignaz von Dollinger: Eine Charakteristik. Innsbruck: Fel. Rauch, 1894.

Möhler, Johann Adam. The Spirit of Celibacy. Translated by Cyprian Blamires. Chicago: Hillenbrand, 2007.

Moloney, Francis J. "Matthew 19, 3–12 and Celibacy: A Redactional and Form Critical Study /1/." *Journal for the Study of the New Testament* 2 (January 1979): 50–53.

Morrisey, Francis G. *The Canonical Significance of Papal and Curial Pronouncements.* Hartford, Conn.: Canon Law Society of America, 1978.

Murray, Robert. *Symbols of Church and Kingdom: A Study in Early Syriac Tradition.* London: Cambridge University Press, 1975.

Neusner, Jacob. *The Idea of Purity in Ancient Judaism.* Leiden: Brill, 1973.

———. "Purity and the Priesthood in the Hebrew Scriptures and Rabbinic Tradition." In *For Love Alone: Reflections on Priestly Celibacy,* edited by Jose Sánchez, 129–36. Slough, U.K.: St. Pauls, 1993.

New Revised Standard Version. Nashville, Tenn.: Thomas Nelson, 1990.

Newman, John Henry. *An Essay on the Development of Christian Doctrine.* London: Basil Montagu Pickering, 1878.

Nyathi, Jerome Rono. "Priesthood Today and the Crisis of Fatherhood: Fatherlessness in Africa with Special Reference to Zimbabwe." STD diss., Pontifical University of St. Thomas, Rome, 2002.

Origen. *Homilies on Leviticus 1–16.* Translated by Gary Wayne Barkley. The Fathers of the Church: A New Translation (Patristic Series) 83. Edited by Thomas P. Halton. Washington, D.C.: The Catholic University of America, 1990.

———. *Homilies on Numbers.* Translated by Thomas P. Scheck. Ancient Christian Texts. Edited by Christopher A. Hall. Downers Grove, Ill.: IVP Academic, 2009.

Ouellet, Marc Cardinal. "Priestly Celibacy and the Life of the Church: Contemporary Values and Challenges." In *Celibacy and the Priesthood: Divine Gift and Cultural Anomaly,* edited by Arthur Kennedy, 1–39. Boston: Saint Botolph Press, 2012.

Peñafort, Raymond. *Summa Iuris Canonici.* Edited by J. Rius Serra. Barcelona: Universidad de Barcelona, 1945.

Peters, Edward, ed. *The 1917 or Pio-Benedictine Code of Canon Law in English Translation with Extensive Scholarly Apparatus.* Translated by Edward Peters. San Francisco: Ignatius, 2000.

———. "Canonical Considerations on Diaconal Continence." *Studia Canonica* 39 (2005): 147–80.

Pope Benedict XV. "Ad R.P.D. Franciscum Kordac, Archiepiscopum Pragensem, Coetum Episcoporum Convocandum Statuens." *Acta Apostolicae Sedis* 12 (1920): 33–35.

Pope Benedict XVI. "Address to the Roman Curia." *L'Osservatore Romano* (January 3, 2007): 5–7.

———. *The Sacrament of Charity: Sacramentum Caritatis.* Washington, D.C.: United States Conference of Catholic Bishops, 2007.

———. "Letter of His Holiness Pope Benedict XVI Proclaiming a Year for Priests on the 150th Anniversary of the 'Dies Natalis' of the Curé of Ars." *Origins* 39 (2009): 116–21.

———. "A Sacrament, a New Life to Make Room for God." *L'Osservatore Romano* (June 16, 2010), 1, 6–7, 10.

Pope John Paul II. *Apostolic Exhortation of John Paul II: The Role of the Christian Family in the Modern World, Familiaris Consortio.* Boston: Pauline, 1981.

———. "Apostolic Letter on the Dignity and Vocation of Women, Mulieris Dignitatem (1988)." In *Theology of the Body.*

———. "Mulieris Dignitatem." *Acta Apostolicae Sedis* 80 (1988): 1653–1729.

———. "Pastores Dabo Vobis." *Acta Apostolicae Sedis* 84 (1992): 657–804.

———. *Post-Synodal Apostolic Exhortation: I Will Give You Shepherds, Pastores Dabo Vobis.* Boston: Pauline, 1992.

———. *Priesthood in the Third Millennium.* Chicago: Midwest Theological Forum, 1994.

———. *The Encyclicals of John Paul II.* Edited by J. Michael Miller. Huntington, Ind.: Our Sunday Visitor, 1996.

———. *Theology of the Body: Human Love in the Divine Plan.* Boston: Pauline, 1997.

———. *On the Eucharist: Ecclesia de Eucharistia.* Washington, D.C.: United States Conference of Catholic Bishops, 2003.

———. *Rise, Let Us Be On Our Way.* New York: Warner, 2004.

———. *Letters to My Brother Priests: Complete Collection of Holy Thursday Letters (1979–2005).* Edited by James Socias. Woodbridge, Ill.: Midwest Theological Forum, 2006.

———. *Man and Woman He Created Them: A Theology of the Body.* Translated by Michael Waldstein. Boston: Pauline, 2006.

Pope John XXIII. "Sacerdotii Nostri Primordia." *Acta Apostolicae Sedis* 51 (1959): 545–79.

———. "Virtutes Dignitati Sacerdotum Necessariae: Caput, Cor et Lingua." *Acta Apostolicae Sedis* 52 (1960): 221–30.

Pope Paul VI. "Epistula Summi Pontificis Pauli VI ad em.mum P.D. Eugenium card. Tisserant Praesidem Consilii Praesidentiae Ss. Concilii." In *Acta Synodalia Sacrosancti Concilii Oecumenici Vatican II.* Vol. IV/I, 40. Vatican City: Typis Polyglottis Vaticanis.

———. "Sacerdotalis Caelibatus." *Acta Apostolicae Sedis* 59 (1967): 657–97.

Pope Pius X. "Haerent Animo." *Acta Apostolicae Sedis* 41 (1908): 545–79.

Pope Pius XI. "Ad Catholici Sacerdotii." *Acta Apostolicae Sedis* 28 (1936): 5–53.

Pope Pius XII. "Menti Nostrae." *Acta Apostolicae Sedis* 42 (1950): 657–702.

———. *Menti Nostrae.* Washington, D.C.: National Catholic Welfare Conference, 1951.

———. "Sacra Virginitas." *Acta Apostolicae Sedis* 46 (1954): 161–91.

Potterie, Ignace de la. "'Mari d'une seule femme': le sens théologique d'une formule paulinienne." In *Paul de Tarse: apôtre du notre temps*, edited by Lorenzo de Lorenzi, 619–38. Rome: Abbaye de Saint Paul, 1979.

———. *Mary in the Mystery of the Covenant.* New York: Alba House, 1992.

————. "The Biblical Foundation of Priestly Celibacy." In *For Love Alone: Reflections on Priestly Celibacy*, edited by Jose Sánchez, 13–30. Slough, U.K.: St. Pauls, 1993.

Przywara, Erich. *Analogia Entis: Metaphysics: Original Structure and Universal Rhythm*. Translated by John R. Betz and David Bentley Hart. Grand Rapids, Mich.: William B. Eerdmans Publishing Company, 2014.

Ramage, Matthew. *Dark Passages of the Bible: Engaging Scripture with Benedict XVI and St. Thomas Aquinas*. Washington, D.C.: The Catholic University of America Press, 2013.

Ratzinger, Joseph. *The Feast of Faith: Approaches to a Theology of the Liturgy*. Translated by Graham Harrison. San Francisco: Ignatius, 1986.

————. *The Spirit of the Liturgy*. Translated by John Saward. San Francisco: Ignatius, 2000.

Revised Standard Version, Catholic Edition. Camden, N.J.: Thomas Nelson, 1966.

Rowe, C. Kavin. *World Upside Down: Reading Acts in the Greco-Roman Age*. New York: Oxford University Press, 2009.

Ryland, Ray. "A Brief History of Clerical Celibacy." In *Priestly Celibacy: Its Scriptural, Historical, Spiritual, and Psychological Roots*, edited by Peter M. J. Stravinskas, 27–44. Mt. Pocono, Penn.: Newman House Press, 2001.

Sánchez, Fernando Benicio Felices. *La Paternidad Espiritual del Sacerdote*. San Juan, P.R.: S.N, 2006.

Sánchez, Jose, ed. *For Love Alone: Reflections on Priestly Celibacy*. Slough, U.K.: St. Pauls, 1993.

Scheeben, Matthias Joseph. *The Mysteries of Christianity*. Translated by Cyril Vollert. St. Louis: B. Herder, 1947.

Schillebeeckx, Edward, OP. *Marriage: Human Reality and Saving Mystery*. Translated by N. D. Smith. London: Sheed and Ward, 1978.

Schnackenburg, Rudolf. *Introduction and Commentary on Chapters 1–4*. Vol. 1 of *The Gospel According to St. John*. Translated by Kevin Smyth. New York: Seabury Press, 1980.

Schneider, Mary R. "The Ancient Tradition of Clerical Celibacy." *Homiletic and Pastoral Review* (July 2007): 18–26.

Selin, Gary. "On the Christological, Ecclesiological, and Eschatological Dimensions of Priestly Celibacy in Presbyterorum Ordinis, Sacerdotalis Caelibatus and Subsequent Magisterial Documents." STD diss., The Catholic University of America, 2011.

Sherwin, Michael. "'The Friend of the Bridegroom Stands and Listens': An Analysis of the Term *Amicus Sponsi* in Augustine's Account of Divine Friendship and the Ministry of Bishops." *Augustinianum* 38 (1998): 197–214.

Sipe, Richard. *A Secret World: Sexuality and the Search for Celibacy*. New York: Brunner/Mazel, 1990.

Sommerfeldt, John R., ed. *Abba: Guides to Wholeness and Holiness East and West*. Cistercian Studies Series 38. Kalamazoo, Mich.: Cistercian Publications, 1982.

Spiazzi, Raimondo. "Annotazioni." *Monitor Ecclesiasticus* 84 (1959): 369–409.

Stafford, J. Francis. "Eucharistic Foundation of Sacerdotal Celibacy." *Origins* 23 (1993): 211–16.

———. "Pope Paul VI and Pope John Paul II: Being True in Body and Soul." November 13, 2008. http://www.catholicnewsagency.com/document.php?n=780.

Steinfels, Peter. *A People Adrift*. New York: Simon and Schuster, 2003.

Stevens, Wallace. *The Collected Poems of Wallace Stevens*. New York: Alfred A. Knopf, Inc., 1991.

Stickler, Alfons. *The Case for Clerical Celibacy: Its Historical Developments and Theological Foundations*. Translated by Brian Ferme. San Francisco: Ignatius, 1995.

Stravinskas, Peter M. J., ed. *Priestly Celibacy: Its Scriptural, Historical, Spiritual, and Psychological Roots*. Mt. Pocono, Penn.: Newman House Press, 2001.

Sullivan, Francis A. *Magisterium*. New York: Paulist, 1983.

Tanner, Norman P., ed. *Nicaea I to Lateran V*. Vol. 1 of *Decrees of the Ecumenical Councils*. London: Sheed and Ward, 1990.

———, ed. *Trent to Vatican II*. Vol. 2 of *Decrees of the Ecumenical Councils*. London: Sheed and Ward, 1990.

Tellenbach, Gerd. *The Church in Western Europe from the Tenth to the Early Twelfth Century*. Translated by Timothy Reuter. Cambridge: Cambridge University Press, 1993.

Theological Dictionary of the New Testament. Volume III. Edited by Gerhard Kittel. Grand Rapids, Mich.: Wm. B. Eerdmans Publishing Company, 1965, 1982.

Thurian, Max. *Mariage et célibat*. Neuchâtel/Paris: Delachaux & Niestlé, 1955.

Tidner, Erik, ed. *Texte und Untersuchungen zur Geschichte der Altchristlichen Literatur*. Berlin: Akademie-Verlag, 1963.

Touze, Laurent. "Married Priests Will Always Be an Exception." http://www.zenit.org/en/articles/married-priests-will-always-be-an-exception.

United States Conference of Catholic Bishops. *The Roman Missal*. Totowa, N.J.: Catholic Book Publishing, 2011.

Vatican Council II. *Acta Synodalia Sacrosancti Concilii Oecumenici Vatican II*. Vatican City: Typis Polyglottis Vaticanis, 1970–1988.

Velati, Mauro. "Completing the Conciliar Agenda." In *The Council and the Transition: The Fourth Period and the End of the Council, September 1965–December 1965*. Vol. V of *History of Vatican II*, edited by Giuseppe Alberigo and Joseph A. Komonchak, 185–274. Maryknoll, N.Y.: Orbis, 2006.

Vendler, Helen. *Wallace Stevens: Words Chosen Out of Desire*. Knoxville: The University of Tennessee Press, 1985.

Versaldi, Giuseppe. "Priestly Celibacy from the Canonical and Psychological Points of View." In *Vatican II: Assessment and Perspectives. Twenty-Five Years After (1962–1987)*. Vol. III, edited by René Latourelle, 131–56. New York: Paulist, 1989.

Vigneron, Allen. "Christ's Virginity: Model of Celibacy and Service for the Diocesan

Priest." In *Celibacy and the Priesthood: Divine Gift and Cultural Anomaly*, edited by Arthur Kennedy, 40–63. Boston: Saint Botolph Press, 2012.

Vogels, Heinz-Jürgen. *Celibacy: Gift or Law?* Translated by G. A. Kon. Kansas City, Mo.: Sheed and Ward, 1993.

Vorgrimler, Herbert, ed. *Commentary on the Documents of Vatican II*, Vol. IV. New York: Herder and Herder, 1969.

Wadham, Juliana. *The Case of Cornelia Connelly*. New York: Pantheon, 1957.

Weber, Max. *Ancient Judaism*. Translated by Hans H. Gerth and Don Martindale. Glencoe, Ill.: Free Press, 1952.

Winkelmann, Friedhelm. "Paphnutios, der Bekenner und Bischof: Probleme der koptischen Literatur." In *Wisssenschaftliche Beiträge der Martin Luther-Universität Halle-Wittenberg*, Vol. I, 145–53, 1968. Halle-Wittenberg: Wisssenschaftliche Beiträge der Martin Luther-Universität.

Wulf, Friedrich Wulf. "Chapter III: The Life of Priests (Articles 12–16)." In *Commentary on the Documents of Vatican II*, Vol. IV, edited by Herbert Vorgrimler, 191–239. New York: Herder and Herder, 1969.

Zizioulas, John. *Being as Communion*. Crestwood, N.Y.: St. Vladimir's Seminary Press, 1985.

INDEX OF BIBLICAL CITATIONS

GENERAL INDEX

Abraham of Nisibis, 128n62
Ad Catholici Sacerdotii (1935), 42–44
Adeodatus (son of Augustine), xviii
Adrian I (pope), 30
Afanasiev, Nicholas, 119–20
African Codex (*419*), 30
Alexander III (pope), 32
Ambrose of Milan, 134; *De Officiis*, 142n106; *De Virginitate*, 11n10, 111n18; *Epistolae*, 14n18, 26n51
Ambrosiaster: *In Epistolam B. Pauli*, 11n10, 14n18, 26n51, 160; *Questiones Veteris et Novi Testamenti*, 144n114, 160
Aquinas. *See* Thomas Aquinas
Arles, Council of (*314*), 24
Ars, Curé of, 150
Augustine, xiii, xviii–xix, 41, 54, 131, 134; *De bono coniugali*, 126n58; *De Trinitate*, xviii, xixn24; *In Iohannis Evangelium Tractatus*, 146n121; *Rule of St. Augustine*, 30; *Sermons*, 131n73, 131n75; *Tractatus in Evangelium Ioannis*, 12n11
Austen, Jane: *Emma*, xi

baptism, 80, 94, 124–25
Basle, Council of (*1417–37*), 33
Benedict XV (pope), 39, 41n95
Benedict XVI (pope): Christmas address to Roman Curia (*2006*), 155–56; on Eucharist and priestly celibacy, 172–75, 180n1; *The Feast of Faith* and *The Spirit of the Liturgy* (Ratzinger), 150n136; *Pastores Gregis*, 135; renewed magisterial teach-

ing on priestly celibacy and, 5; ritual purity language used, 150; *Sacramentum Caritatis*, xii, 173–75, 177; at vigil of end of Year for Priests (*2010*), 162, 180n1
Bernard of Clairvaux, xii, xiii
Bertram, Jerome, xviin18
Bertrams, Wilhelm: *The Celibacy of the Priest*, 48–50
biblical foundations, 7–17; of Christological dimension, 107–11; *Directory for the Ministry and Life of Priests* on, 100–101; of ecclesiological dimension, 121–27; of eschatological dimension, 152–54; New Testament origins of clerical celibacy, 9–16, 43, 57, 179; Old Testament origins of clerical celibacy, 7–9, 25, 46, 179; of ritual purity, 139–42; of spiritual fatherhood, 133–34. *See also Index of Biblical Citations*
Bickell, Gustav, xvi, 38–39
bishops: celibacy of, 116–20; as friend of bridegroom, 130–32; rings worn by, 128; Trinitarian and communitarian foundation of ministry of, 164–65. *See also* Ordinary Synod of Bishops
Blessed Virgin Mary, 37, 88, 114, 123
Bonaventure: *Liber II Sententiarum*, 126n59, 129–30
Bridegroom of Church. *See* nuptial aspect of priesthood
Brown, Peter, 18n29, 142
Burgess, Council of (*1031*), 31
Butler, Sara, 83n65, 94n98, 94n100, 127, 135, 137

Priestly Celibacy: Theological Foundations was designed in Frutiger Serif and composed by Kachergis Book Design of Pittsboro, North Carolina. It was printed on 50-pound Natures text stock and bound by McNaughton & Gunn of Saline, Michigan.